LEWIS S. MUDGE

THE SENSE OF A PEOPLE

Toward a Church for the Human Future

Trinity Press International   Philadelphia

First Published 1992

Trinity Press International
3725 Chestnut Street
Philadelphia, PA 19104

Cover design by Brian Preuss

Library of Congress Cataloging-in-Publication Data
Mudge, Lewis S.
The sense of a people : toward a church for the human future / Lewis S. Mudge.
    p.   cm.
Includes bibliographical references and index.
ISBN 1-56338-040-4
1. Church. 2. Sociology, Christian. I. Title.
BV600.2.M83   1992   92-7926
262'.7—dc20   CIP

Printed in the United States of America

Table of Contents

Foreword

"The important thing," a wise friend used to say, "is to be in the dialogue." Of course it is not easy to decide these days which dialogue is the one to be in. I hope that the vision embodied in this book will find its place in what is being thought and said in today's theological world. If attention to these ideas also comes from persons outside that particular circle, I will be pleased. Perhaps these pages may even catch some sense of a still more inclusive conversation: what Michael Oakeshott, followed by Gilbert Ryle, Richard Rorty, and others, has called "the conversation of humankind."[1]

One can truly enter a dialogue only by bringing some part of it to critical and, hopefully, fruitful focus. I have sought to do that in several ways over the years as a Christian theologian. I have found, of course, that theologians are no more sure than anyone else today what their field involves and how they should go about pursuing it. Yet there can be little doubt that a central theological issue of this decade will concern the public role and purpose of churches and other faith communities in a rapidly changing and deeply troubled global civilization. I want to pursue this question not only as an issue for church strategists and social ethicists but as a fundamental question of *ecclesiology*.

I believe, as the sequel will show, that this concern has serious implications beyond the boundaries of religious communities as such. The way these bodies conceive humanity's conversation as a factor in their own internal dialogues should be a matter of public, not merely ecclesiastical, interest. If the question of the churches' role in the human community can be pressed to the level of fundamental ecclesiological assumptions, the consequences will be deeply felt both within the churches and beyond.

I come to these broad questions from involvement in three more specific arenas of discourse and action. First, there has been the *professional* dialogue related to my responsibilities as a theological educator. This has not been limited to concerns for ministerial education as such. It has included an effort to think about the churches' thinking: to ask how and with what conceptual resources churches need to do their practical reasoning in the late twentieth century. Second, there has been the *ecumenical* conversation, focused on issues related to the churches' unity, catholicity, and testimony to the world. This concern has led me to participation in the writing and editing of confessional bilateral and multilateral reports and documents designed to bring the churches closer to one another and to their common calling. Third, I have had an *academic* preoccupation with philosophical hermeneutics as applied to the Bible and other texts. This inquiry has begun of late to concern the hermeneutical nature of the human sciences. In each of these fields I have had many good companions, more than I can now name. Many are known personally to me. Others I know only through their writings. I am grateful to all of them.

These three dialogical currents now flow into this quest for a new ecclesio-social vision. In one sense, this confluence is a reflection of my own life: I have wanted to find the unity—if there is any—of the streams I have been swimming in all these years. But I am also convinced that the dialogues I have shared *need* to meet in this day and age. Theological educators, ecumenists, and hermeneuts have tended to go their own separate ways. But they could learn a great deal from one another. The risk of trying to bring them together in one volume, of course, is that I will do less than justice to each, fail to make adequate connections, and as a result please no one. But the experiment is worth making. I sense that in these pages I am introducing some of my dialogue partners to one another for the first time. I hope they will pause to receive the proffered companionship and even come to enjoy one anoth-ers' company, even if it is not in *my* house that they next choose to meet!

It is a happy task to thank those companions in conversa-tion who have read drafts of this book early and late, offering me comments and criticisms from which I have learned much. First, I am grateful for exchanges of ideas—centered on frag-ments and early chapter drafts—with Martin Conway, John Ford, Günther Gassmann, Thomas Best, John Radano, Ed-ward Farley, Alasdair Heron, Alan Lewis, and James Fowler. A penultimate version of the whole work was read by George Lindbeck, Richard Norris, Don Browning, Gary Comstock, Herman Waetjen, and Robert Coote. These friends did much to help me trim, focus, and reflect. Many of the ideas in this book also figured in conversations Don Browning and I had on our morning walks from Ross Stevenson Circle to the Center of Theological Inquiry in Princeton in the winter and spring of 1990. And finally, Richard Norris, Thomas Parker, Peter Hodgson, Jack Stotts, and Alasdair Heron were good enough to go through a nearly ultimate draft, helpfully reacting to my ideas, pointing to obscurities, saving me from mistakes. W. D. Davies challenged me with his response to a draft of the introduction, and George Kateb commented most helpfully on the final chapter. I wish I could find some truly original way to thank all these colleagues while relieving them of responsibility for the outcome. No such luck. But I *am* grate-ful, and I *do* grant the needed absolutions!

I also remember several institutions and persons for sig-nificant courtesies. Thanks go to the Trustees of McCormick Theological Seminary and to former President Jack L. Stotts for periods of leave from deaning. Thanks also to McCormick colleagues Marc Priester and Robert Boling for sitting in, and to Shirley Dudley and Kathy Wohlschlaeger for encourage-ment and administrative support. I am grateful to the Trust-ees of San Francisco Theological Seminary and to President J. Randolph Taylor for a sabbatical semester. Walter Davis oc-cupied the Dean's chair during that time, an act of friendship I value greatly.

Appreciation is due former Director Martin Marty for

research and office facilities for a time at The Center for the Advanced Study of Religion of the University of Chicago Divinity School, and to Acting Director James Armstrong and his Board of Directors for research, office, and residential accommodations for a semester at the Center of Theological Inquiry. I also thank the Faculty of Theology of the University of Lausanne, in particular Professors Bernard Reymond and Dennis Müller, for an invitation to a session of the European seminar on Ernst Troeltsch directed by Trutz Rendtorff; and Don Browning for invitations to conferences on practical theology at Elspeet, the Netherlands, and at the conference center of Tübingen University in Blaubeuren, Germany. The latter meeting was assisted by a grant from the Volkswagen Foundation.

I have been helped in manuscript editing by the splendid close-reading abilities of recent SFTS graduate, Debra Baker. But indispensable to me has been the all-around administrative competence, the cheerful willingness to bear any burden, and the skill in manuscript preparation of my extraordinary assistant, Mary Poletti. Joanne Baughan, also of the SFTS staff, helped me with the index. I reserve a special word of thanks for my editor, Harold Rast, the enterprising and resourceful Director of Trinity Press International. He believed in this book from the start. He has been a source of moral, material, and editorial support throughout.

I realize that for some time now I have owed my family, colleagues, and myself an end to this overly preoccupying project. My grown children—Robert, William, and Anne—as well as my son-in-law, Jim Mittelberger, have been genially bemused yet loyally encouraging. My wife, Jean, with a writing and filmmaking career of her own to attend to, has borne the brunt in more ways than I probably know, and I know enough. But she has also done more. She has looked with her writer's eye particularly at the early chapters, leading me to simplify where I could, to be direct when my tendencies apparently ran to obfuscation. And I think she never lost confidence that something would eventually appear. This work is affectionately dedicated to her and to my new granddaughter, Alison, who as yet knows nothing about this book, but who represents in her own special way the human future for which it is written.

L.S.M.

San Francisco Theological Seminary
The Graduate Theological Union
Martin Luther King Day 1992

Introduction

Religious Communities and the Future of Faith

Will articulate expressions of religious faith play a significant role in the complex human commonwealth now emerging on this planet? We cannot see the future clearly enough to be sure. But faith's persistence in recognizable forms will surely depend in no small part on the evolution of its communal embodiments. The social forms and relationships of religious communities will decisively influence the way faith itself is construed and understood. Without communities to express and live out coherent religious traditions, people will not be able to put words to ultimate concern or primordial trust, let alone follow the life paths to which such experiences in the past have led. Shared symbolizations of faith will be needed, in short, if faith itself is to remain consciously alive in the world. The theologies of the future will be grounded in the self-understanding and practical reasoning of believing communities. These communities, Christian churches among them, need to consider the forms of life in which their insights can best be pursued in the new human situation we see coming into being all around us. It is important to humanity—to

believers, agnostics, atheists, and even to those increasing
numbers who do not care one way or another—that religious
traditions should learn how to live with depth and integrity as
parts of this human scene, yet share the task of *representing*,
in their many ways, the people of earth as a spiritual community.

1. *The Emerging Human Condition*

Many features of the world in which our children and
grandchildren will live are already apparent. Humanity today
has reached an unprecedented and multidimensional degree
of interdependence. And yet our worldwide networks of information exchange and interlocking economic relationships
have virtually no spiritual dimension.[1] This combination of
material interdependence with spiritual fragmentation will
likely become more marked as the twenty-first century unfolds.

Consider the linkages in which we all live. Ours is a world
system which has come to rely on the instant transmission and
reception of data as well as a worldwide interchange of goods
and services. A movement on the Tokyo stock exchange has
virtually instant ramifications in London and New York. The
announcement of a scientific discovery in one nation has laboratories on other continents trying to duplicate it within hours.
The news media bring sounds and sights from every corner of
the earth into our living rooms. The information horizon of
any happening moves outward in all directions with the speed
of light. We belong to an enormously complex and interactive
human whole.

But this whole has little spiritual substance. Participants
in the world's information and control networks generally
understand at least some of the far-flung ramifications of what
they do, but they usually have little sense of solidarity with
those who feel the impact of their actions. The communication networks which make such impersonal patterns of interaction possible transmit messages which are mainly technical
or pragmatic in character. Even the plain-language vocabu-

laries of public life are nearly incapable of human communication in depth. Neither our information systems nor our broadcast journalists truly convey our vulnerability, our finitude, our fears, our joys, our humanness. The interviewer's questions at the scene of the disaster are more verbal voyeurism then genuine concern. They carry little feeling that the human race is composed of family members about whom we might care if given the chance. Publicly maintained meanings are largely limited to the literal and the useful. We keep to the right, except in places where we keep to the left. A standardized array of directional symbols has begun to emerge along highways and another has begun to appear in airport concourses. A limited range of graspable ideas and imputable motives is available to journalists and newscasters who try to interpret complex events, and who, in doing so, nearly always miss something utterly essential to those who know the facts at firsthand.

It will be said, of course, that the literary and artistic worlds, including the worlds of popular culture, provide depth languages of a sort. For many, these newer languages have replaced systems of spiritual expression sponsored by the older religious traditions. But such contemporary symbol systems are often as sectarian as the different competing worlds of religious faith. They depend in their own ways on various traditions, conventions, and genres which are available mainly to literary and artistic elites who understand the codes. The more popular arts—song lyrics and comic strips for example—are also capable of serious comment on the human condition. Yet such faith expressions for the masses tend to be evanescent and ultimately incoherent in their total effect. They come and go with the commercial fortunes of creators and performers in a fiercely competitive market.

We live, moreover, in a time when confidence in Enlightenment reason as a potentially universal, if secular, perspective sustained by the march of democracy, technology, and science has drastically waned. Enlightenment claims are not only going out of style, but today they are also under devastating philosophical attack from deconstructionists, neopragmatists, theologians, and others.[2] For many it now appears that the rational style that in various ways inspired French *philosophes*, founding fathers, and two centuries of different sorts of secular humanists, is more the expressive artifact of a particular tract of human experience than it is a way of thinking characteristic of the human as such. Something more, even, than the West's body of literary, political, and scientific achievement, must underlie our confidence that language and reasoning are not in vain: that our words somehow have a relationship to what is ultimately true about the world.

In this situation religious bodies have an enormous opportunity to serve human well-being and thereby their own. Only religious traditions and the communities that sustain and are sustained by them can articulate depth concerns for the many with coherence and staying power. There is, in fact, a widespread impulse today to revisit ancient traditions in search of symbols capable of binding communities together and sustaining a moral vision of the universe. In a world whose communication networks are allergic to spiritual substance, faith communities can become the social spaces in which questions impossible for secular human beings even to formulate on their own can continue to be asked. If religious communities do not keep ultimate questions alive as issues for human beings, there will be no one to listen to the answers they have to offer.

But there are dangers that go with this opportunity. The impulse to recover tradition may lead only to new and fractious fundamentalisms. What comes out may be unimaginative parochialism or religiously tinged ethnic awareness, functioning largely for self-protection and self-esteem. If ancient traditions are to be recovered, they must come to be understood in a new way. Historic faith traditions can no longer represent themselves as one-possibility interpretations of the world, standpoints which make their adherents superior to others or give them special access to truth. It is plain, even for many of those seeking to repristinate the old ways of life, that no such way is the sole valid possibility for human beings. The closer one is to the life of actual people, the clearer this is.

Christians live on the same city blocks with Christians of quite different traditions, practices, and confessional positions, not to speak of Moslems, Jews, "new age" cultists, secular humanists, and a host of others. This fact confronts us anew with the need to live our own particular tradition of faith with full respect for those who live other traditions or no apparent tradition at all. Particularity in faith expression must coexist now with knowledge of the relativity of all such forms of faith. But *can* religious communities mediate their traditional content and sustain their members' loyalty while acknowledging that their versions of truth are not absolute? *Can* anyone really live with devotion and commitment in such a "second naiveté"?[3]

Our answers to these questions, whatever forms they may take, need to press toward a new, post-Enlightenment conception of human universality, one that does not depend on the notion that all educated human beings will believe and think in the same way. We must now think in terms of an unending *conversation* between divergent yet interacting symbolizations of human depth and destiny. The human world, not merely the world of religious communities, needs to think of itself as a dialogical communion of many spiritual cultures. Final truth can only be a truth about this dialogue itself, not a fixed conception of reality sustained by some one culture which holds symbolic and technological hegemony over all the others.

2. Ecclesiology in a New Key

How may Christian churches prepare themselves for a constructive role in this new situation? How may Christian thought and practice generate ideas which can be fruitful, yet not prescriptive or dominating, for the dialogue of all religious traditions? The issues involved here engage the whole range of theological disciplines: anthropology, Christology, ethics, eschatology, and more. But the heart of the matter, I argue, lies in our conception of the socio-historical reality, the concrete form of life, which mediates faith in the God of Jesus

Christ. In theological shorthand, the indispensable question has to do with *ecclesiology*.

My use of this word needs some explanation. The term has connotations of institutionalism and prelacy, and perhaps also of precious self-concern.[5] Many persons will think of competing claims by religious bodies to be the "true church," or of the "marks" which are said to make a communion or congregation authentic. Others will think of conceptions of church governance, or of the relationships between the church and the civil order, or of the strategic and programmatic considerations which occupy church leaders. Some will even think of the claim that the church is a body "outside of which there is no salvation." The classical categories for speaking of the church—visibility and invisibility, validity and efficacity, "right" preaching and celebration, apostolicity as episcopal succession or faithfulness to teaching, and so on—were formulated to address questions such as these. We dare not fail to learn the lessons they teach. But the ecclesiology I have in mind is defined in fundamentally theological, rather than largely institutional, terms. It is a discipline which asks what the message of Jesus Christ means as expressed in the form of a community. Such an ecclesiology looks at the churches' forms of governance, life together, and corporate witness as a primary means by which the gospel is lived and communicated. Ecclesiology becomes the normative study of communities which make social and symbolic space in the world for the message of Jesus Christ. In such a perspective, ecclesiology becomes far more than an afterthought—far more than the institutional outworking of truths reached in other ways. It becomes fundamental to Christian theological reflection as such.

Seen as "fundamental theology,"[6] ecclesiology concerns the nature of the social space which makes language about God, and therefore faith itself, possible. What sort of community can sponsor and sustain a kind of discourse which employs, but transcends the limits of, that space's characteristic imagery, concepts, language, and action patterns toward some sort of signification of the absolute? If theology itself, by definition, is discourse which regulates the language and activity of a religious community, then there must be some quality of the social space that the community defines and represents which permits us to understand this discourse as pointing beyond itself. Theology does not become "language about God" on the basis of its contents or argumentative strategies alone, as if human discourse could lift itself to God by its own bootstraps. It becomes language about God because it is the language of a certain kind of community. Hence theology's root question is whether, in the light of what we know today about the relativity of cultures, a community in and through which the God of Jesus Christ becomes present within history's contingencies can even be *conceived*. Only then can we ask if such communities are *possible* under the conditions of postmodernity, and, if so, whether such a community actually *exists*. Ecclesiology becomes a radical, front-of-the-book inquiry. It pursues the nature of and the conditions of possibility in history for the "beloved community"[7] itself. What sort of human gathering, if any, can possibly make space for God in the world today?

Churches provide the world with language and symbols that keep the *question* of God open. In that respect their function is indispensable. But the validation of what these expressions assert about God must rest on something more. I will contend that this "more" is the notion of humanity as a spiritual communion, a space of God's dwelling, which transcends not only the churches but also all other bodies and institutions which make religious claims. I conceive of this notion of a spiritual communion, signified in many different ways, as an alternative to the discredited idea of a humanity defined by participation in Enlightenment-style rational discourse. Churches need to see themselves as participating in this larger communion in such a way that they can be signs, sacraments, or instruments of it. In that way specific vocabularies of transcendence cease to be seen as absolute in themselves, but can be understood as expressions *of* the absolute. Particular religious symbols are validated through participation in a larger dialogue of symbols whose truth inheres in the trajectory of the dialogue itself. The *idea* of a human communion in God, which provides a frame of reference for this dialogue, needs to be present *in* the self-understanding of each participating body.

The possibility of a genuine dialogue of traditions (not belief that all religions are ultimately expressions of the same thing) requires a transcendental ground: a theism both needed to "underwrite" the coherence of such dialogical relationships and yet beyond our ability to comprehend fully. I believe that a theology of the Word of God, which sees humanity and indeed all creation as *creatura verbi divini*, has the potential for precisely this insight. A theology of the Word can grasp the sense of such "underwriting." It is a theology that guarantees, on the ground of its belief in Christ as *logos*, that the realm of human discourse is a world of ultimate sense and that it is not fruitless to pursue a dialogue of metaphors of ultimacy on this basis. Christians will say that this is because humankind is called to be a spiritual community in which God dwells as Word incarnate, incorporating human spirit into Holy Spirit. Churches need to see themselves as expressive embodiments of this truth. To be prepared for a human future, to make a worthy contribution to it, the churches must learn to live with passion and conviction as distinctive faith communities which signify this truth alongside communities whose traditions also do so in very different ways. To claim that the faith stories of different religious groups are distinctive subplots within a single cosmic narrative is itself an act of faith—that God is somehow the sponsor of the dialogue of faith expressions.

3. *The People of God and Their Institutions*

The notion of humanity coming-to-be as a spiritual community needs a metaphor. Good metaphors can instigate conceptual models of the reality they are meant to reach. The biblical tradition offers several possibilities: kingdom of God, household of God, city of God, people of God. There are other expressions derived at least in part from biblical insights: the

fullness of humanity (Gregory of Nyssa), a kingdom of ends
(Immanuel Kant), the beloved community (Josiah Royce), the
spiritual commonwealth (Walter Rauschenbusch), a coalition
of hope (J. B. Metz), the household of life (Konrad Raiser).[8]
Each of these metaphors sees God's purpose for humankind
as represented, one way or another, by a vision of community
or commonwealth. Each with its particular pattern of usage,
related imagery, and associations offers advantages and
disadvantages for our purpose. For this book, I have chosen
the last-named biblical possibility: the notion of a *people*
representing God's gathering and covenanting presence on
earth. My reasons for this choice will become clearer as the
exposition unfolds. Suffice it to say now that "people of God"
seems the most concretely (as opposed to idealistically) inclusive of the possibilities, the most sociologically realistic, and at
least as resistant as most of the other images to monarchical,
imperial, or patriarchal overtones.[9] I am aware, of course,
that even this image has drawbacks, mainly related, I think,
to certain patterns of misuse. Obviously I do not take "people
of God" in the "German Christian" sense of *Volk* or in the
long-standing American or the more recent Afrikaans sense of
being a "chosen people" over against other people. People of
God for me is the human race to the extent that it belongs to
God by being a place of God's dwelling in the Spirit. I reach
this point by following the trajectory of the scriptural notion
of God's people, from its parochial beginnings in certain
strands of the literature of early Israel, and its equally parochial usages in some of the literature of early Christianity, to
reach the vision of a human community which is the habita-
tion of God on earth. If there is a passage which puts words
to this fulfillment, it is Rev. 21:3:

> Behold, the dwelling place of God is with human beings. God
> will dwell with them and they shall be God's people. And God
> in person shall be with them and be their God.[10]

In the light of this promised fulfillment, I bring a particular
sense of the term "people of God" to focus. I see in this

expression far more than a useful synonym for the institutional church, more than a term for all the Christians who happen to live in a particular place, or even for all the Christians on earth. Yet I do not simply say that all human beings are people of God by virtue of their having been created for that destiny. By "people of God" in this book I intend that company of human beings which at any given moment and in any particular circumstance anticipates the vision of Rev. 21:3 by embodying the gathering, shaping energy of the Holy Spirit of God in history. The meaning I intend comes close to that of the "communion of saints," provided we understand that no faith community, Christian or otherwise, has a monopoly in the task of making the saints of God visible on earth. In this usage, the expression "people of God" points not to the church as institution but rather to a gathering of human beings which transcends that institution and all other such bodies making religious claims.

Joseph Haroutunian would often speak of "the people of God and their institutions."[11] The institution belongs to the people rather than the other way around. While the institution as such may be rather closely defined, the people are those called by God and energized by the Holy Spirit in ways our categories cannot fully comprehend. Christians have understood the precise relation between visible churches and the grace-filled community of the Holy Spirit in many different ways. They have expressed their insights in many different and sometimes conflicting vocabularies. It could be that today we are beginning to transcend these fields of battle toward a new, universal understanding of the "people." Clearly the "membership" (if that is the right term) of such a "people" can never be precisely or even approximately known. Its composition may well change from one occasion to another. Nevertheless, the "sense" or notion of such a people becomes very real to those who seek to grasp the calling of religious communities in a global human community searching for spiritual communion in a struggle for justice and peace.

Here, perhaps, is a Christian contribution to interreligious dialogue which could help all religious traditions take part in that dialogue in a way that could serve their own interests and those of humanity as well. I see Christian congregations living side by side with communities belonging to other religious traditions in the conviction that they are called to make such a communion of humankind in the Spirit tangible in diverse but ultimately compatible ways. The different religious bodies will no doubt express this conviction, if they hold it at all, in a variety of vocabularies and symbolic expressions. The sense of "a people" plays a role, for example, in both the Jewish and Islamic traditions. It is important in this invitation to dialogue that no tradition seek to impose its sense of the term on any other, and indeed that the framing of the question itself not presuppose any one tradition's vision. I trust that "the sense of a people" will be embodied best in the end not by watering down each tradition but by going deeper into its fundamental intentions. I cannot speak, of course, for any religious tradition but my own as I understand it. But I consider persons of other faiths to be my brothers and sisters in a common search for spiritual community. I hope they will understand me, and I them, but I cannot speak *for* them. Whether anything like this sense of universal peoplehood in the Spirit can find resonance in the other great religious traditions of humankind remains to be seen. I hope that it can. Here lies a topic for further serious inquiry, hopefully inquiry pursued in a shared dialogue based on mutual respect and serious listening.

4. An Overview of the Argument

The issues I have raised tend to ramify uncontrollably. No single volume can do justice to them, and this book will certainly not try. Instead, I will seek to traverse these fields of concern along a particular path: one designed to find a way to think ecclesiologically in and for the global human civilization that, for good or ill, is coming into being before our eyes. My argument assumes that the churches as we know them still have the potential for making faith articulate for such a world, and thereby for influencing that world profoundly. It also assumes that it is important how the churches *think* about what they do. The way in which a question is initially framed has impact on what is eventually done about it. This book is organized accordingly. From an interpretation of the situation of the churches and their people as they are (chapters 1 and 2), I move to new ways of seeing some old theological questions (chapters 3 and 4), and eventually to some of the ecumenical (chapter 5) and public (chapter 6) consequences of seeing matters in this way.

One needs to begin with an image which can hold the appropriate perspectives and questions together. A picture which suggests itself is that of the enormously diverse crowd in St. Peter's Square, gathered in architectural precincts which speak eloquently of Rome's historic claim to universality (chapter 1). Yet, if our imaginations can shake loose from the symbolism of the stones, we can begin to see the actual character of the crowd—its many patterns of belief, the variety of situations from which its members come, its connections with myriad others inside the institutional church and without. From the perspective of this people, as it were "from below" (Leonardo Boff), I try to reinvent the very idea of a universal church. How well does the term "people of God" serve as a vehicle for this purpose? There are warrants for such a usage in the history of the term in the Bible, and also in the valuable treatments of this subject in the Vatican II documents *Lumen Gentium* and *Gaudium et Spes*. In these texts a new ecclesiology stands alongside an older one. The full import of the new still waits to break upon the consciousness of the *oikoumene*. If the many churches are to become the one church in a great "communion of communions," and if they are to serve the coming of a truly human future, then the notion of a global people articulating God's reign in the very character of its theological and ethical discourse needs to play a regulative role in and for the thinking of each participating traditioned community.

An approach to ecclesiology which takes into account the actual people, as well as their myriad connections to worlds beyond the churches' borders, requires a large measure of sociological realism (chapter 2). For this purpose, the vision of

Ernst Troeltsch, and especially his way of wrestling with the problems of historical relativity, is still valuable. Much of what Troeltsch saw in 1912 is still true of our situation today. The notion of tradition itself has become difficult and problematic. Pluralism of religious expression reigns both within the churches and outside. Theological conceptualization, especially in Protestantism, is in disarray. Yet at the very same time, new forms of religious community, some possessed of great vitality, are springing up: neomonastic communities, base communities, politically engaged congregations, and liturgical gatherings. These form around the agendas of women, of movements representing Native American, African, Hispanic, Asian and other identities, and of special interest groups of many kinds.

These circumstances demand an ecclesiology based not on the self-understandings and needs of ecclesiastical institutions as such, but rather on the character of God's humanity in process of being gathered (chapter 3). The ecclesiology we need will be one capable of detecting and honoring the gathering work of the Spirit of God among the people, a discovery that will quickly require us to think about human life and history irrespective of ecclesiastical boundaries. When we find the needed perspective we will also discover traces of a much larger spiritual commonwealth, a global community of moral discourse corresponding to the reach of God's reign and worthy of the term "people of God." Pursuing such traces, we will need to enlist several kinds of hermeneutically informed social theory (Pierce, Mead, Wittgenstein, Geertz, Lakoff and Johnson, Ricoeur). The signs of peoplehood under God are undetectable to objectifying and positivist forms of social inquiry. The signs which the churches are called to gather to visibility lie rather in the subtle things that gatherings of human beings "say" by being what they are. In the perspective of this book, the churches are seen as spaces of signification which selectively discern patterns of the transforming presence of God in society and articulate them for the world's understanding. The churches can become signs of the coming people of God by decoding the messages of that people's reality inscribed in the society both in them and around them, and by combining those messages in liturgy, proclamation, and moral witness in such a way that they can be seen and heard both within the faith community and beyond it. The churches can be like seismic detectors of the gathering work of the Spirit in human life. Indeed, ecclesiology itself can become a kind of critical social theory. It can explain how the human community can be *interpreted* in its potential for peoplehood by being gathered into congregations. These congregations maintain their identities through a kind of practical reasoning or *phronesis* in which this critical hermeneutic of society is put to use.

Such a direction in ecclesiology is bound to have important consequences. As a new kind of fundamental theology, it joins contemporary "postliberal" thinking about the nature and function of doctrine (chapter 4). The problem of the reality reference of theological propositions can now be seen in fresh perspective. "Real presence" is located in the social reality of the church itself. The argument joins forces with the view (George Lindbeck) which sees doctrines as rules for communal thought and action. Doctrines become regulative ideas which "appresent," in Husserl's sense, the full meaning of realities which each faith community makes partly present in its life. These communities are like texts. The "necessary possibility" of God is needed to "underwrite" (George Steiner) the coherence of a dialogue between them. A further development of thinking about the "economic" Trinity, overcoming monarchical and patriarchal metaphors for God (Thomas Parker), is needed to see how human spirit is taken up into Holy Spirit in visible figures, shapes, or gestalts (Peter Hodgson). We can see that the Holy Spirit generates realms of "resonance" (Michael Welker) in which faith communities may have a dialogue of depth languages through which the sense of a people of God begins to appear.

Such a perspective has important implications for ecumenism (chapter 5). We need to press toward a truly inclusive understanding of the notion of catholicity, of the wholeness of

God's gathering of a people in history to which particular faith communities bear witness. Such insight is already present in the work of the World Council of Churches Commission on Faith and Order. Here we have not only a dialogue among existing ecclesiological perspectives, but also the emergence of a new "tradition" marking progress in realizing and embodying the *Una Sancta*. This headway results in part from the use of an "intercontextual method" that brings into the dialogue the actual experience of faith communities formed in particular places around particular issues: racism, sexism, the attainment of a peaceful and just society. These inquiries show what it means to see the churches as sacraments, signs, and instruments of humanity's potential for union with God and for unity as a spiritual community. The sense of a people of God is implied in this progress and has the potential for opening the way to a genuinely conciliar relationship among the churches.

Finally, these perspectives bear on the role of the churches in a wider human conversation (chapter 6). The memory of the Holocaust casts its shadow over all visions of human mutuality. Adolph Eichmann's "thoughtlessness" (Hannah Arendt) meant that he and countless others lacked the symbolic means of linking persons of other religions and cultures with themselves in fields of spiritual resonance. Today's technologically interdependent world institutionalizes individualism and selfishness, particularly in the West. This in turn undercuts covenantal responsibility and communion. Now we are challenged by the "theory of communicative action" (Jürgen Habermas), an Enlightenment-based projection of human rationality upon the social sphere. What role might religious communities have in such a vision of the human world? Far from being marginalized, or even excluded, traditioned communities capable of symbolizing the human condition in depth and also capable of communicating with one another are needed for the success of "communicative action" in any form. The human conversation is not a matter of determining who "has the better argument." It is a matter of acting out relationships of such quality that truth inheres in the fact of the conversation itself. The dialogue fragmentarily discerns gestalts and configurations (Peter Hodgson) of the Spirit in the human life world, coming at certain times and places to manifest a fragile communion. The church-based network of responsibility which saved Jews from the Gestapo in the French village of Le Chambon-sur-Lignon in World War II is an example. We try to embody this fragile communion of human beings in political institutions, but institutions as such cannot guarantee that justice and compassion will be present. The presence of churches and other religious communities in the human conversation keeps alive the vision of that conversation's ultimately spiritual goal.

The next step in this argument lies beyond the limits of the present book. Given the vision of a Christian ecclesiology embodying the "sense" of a much larger, more inclusive people of God, we must begin to ask about the distinctive Christian contribution to the dialogue. In what particular ways do Christian communities act as signs, sacraments, or instruments of humanity's union *with* God and of humanity as a global communion *in* God? The first answer, of course, is that they do so in as many ways as they interact with the many cultures of humankind. But is there not some particular content, something unique in the relationship to Jesus Christ? Does it not mean something specifiable that the sign of the Spirit of God is Jesus Christ "come in the flesh" (1 John 4:2)? Yes, I believe it does. And I believe that, once articulated, that specificity will be very recognizable to those who know Jesus as the infinitely attractive place-holder for God in human history. But this recognizable identity needs to be verified by means of a socio-hermeneutical inquiry into the nature of the early "Jesus community," and of the apostolic gatherings which followed from it, as social spaces in which God became present as Spirit and Word of life. This is a project beyond the scope of these pages. But I intend to try something like it in the near future.

5. A Vision: To What Ends?

A friend of former years, having listened to a colleague's presentation quite long enough, would sometimes mutter, "Ach, was *wünchst* der Mann?" By this I think he meant: "What does this person want to see *happen* in the world, in the wake of all these words?" Readers who have come this far deserve my own answer to this question.

I want to see a vision of the people of God grasped by the churches and then lived out. The essential point is that the churches and other religious communities should go deeply into their resources for ways of living distinctively *traditioned* lives for the sake of the *whole* of human life. I believe that living for the vision of a human community understood as God's dwelling place on earth requires neither the subjugation of all other religious traditions by one, nor the watering down of all particular faiths into a vague global spirituality of the many. I believe that particular traditions can discover in their own identities and resources a way to share the vision of a human future together.

It will be said that the churches are far from ready for such a message. In North America at least, their numerical decline, their own internal problems, are such that they may not be able to hear, let alone respond, to such a vision. Yet this could be a propitious time for a global ecclesiology grounded in a wider vision of peoplehood, if one could be clearly stated. The churches, problems notwithstanding, seem to be yearning for clarity about their reasons for being. In the midst of fragmentation and mutual distrust between ideological caucuses, racial/ethnic communities, and special interest groups, in the seeming absence of vision and often of adequate leadership, we desperately need a new sense of what the churches are called to be and do. We are witnessing the retreat of many church bodies into confessional isolation, into nostalgic wallowing in half-understood traditional formulas. Might something better emerge from this than what we probably deserve? Could the return to tradition deepen rather than undermine the churches' sense of calling to become a church for the future of humankind?

The only way for a faith tradition to test such a vision, or even to learn what it really means, is to try to practice it concretely. Neither for Christians nor for others is this something that can simply be arranged administratively. In such matters it is hard to design and carry out controlled experiments! History itself is the judge, and that is not in our control. The adoption of new creedal and liturgical formulas in the early church could take hundreds of years. But short of that, I think that the position sketched here, if indeed it is cogent and coherent, could at least be tested provisionally by Christians at two levels of the churches' life. There could be a local, congregational testing of "the sense of a people," and a more ecumenical, universal working out of the implications of the idea.

Evaluation of the vision at the level of local practice would begin with translation into the language of the people themselves. Could one design a workable program of congregational catechesis around this proposal? Could the idea be coherently embodied in a form of life? Could that form of life function persuasively as a vehicle for the Christian message in its fullness in a manner also open to the claims of other faiths? One might try to answer this question out of one's head, but the only real answer would come from practical experimentation. Would the actual people, those constituting today's *sensus fidelium*, such as it is, recognize something authentic, something ringing true, something energizing here? Much would depend on the skill of pastoral leadership: something that theologians in their studies ought to respect more than they do. Without actual congregations led by skilled pastors, theological ideas have no tangible place to be in the world.

I hope that what I say in this book will also have some resonance in the ecumenical movement. That movement, of course, appears at the moment to reflect some of the theological amnesia combined with institutional self-destructiveness of its participating bodies. The National Council of Churches in the U.S.A. has been busy for the past few years shaking itself apart with internal strife and public dispute. Initiatives, such as the Consultation on Church Union, have lived on, unfulfilled, into a situation in which their theological motivations are little understood.

The recent World Council of Churches Seventh Assembly at Canberra, Australia, seems to have been both a great spiritual experience for those present and a further step in the decay of the distinctive theological and ecclesiastical understandings generated by a half-century of devoted dialogical work, understandings on which the Council as such has been dependent over the years. A daring keynote address by a young Korean Presbyterian woman theologian lifted hearts and spirits, yet threatened to divide the Assembly over what some took to be a threat to orthodoxy.[12] Worship under the great "tent of meeting" movingly invoked the work of the Spirit in all creation. Nevertheless, the Assembly marked a seeming abandonment of, or at least failure to understand, the goal of visible unity-in-diversity of the global church. Engagement with the problems of the world—injustice, oppression, the war in the Gulf—seemed to overwhelm serious thought about the community of faith in whose global reality alone such problems might effectively be addressed.

The Roman Catholic community at least has the advantage of sustaining a more coherent context for theological discourse than any to be found in Protestantism. The deliverances of Vatican II still function as a point of reference when the conclusions of several World Council of Churches assemblies have long since been forgotten. By far the most important and authoritative treatment of the "people of God" theme occurs in *Lumen Gentium* where much of the potential of that theme drawn out in these pages is hinted at or present by implication. The relative coherence of Roman Catholic dialogue, of course, does not mean an absence of diversity and controversy. In some ways the division between the conservative and progressive wings of Roman Catholicism is as deep as any such rift in Christendom. But the structure of the Church, its tradition and teaching authority, tends to keep the different positions at least within shouting distance of each other, an advantage that Protestantism has largely lost.

Perhaps it is providential that the World Council of

Churches Commission on Faith and Order is in the early stages of a new study of the nature of the church itself. That study needs to stay in touch with the churches' traditions and with recent hard-won achievements in interchurch dialogue and yet also listen to new voices. Above all, the study needs to seek clarity about the historical role of the churches, and of the universal church to which their existence points, in the providence of God. If the gathering and sustenance of the church is the work of the Holy Spirit, then ecclesiology needs to be rooted in an understanding of God's presence in history through the Spirit's culture-transforming power. This book seeks to make a contribution to that Faith and Order study.

As I write, less than a decade separates us from the end of one Christian millennium and the beginning of another. In one sense, of course, the turn of the millennia is only an accident of our base-ten numbering system. But human beings have a way of thinking in terms of decades, centuries, and even longer epochs. Indeed, in the minds of some, the "third millennium" has already begun, with signs and portents we only partly understand. Certainly we wonder where the world will be, spiritually and intellectually, when January 1, 2001, actually dawns. The present Pope refers to the millennial moment repeatedly in public statements.[13] We think he means to be alive when the time comes!

Is it possible to hope that the Roman Catholic Holy Year already being prepared for that time could be cooperatively accompanied by a genuinely ecumenical series of events? Could a Roman Catholic synod of bishops, an Assembly of the World Council of Churches, a pan-Orthodox Congress, a world meeting of evangelicals and Pentecostals, gatherings of the world confessional bodies, and perhaps other events take place at the same time in ways both independent and interrelated? Could there be an element of common agenda, as well as distinctive items of business, in these meetings? Could there be Kirchentag-type assemblies, including a few in St. Peter's Square itself, in which Christians of all communions could be joined by representatives of other world faiths?[14] What new way of thinking about God's people might such encounters make possible, as well as meaningful for the human race?

I

A Meditation in
St. Peter's Square

In my mind's eye, I am part of an immense throng assembled in what is arguably the greatest outdoor architectural space in the Western world. Bernini's semicircular colonnades march four abreast on both sides of our multitude, enclosing us as if in parentheses. Before us stands the massive facade of St. Peter's Basilica. In the opposite direction is a broad opening, through which one may catch glimpses down the hopefully named Via della Conziliazione, toward the dirty Tiber and the busy metropolis beyond.

This is liminal space. We are gathered on a cobblestoned threshold which links the sacred with the secular, the *templum* with the *pro-fanum*. And this is also liminal time. We are waiting in a suspended moment, in a "now" abstracted from the diurnal stream, for a figure in white to appear at an upper window and say a few words of greeting and blessing which will seem for an instant to turn this milling mass into something more than a motley gathering of tourists and pilgrims. But the moment will quickly pass. We will disperse, leaving the Square once more to its knotting and unravelling

skeins of visitors, its souvenir sellers and bus drivers, its occa-
sional minor functionary enroute with no visible means of
support (black rain poncho draped nearly to the ground over
Vespa scooter), its sense, especially when nearly empty, of
centuries-long tradition, and yet also of daily rejuvenation as
new throngs arrive to wait and to share the moment together.

Who are we here today? I am struck by the many human
worlds we represent. The Berninian colonnades are permeable: pedestrians of every persuasion freely come and go.
Priests from Chicago, women religious from Germany, bus-
loads of pilgrims from Spain, Protestants returning from "ho-
lyland" tours, seminary professors on sabbatical leave, tourists of every description. Of one thing I am certain: for most
participants in this aggregation of humanity, drawn here by
some strange attraction, the ecclesiastical tradition which this
place formally represents is only half the story. Each person
has his or her own particular reasons for being here. Some are
on pious pilgrimages. Others' faith is mainly a love of Renais-
sance art. For still others, this may be just a prearranged stop
on the tour itinerary. Even if we are active Catholics, or
Protestants, or Orthodox, we represent almost as many private or familial versions of Christian faith as we are in number. We have different degrees of faith commitment, different
kinds of relationship with the organized church. We represent
different interactions, and often syncretisms, with a variety of
cultures. We have profoundly differing views of what ways of
life and witness in the world our faith requires. Some of us are
obedient to the teachings of our communions and some are
not. Some of us come from homogeneous neighborhoods.
Most come from places where Catholics, Protestants, Jews,
Moslems, Buddhists, secular humanists, new age religionists,
various sorts of atheists, and persons of many other religious
or irreligious commitments live side by side as neighbors. We
are, in short, an incredibly diverse assembly whose many
ways of life have somehow brought us, at least for a moment,
into proximity with orthodox traditions of faith as taught by
prelates and theologians. The people of God, insofar as they

can be seen in a crowd like this one, are an aggregation of diverse lives, cultures, nations, worlds. Through their human links across the globe they are in touch with myriad other such communities and gatherings. Each of these forms of life is *sui generis*. Each has its own relation, or lack of relation, to what the church and the churches have for centuries formally believed and taught.

Yet all these people are gathered today in a space heavy with historic and symbolic import. For Roman Catholics, diverse as they are, this place remains a kind of holy ground, a setting for resplendent ceremonial occasions, an extraterritorial terrain between the Basilica and the city beckoning all comers to the communion of the See of St. Peter. This is, after all, a space which bears a universal claim. Here as nowhere else on earth the very stones proclaim the unity possible to human beings if they will submit themselves to that spiritual jurisdiction. But not all do. Protestants in this city and elsewhere have been heard to compare Bernini's colonnades to the claws of a crab, ready to trap the unwary who gaze upward so steadily that they forget the dangerous ground on which they are standing. Between these spiritual worlds there remains a gulf whose implications cannot be ignored.

But there is another way altogether of seeing this place with its variegated crowd of pilgrims. If there *is* a universal church, if the idea makes any sense at all, we will more likely begin to find its reality down here among the people than in the stones and statues around them or in the prelatical apartments above them. After all, one can imagine the ground plan of this sheltering space (its narrow portals leading upward into the basilica, its wide opening leading downward to the city) as a womb. This space, and others analogous to it, could give birth to a new humanity made alive in the Spirit, a humanity needing a spiritual dwelling place on earth perhaps very different from this one: a church open to a universality given by God's own transforming presence in the world.

1. Revisioning the Universal Church: The View from Below

I want, if I can, to imagine this crowd of pilgrims, tourists, souvenir hawkers, and pickpockets as something more than the mundane reality it now is. I will try to portray it as having the potential to be a representative assembly of that global people which, in the trajectory of biblical vision, the Holy Spirit is calling together through history as the visible expression of God's reign. Within this larger perspective, I hope to construct an understanding of the church—an ecclesiology— in which the *sense* of such a universal people functions as the essential regulative idea. Instead of beginning our reasoning with the position of any one of the great communions, or even with the promising yet frustrating ecumenical conversations going on among them, I want to reconceive the very *idea* of the universal church from down here on the cobblestones, from a place among the people.

Joseph Haroutunian, we have already seen, liked to speak of "the people of God and their institutions."[1] Carrying forward that theme, we should think of the term "people of God," not as a genial synonym for members and adherents of churches, but as a much more inclusive ideal of human community—including persons of many cultures and commitments—in process of becoming visible, however partially and fragmentarily, *through* churches and, perhaps, in other ways as well. We should conceive this larger human community as the work of the Holy Spirit in history, as a trans-institutional communion of saints seeking various forms of concrete expression. The sense, the idea or notion, of such a people could begin to play its role *in* ecclesiological reasoning. The *idea* of such a people of God, transcending church institutions, but especially manifest in them, could in time transform the way the churches think about themselves. In such a changed perspective could lie a way for the many churches to begin to see themselves as the church, a universal communion of communions living for the human future.

In St. Peter's Square we can see both what is and what

might come to be. What is actually going on among people and communities of faith today is hardly describable or containable within the churches' traditional self-understandings. But out of this confused situation could come a much wider and richer understanding of the Spirit's work in history. Let us first look at the reality and then at the possibility.

If we describe analytically what has just been presented imaginatively, we will sense the distance that separates the people from the ecclesiastical polities in whose precincts they gather. We find a poor fit between the doctrinal and ethical teachings of the churches on the one hand, and the actual beliefs and practices of many who consider themselves among the faithful on the other. Classical doctrinal formulas and canonical regulations play little role in the minds, not to speak of the lives, of most Presbyterians, Episcopalians, Lutherans, Roman Catholics or other kinds of Christians. Many communicants may not understand, let alone follow, the teachings of their churches about contraception or abortion or economic justice or just war. Moreover, we see that many who hold some form of belief in Jesus Christ have no form of participation or membership in a church. As Wolfhart Pannenberg has argued, there are vast numbers of "churchless Christians" who, in their own ways, are as serious and devout as those inside, but do not find organized churches to their liking.[2] These are often persons whom we would have difficulty ruling outside the faith if the basis of comparison were the faith and practice of actual communicants or "members."

There are "churchless Christians" inside the churches, too. Many of those who do affiliate with congregations do so with no particular loyalty to any given communion, or even to those in the parish around them. They consider themselves to be Christians in a general sense and join the congregation that suits them at any given place or time. This is true especially among mobile Protestants in North America, although the phenomenon is spreading, especially among those who understand themselves to represent a non-denominational or transdenominational evangelicalism. This adaptable form of Christian life, among other things, unreflectively acts out the truth that baptism is a rite of entry into something more inclusive than the institutional church, congregation, or communion in which the sacrament is administered. While the notion of a community of the baptized may play little role in the thinking of these individualistic nomads, it points to a reality with which the churches have not as yet been able to come to terms.

Life within the church, furthermore, if seriously thought through, tends to point people beyond the institution. For many of the most reflective it is clear that networks of concern and activity in the spirit of Christ extend beyond the visible boundaries of the churches and even of identifiable Christian faith. To profess this faith today is often to be involved with one's neighbors whatever their faith or unfaith, and often to discover deep communion with persons with religious commitments quite different from one's own. More and more congregations, especially in liberal circles, have come to be meeting places of persons with various sorts of specific concerns in which they are allied with persons and movements outside the church as such. One cannot be serious about peacemaking, or environmentalism, or justice issues, or medical ethics, or any of a hundred other concerns, without forging spiritual alliances with others who have the same commitments outside ecclesiastical boundaries, and without bringing the concerns of those outside inside.

And finally, there are new Christian communities springing up which stress such relationships: which identify the work of the Spirit with the liberation of "the people" in new senses of that term. Christian gatherings specifically focused on this or that agenda for social transformation have begun to abound. One thinks of Christian feminist and womanist groups, worshiping communities focused on the liberation of racial/ethnic peoples in North American, Latin American, African and Asian "base communities," and all the rest. In each of these cases, it is clear that Christian tradition is being reformulated around one or another vision of who the people of God really are, of how and where the Spirit is at work. The poor and oppressed in general, or some particular community such as the Korean "Minjung" (which literally means "the people") are identified as the peculiar locus of God's saving work in history, the standpoint from which the gospel may most authentically be understood.

All this leads us to question whether the future of faith on this earth is safe in the hands of our traditional ecclesiastical institutions, or whether we must look to new social expressions of faith for the years to come. Of course it is clear that without the life of institutional churches over centuries there would be neither language in which to raise the questions we are now asking nor social space in which answers to these questions could begin to take form. There would be no tradition about a "people of God" to begin with. Josiah Royce would not have been able to write about a "beloved community."[3] The diverse gatherings of human beings we have described as standing in various relations to Christian faith would not be identifiable as such. Thus the object of this inquiry is not to idealize what is going on among the people or to assume that the present confused situation is itself an object of hope. Our intent is rather to ask some traditional ecclesiological questions, which only exist because the churches exist, from the people's *perspective*. It is to test certain traditional meanings from a standpoint down in the crowd and among the other multitudes this crowd represents.

By adopting such a new angle of vision for ecclesiological reasoning I hope to move that thinking toward a mode of openness to what the Holy Spirit is doing in unlikely persons and places. Above all I mean to bring the notion or *sense* of a people of God transcending the institutional churches *into* the reasoning processes *of* the churches. By thinking ecclesiologically in new social locations we may generate insights which will serve the churches' thinking about their own nature and mission. We will come closer to seeing the churches as institutions belonging to a larger movement of the people of God in history energized and directed by the power of the Holy Spirit.

In proposing this direction of thought, I am invoking precedents both ancient and modern. In many ways this proposal is a revised version of the ancient notion of the *sensus fidelium*, the conviction that the people possess an inherent wisdom borne of years of hearing the scriptures read and of participating in the liturgy, wisdom that enables them to judge what is and is not authentic teaching. This historic notion has played an important role in Christian thought and action. It is preserved today in the more democratic church polities. We also see it ritually in several liturgies for the consecration of a bishop, where the assembled people cry out, "He is worthy." Today, of course, we need an understanding of *sensus fidelium* that can speak to the new forms of disjunction between church polity and faithful people in the world: an understanding in which the "faithful" are both within the institution and beyond it and in which their understanding of the faith may be more a challenge to orthodoxy than a defense of it.

There are also contemporary parallels to this proposal. Intended here is a project very like that undertaken by several Latin American liberation theologians in relation to the well-known "base communities."[4] An example is the work of Leonardo Boff in *Ecclesiogenesis*.[5] Boff is not merely describing how base communities come into being. From the perspective of these communities, he is writing about the rebirth, the *palingenesia* of the church universal itself. Boff's work challenges his own communion, and particularly the Roman curia, because by its very nature it questions the prevailing conceptions of teaching authority and governance in Roman Catholicism. Boff's thinking implies an ecclesiological revisionism which is, for some, worse than mere heresy because it has dangerous implications for prevailing structures of ecclesiastical power. The present book, of course, is written from a North American Protestant rather than a Latin American Roman Catholic perspective, and takes into account a wider range of phenomena among the people of God. Base communities are not the only manifestations of peoples' faith with which we have to deal. We need to consider all the people-forming consequences of the presence of the gospel in the world. The churches have instigated forms of life together in the Spirit beyond their formal boundaries with which they now must come to terms.

What are the chances of success in such a project? There exist today conceptual resources not before available to the churches which may help us understand how a people of God can be discerned through criteria other than those of formal membership, admission to communion, or submission to authority, as defined in established ecclesiastical polities. Up to now, our thinking about persons, inside the church or out, whose patterns of association in faith do not fit the normal canons of ecclesial communion, has tended to run toward categories of religious individualism. It has been hard to think of those outside as belonging to a people of God in common with those within. Yet there are styles of sociological inquiry today which press beyond routine categories of institutional identity to ask about other kinds of human association which could be more expressive than routine parish participation of what it is to be a people under God. We can seek to sketch out a sort of "depth sociology" capable of finding the spiritual bonds—the forms of community in the spirit—which underlie, appear within, and at the same time encompass the visible churches we know.

One kind of depth sociology, as we shall see in chapter 3, is hermeneutical: it treats human association as inherently expressive, as text-like, and hence capable of being "read." With the Word become flesh as a key to decoding such associational texts, we can detect the gathering work of the Holy Spirit by *reading* the messages which various social realities transmit to their participants and to the world around them. Such a hermeneutical or interpretative style of social inquiry can help us detect people-formation in a variety of settings, within the precincts of the churches and also beyond, without being dependent on criteria for inclusion or good standing embodied in codes of canon law or in books of ecclesiastical discipline. When we are able to detect the expressive styles or life-forms of such peoplehood in the spirit, we will find that church polities and systems of doctrine as we know them fall well short of defining the limits, or even the essence, of this citizenship. Yet it is in the churches that the *question* of God's beloved community is raised and kept alive. And it is in the church that the question must in the end be answered.

2. People of God as Ecclesiological Metaphor

I have begun to use the term people of God to mean the whole communal reality, in the churches and beyond them, generated in the world by God's presence in Jesus Christ through the power of the Spirit. Christian congregations, I argue, hold open social and symbolic spaces in which this blessed community of humanity can become partially, fragmentarily, visible. The churches are not identical with God's people either as separate bodies or as taken together. The notion of a people of God is rather the context or horizon for practical reasoning in each specific community of faith. The *sense* of such a people should function as a regulative idea *in* the churches' thinking. It should be understood as a principle pointing the reasoning of congregations toward this larger horizon of God's people-gathering activity in the world.

But before going further we must ask, can "people of God" language, as found in Scripture, really bear this intended meaning? The terms people (*laos*) and people of God (*laos tou theou*) are common in both the Old Testament and the New, and the literature about them is well-known. Still, I believe there is something to be learned by looking at these passages once more. The biblical usage speaks of *a* people (*laos* or *ethnos*) as an ethnic or national community having its own culture and territory, its own collective identity. The individual is identified by the people to whom he or she is related. Humanity as such is "all the peoples" (plural) of the earth taken together. To identify one people as people of God is on the face of things to set it over against all other peoples in an exclusive sense.

This is exactly what happens in scores of Old Testament passages in which the people or God's people simply means Israel: this particular ethnic, political, or military reality. There is no use idealizing the intended meaning in most of these contexts. The best-known passage may be the words of Yahweh to Moses at Exod. 6:6-7:

> Say, therefore, to the people of Israel, "I am the Lord, and I will bring you out from under the burdens of the Egyptians, and I will deliver you from their bondage, and I will redeem you with an outstretched arm and with great acts of judgment, and I will take you for my people and I will be your God.

In all likelihood this, with other similar formulas, is part of the "J" epic edited by the scribes of the early monarchical period to legitimize Israel's national and cultic existence against other ancient Near Eastern "peoples."

But I will argue that the trajectory of biblical thought is toward increasing realization of what is really meant by a people *of God*. If one takes the latter words in their full force they mean not that God has chosen a particular nation for special privilege but rather that the presence and work of God in history has the effect of gathering a human community whose basis is God's mercy, and in which Torah is an instrument of justice and communal cohesion, not merely a monument to nationalistic particularism. The prophets constantly call Israel back to the original terms of the covenant. They dramatize the people's calling in the perspective of God's present and future rule over the nations.

For Hosea, the relation of the Lord to his wayward people will be like a new betrothal, an act of mercy (2:16-23). The basis of this new peoplehood will be steadfast love and knowledge of God, not sacrifice or burnt offerings (6:6). Jeremiah has a similar vision, if different language. "The days are coming" when God will make a new covenant with the houses of Israel and Judah: one in which the law will be within them and upon their hearts (31:31-34). Torah will no longer need to be taught or enforced in the ordinary social and juridical ways, although the intent to address concrete political realities will remain. Hosea and Jeremiah are moving toward a spiritual understanding of peoplehood which cannot simply be identified with existing forms of religious community. Historic Israel, in the prophets' vision, points toward this possibility but does not yet embody it. The people of Hosea's or Jeremiah's new covenant is *like* a political or ethnic community with its coherence and cohesiveness. But the vision transcends the possibility of communities founded on the basis of ethnic or legal or geographical affinity. Already in these prophets, and in others, the usage of the word "people" moves from being literal to being figurative or metaphorical.

New Testament usage moves further in the same direction. Paul wrestles with the implications of his Gentile mission by reframing and reinterpreting Hosea's words. In Rom. 9:25-26, we read that God has called his people not only from historic Israel, but also from other nations.

> Those who were not my people I will call "my people". . . .
> And in the very place it was said to them, "You are not my people," they will be called sons of the living God.

Paul's move is logical. If the essence of the new peoplehood is no longer historic, cultural, or legal, if the people of God is now a work of divine grace and mercy which transforms the fabric of relationships, then there is no reason not to include those Gentiles in whom this divine work may be discerned. The Gentiles who did not pursue righteousness in the sense of obedience to Torah have nonetheless attained it by God's grace received in faith. Paul works out the astounding implications of all this in Romans 9-11. The essential point is that there is no way of grasping all that people of God now means within the limits of any one community of faith. The ongoing dialectic between Gentiles and Jews within God's gracious purpose of gathering the elect (Rom. 11:7) means that, for now, no single religious body is sufficient to make visible all that God is doing. Judaism as such remains in the picture, and the new Jewish-Gentile community in Christ is only beginning to find its appropriate forms of life.

To somewhat the same effect the Epistle to the Hebrews both idealizes and decenters the "new covenant" passage of Jer. 31:31-34. Jeremiah has already interpreted Torah as something inward and hence not defined in terms of any given community's capacity for teaching or group reinforcement. The writer to the Hebrews now sees such earthly forms of Israel's life as mere copies of heavenly originals. The law and priesthood of the new community are no longer those of historic Israel. We have a new high priest, the ascended Christ. The words "I will be their God and they shall be my people" now refer to a gathering grounded in God's freely bestowed mercy and grace. It is made clear furthermore that this people will not be confined within the old boundaries. Jesus sanctified the people with his blood "outside the gate." And the writer continues:

> Therefore let us go forth to him outside the camp, bearing abuse for him. For here we have no lasting city, but we seek the city which is to come.

God's community still bears the name of Israel, but the meaning is not the same. The cohesiveness, the coherent lived sense, of this people now lies in its relationship to Jesus Christ who thus is made present in the power of the Holy Spirit. There is no way of simply identifying this people as a known or, even in principle knowable, population. It is the community that at any given time is configured by a fabric of relationships that articulate God's gracious presence in the world in Christ. In this theological perspective, the word "people" takes on a metaphorical sense. The word retains its ancient realism and power by reminding us of its roots in the Israel of old, but it no longer functions as it once did. The transition from literal description to metaphor is evident in 1 Pet. 2:9-10:

> But you are a chosen race, a royal priesthood, a holy nation, God's own people, that you may declare the wonderful deeds of him who called you out of darkness into his marvelous light. Once you were no people but now you are God's people; once you had not received mercy but now you have received mercy.

None of these terms—"race," "priesthood," "nation," or "people"—can now be taken to mean what they formerly did in historic Israel. Their meaning is now figurative. Becoming "God's people" is now a consequence of "mercy," or as Paul would have said, the free outpouring of grace. It is significant that mercy here is *not* merely an individualizing indulgence on God's part which transforms the lives of particular persons. Mercy now has people-forming, not merely person-transforming, consequences.

Possibly the most far-reaching social metaphorization of God's actions toward humankind is to be found in Rev. 21:3. We read of the "dwelling" of God with human beings in the "holy city, new Jerusalem, prepared as a bride adorned for her husband." And the great voice from the throne speaks,

> Behold, the dwelling of God is with human beings. He will dwell with them and they shall be his people, and God himself shall be with them.

Now the people metaphor becomes a figure for, describes the manner of, divine presence in human affairs. This is, to be sure, an eschatological vision. But we are not dealing with another world entirely. We look forward to "a new heaven" *and* "a new earth." The image implies transformation, but not an abandonment of historical categories. It is important to grasp the context of this imagery of the "holy city." The writer of Revelation intends a contrast with the power and pretension of Rome. Rome is portrayed in Revelation 13 as the great "beast." Its power, wealth, and pretension are described with disdain in chapters 17 and 18.[6] By contrast, the holy city of Rev. 21:3 becomes the space, and its people become the living context, for God's true involvement with creation and history. It is notable that this holy city coexists with the many other peoples of humankind. Indeed it finds its calling in relation to them and may be intended by the writer to include them. "By its light shall the nations walk" (Rev. 21:24). There is much of human value outside which is *worthy* of being inside. "The kings of the earth shall bring their glory into it . . . they shall bring into it the glory and honor of the nations" (Rev. 21:25-26).

Perhaps there remains a trace here of the old ideology of tribute. But Walter Wink argues that in the biblical view the nations "are not . . . historical accidents or human contrivances. They are an integral part of the divine creation."[7] Gerhard von Rad (Wink notes) has argued that "the creation stories of Genesis do not end with the creation of humanity in chapters one and two, but with the creation of the nations in chapter ten." "In the same way," he continues, "the story of the fall does not conclude with the story of the exclusion of Adam and Eve from the garden in Genesis 3; it concludes in Genesis 11 with the confusion of tongues at the tower of Babel and the scattering of the nations. This 'fall' of the nations is placed in parallelism with the 'fall' of humanity."[8] Wink elaborates,

> One would have thought that the nations had been finished off once and for all at Armageddon (Rev. 16:16) or in the great War of the Lamb (Rev. 19-20). But the biblical view of the nations is more subtle than that. They are not demonized. They are not considered irremediably evil. Perhaps what we witness in the surrealistic violence of Revelation is their purgation from short-term views of their own self-interest and the destruction of the egoism of their collective personalities. In any case these smitten nations, trod upon in the wine press of the fury of the wrath of God the Almighty and devoured by vultures (19: 15, 17) are integral to the Holy City. Even these shall be transformed at last by the tree of life, whose leaves Ezekiel has said were "for healing" (Ezek. 47:12)—to which the Seer of the Apocalypse has added "of the nations" (Rev. 22: 2).[9]

These are the peoples who now bring their gifts: their "glory" and their "honor." Such gifts imply inclusion, not groveling, and therefore a transformation of royal imagery into something it has not been before.

Both Paul Minear and Avery Dulles discuss the importance of such images or models in thinking within or about the church. In *Images of the Church in the New Testament*,[10] Minear lists people of God as one of four major New Testament "images" (the others are "the new creation," "the fellowship of faith," and "the body of Christ") among a host of less important ones. Minear's work is in the "biblical theology" tradition of the fifties and sixties. The treatment of people of God is illuminating, especially in its very Protestant emphasis on God's sovereign initiative, which transforms the people from being merely an ethnic or geographical community. But for Minear people is merely one of many images *of* the church: it is not seen as a dynamic reality in the world within whose frame of reference the church as institution is to be understood.

In *Models of the Church*,[11] Dulles does not treat people of God as a "model" in its own right. Rather he sees this expression, together with the "body of Christ" image, as a biblical warrant for understanding the church as "mystical communion." Dulles's placement of the people of God discussion in the context of the mystical communion model has important consequences for his interpretation of its meaning. People of God becomes a democratic and even intimate expression for the interpersonal aspects of communion. The emphasis here is upon face-to-face relationships, upon the "we-relation" (*Gemeinschaft* in Tönnies's well-known phraseology) as opposed to the institution (Tönnies's *Gesellschaft*). This is not wrong in itself, but it misses the sociological realism and the trans-institutional reach of the biblical people of God usage at the end of its eschatological trajectory.

It is important that we be clear how images and models of the church actually work. These are not just synonyms which might be looked up in a thesaurus to avoid tiresome repetition. They are evocations of specific *metaphorical* contexts for concept formation and reasoning both in the church and about the church. We will see in chapter 3 how metaphors shape or "rule" (as Paul Ricoeur says)[12] whole contexts of discourse. It is not just a matter of finding the appropriate simile or figure of speech. It is rather a matter of placing the church's thinking in a particular frame of metaphorical reference, which in turn determines what lines of reasoning are likely to be felt as persuasive, and what courses of action flowing from that reasoning are apt to be seen as appropriate. The image or model is not simply a figurative device for making ecclesiological discourse more vivid than it would otherwise be. The image or model functions metaphorically to shape the character of the discourse itself.

It is important to grasp how important the ruling image is, and how pivotal it can be in any given situation that the metaphorical frame of reference be an authentic one. In *Images*, Paul Minear says of the church that

> its self-understanding, its inner cohesion, its *esprit de corps*, derive from a dominant image of itself, even though that image remains inarticulately embedded in subconscious strata. If an unauthentic image dominates its consciousness, there will first be subtle signs of malaise, followed by more overt tokens of communal deterioration. If an authentic image is recognized at the verbal level but denied in practice, there will also follow sure deterioration of the ligaments of corporate life. The process of discovering and rediscovering an authentic self-image will involve the whole community not only in clear-headed conceptual thinking and disciplined speech, but also in a rebirth of its images and its imagination, and in the absorption of these images into the interstices of communal activities of every sort.[13]

What are the particular metaphorical tendencies of the people image? In what situations might it be "authentic?" The trajectories explored here suggest that to take this image as a root metaphor is to place one's community of faith in the context of a *comprehensive vision of God's gracious people-forming presence in human history*. It is to adopt an eschatological perspective for reasoning about God's relation to human life which stresses categories of relationship, of communal coherence, and ultimately of justice and peace. The sense of a final human gathering in the context of God's reign—the beloved community—decisively shapes our understanding of the nature of God's gracious "dwelling" among us and, hence, our understanding of congregations and base communities as real, if flawed, expressions of this dwelling.

People of God, moreover, is the most *generic* expression for the community resulting from God's covenanting initiative. By this I mean that it is the most available of the images in terms of ordinary language, and that it has the least tendency to carry a particular confessional or denominational agenda. But there are certain consequences which therefore go with its use. On the one hand, this image calls special attention to the church's relationship with historic Israel. This is a relationship which remains to be fully explored and understood. When it is, ecclesiological reasoning will be transformed and the churches' sense of themselves will be very different. On the other hand, the people metaphor raises the question of God's community-forming work among all those other human beings who seek justice and peace, the "gentiles" of our own age and every age who have no visible relation to Israel or the church. Can the churches be meaningfully related to them without bringing them within the visible bounds of "communion" or "membership" as such? Rightly pursued, these questions too will lead the churches to new self-understandings.

Above all, the biblical "people" metaphor carries with it a note of *historical and sociological realism*. Unlike terms such as "body" or "temple" or "sacrament" or even "servant," it requires relatively little translation into operational terms. It simply means what it says, that the consequence of God's gracious action in history is a kind of community in humanly graspable time and space. There are constant warnings against equating this community with any single visible institution, or even with the membership of such an institution seen as a network of interpersonal knowledge and concern. Yet we are not permitted by the biblical texts to idealize the people of God as something beyond history or as in principle "invisible" or "mystical." We are rather challenged to understand what this people means as a reality coming to be within space and time. Sociological inquiry is relevant to understanding it. We are speaking of a reality whose traces we can see: something capable of being made concretely visible if we can grasp the way to do so.

But the road to such understanding is fraught with peril. Only with great difficulty do we seem to overcome parochial understandings of peoplehood. In fact the generic, unspecific character of the image positively invites the sort of presumptuous misuse that occurs when a particular nation or culture or class thinks of itself as God's people, or "chosen people" in some unique sense. One can see, for example, that a sense of exclusive chosenness runs through the history of American Protestantism like a leading thread. That sense of special calling was responsible for energizing the early American republic, but also for many forms of racial and imperial presumption. Lincoln, appreciating the irony, spoke of his nation as an "almost chosen people," and Robert Bellah has brilliantly analyzed the historical travail of the metaphor in *The Broken Covenant*.[14] An unbiblical interpretation of chosenness also evolved in the thinking of the Afrikaner settlers in what is today South Africa. It gained impetus in its combination with a misunderstood Calvinism and the "Laager mentality" of cultural beleaguerment to found the ideology of *apartheid*. These are, of course, only examples near at hand. The history of the church offers numerous dismal parallels.

The sense of a people for which this book argues stands at a great distance from these sorts of misuse. Its point is that under God the human race has the potentiality of becoming a people under God's reign and by the power of the Spirit. I argue that this universal articulation of peoplehood is the vehicle or form of God's presence in history: that such peoplehood, even if it appears in fragmentary and partial forms, carries the *sense* which God makes in the human world. And yet I am arguing that under present conditions of history this sense cannot find expression in any sort of dominating state or church, least of all any that claims symbolic universality. Any such totalizing expression is bound to be dysfunctional, if not sinister and abortive. Humankind has the potential of being a universal people under God and in God. But this potential will become visible only as less pretentious, more local gatherings of humanity devote themselves to maintaining spaces in which signs of that possibility may appear.

3. A Case Study: People in the Ecclesiology of Vatican II

How may the "sense of a people" actually play a role in the self-understanding and practical reasoning of the churches? This, after all, is the crucial question. However biblically based it may be, if this sense of a people of God remains merely a theological construct it will have no influence in human lives. Only by finding a home in the actual discourse and action of religious communions will this sense of God's blessed community of humankind achieve objective historical form. Only so will it fulfill the purpose inherent in the Spirit's nature: that it is to become concrete in a people whose forms of life bear witness to a Messiah come "in the flesh."

An example will clarify this point. A people of God ecclesiology can be found in the documents of the Second Vatican Council: first in the great "Dogmatic Constitution on the Church," known as *Lumen Gentium*,[15] and further in the "Pastoral Constitution on the Church in the Modern World," *Gaudium et Spes*.[16] These documents exemplify one way in which the sense of a people may function in ecclesiological reflection. They demonstrate the possibilities, and also the limitations, of what can be accomplished in this regard given the dominant political conceptions at work in the present structure and governance of the Roman Catholic Church.

As conservative commentators from Cardinal Ratzinger on down have done, one can view the Vatican II documents mainly as reinforcing traditional positions. These writings indeed contain much that is very old. They must if they are to accomplish their re-traditioning yet re-forming purpose. But I agree with George Lindbeck that what is significant here is what is new.[17] And so far as official Roman Catholicism is concerned, this people of God ecclesiology is without precedent. No trace of any such thing is to be found in the unfinished work of Vatican I. Avery Dulles goes so far as to say that people of God is "the principal paradigm of the Church" in the Vatican II documents read as a whole.[18] More recently,

Paul Lakeland has written that *Lumen Gentium* is literally "built around" the people of God metaphor.[19] I believe that these judgments are both true and yet not quite true. The "people of God" paradigm indeed appears here for the first time in formal conciliar documents. But it does not dominate to the extent that Dulles, Lindbeck, and Lakeland claim. Other paradigms, particularly institutional and hierarchical ones, limit its reach.

Much of *Lumen Gentium* is given over to exposition of the church's hierarchical structure. I would argue that the people of God theme stands alongside the themes of mystical body and visible hierarchy so as to offer an alternative mode of ecclesiological reasoning, a mode not yet fully integrated into the rest of the document. The essential nature of the church as expounded in this document is "mystery."[20] The opening thematic has to do with the mystical body, which is portrayed as related to the church's historical nature much as the divinity of Christ is related to his humanity. The human mind cannot fully grasp the mystery. Hence, we are told, Scripture gives us graspable images. *Lumen Gentium* points to a series of scriptural metaphors that have this purpose: the sheepfold, the tract of land to be cultivated, the edifice of God, the city above. These are metaphors for "the constituted and organized society" which "subsists in" the Roman Catholic Church.[21] Only after this last-named formula of near identity between the mystical body and the visible institution, and only after a number of other doctrinal points have been made, does the people of God theme come on stage. But then it is given a chapter of its own.[22] What conclusions should we draw? What explicit influence does the people of God theme have on the whole presentation? What is its role as underlying metaphor?

Where the people of God theme is present, I have the distinct impression that it is not merely an inclusive, democratizing, historicizing image for thinking about the church. It is all that, but it is also a term for a larger human communion corresponding to the totality of God's work in the power of the Spirit. The key passage occurs at the beginning of chapter 2:

> At all times and among every people, God has given welcome
> to whoever fears Him and does what is right (cf. Acts 10:35).
> It has pleased God, however, to make men holy and to save
> them not merely as individuals without any mutual bonds, but
> by making them a single people, a people which acknowledges
> Him in truth and serves Him in holiness.[23]

The text that follows indicates that this people includes historic Israel, the people of Jeremiah's "new covenant," the
people gathered around Jesus, the faithful of the Roman
Catholic Church, the faithful of other Christian churches. The
people of God theme permits certain theological moves that
other metaphors do not. The relation of other Christians to
the church of Rome, both in *Lumen Gentium* and in *Unitatis
Redintegratio*, the "Decree on Ecumenism," is treated under
this rubric rather than under that of the mystical body. As
Avery Dulles comments, the document is thus "able to avoid
various subtle and controverted questions concerning "degrees' which have been much discussed since *Mystici Corpo-
ris*."[24]

Even Jews and Moslems and those who have not yet
heard the gospel are at least "related" to this people. The
people intended here is evidently not simply the Roman Catholic Church, or all the churches put together. It is more: it is
those persons across the globe who, consciously or not, are in
communion with each other in the Holy Spirit, who share "a
sense of faith which is aroused and sustained by the Spirit of
truth."[25] The people image is clearly the visible church *and* a
human-divine reality which transcends the institution. Unlike
the mystical body it is not the church in its "divine nature,"
but a human gathering in history corresponding to God's gracious presence. We read:

> All men are called to be part of this catholic unity of the People
> of God, a unity which is the harbinger of the universal peace
> it promotes. And there belong to it or are related to it in
> various ways, the Catholic faithful as well as all who believe
> in Christ, and indeed the whole of humankind. For all men are
> called to salvation by the grace of God.[26]

The words "related to it in various ways" cover a multitude of possibilities which the Council Fathers evidently preferred to leave undefined. We note only that *all three* categories of persons—Catholic faithful, other believers in Christ, and the whole of humankind—are "related to" the people of God. None is simply identified with it. Is the link between the "Catholic faithful" and God's whole people different in kind, or only in degree, from that of the other groups? Here there is room for more thought. What distinguishes the relation of conscious believers to God's people from that of others in whom the Spirit may also be at work? Visible church membership? But what in this context does that mean?

The "Constitution on the Church in the Modern World," *Gaudium et Spes*, builds on *Lumen Gentium* and carries the argument further in a world-related direction. The Fathers write:

> Presupposing everything which has already been said by this Council concerning the mystery of the Church, we must now consider this same Church inasmuch as she exists in the world, living and acting with it.[27]

The people theme now shows its usefulness: both in setting forth the historical reality of what God is doing and in relating that to the presence of the Holy Spirit. This existence of the people "in the world" brings us closer to the complex and confused social reality that we know. In this setting,

> the People of God believes that it is led by the Spirit of the Lord, who fills the earth. Motivated by this faith, it labors to decipher authentic signs of God's presence and purpose in the happenings, needs, and desires in which this People have a part along with other men of our age. For faith throws a light on everything, manifests God's design for man's total vocation, and thus directs the mind to solutions which are fully human.[28]

Here, especially in the notion of "decipherment" of the patterns of God's activity in human affairs, the people of God ecclesiology suggests the attempt to make sense of the world's confusing signs. May the church not only carry out a decipherment of the world but *be* in its own way a decoding of the Spirit's people-gathering work? Early in *Lumen Gentium* there is a statement on this subject which has proved to be of considerable ecumenical importance and whose full implications remain to be drawn out.

> By her relationship with Christ, the Church is a kind of sacrament or sign of intimate union with God and of the unity of all humankind. She is also an instrument for the achievement of such union and unity.[29]

These words clearly refer to the larger spiritual reality of what God is doing in the world, and hence, without saying so, to the forming of God's people by the power of the Spirit. The visible church is a "sacrament" or "sign" in the world that such a people is coming into being. Perhaps one could say that by gathering all sorts and conditions of human beings, those in formal communion and those not, the church makes the larger people of God become provisionally visible. It also sacramentally signifies what the people is and means.

It is true that some have read these words as merely imperialistic in the old sense: the Roman Church will bring humanity together in union with God by imposing her order on the world by cunning and force. One understands this suspicion. There is much in the past which lends credence to it. But these words, in their context, reduce the temporal claims of the church instead of reasserting them. The church is a sacrament or sign of a larger reality. Here are the seeds of a new conception of ecclesiastical life in relation to the world, seeds which have not yet fully sprouted. Indeed, many of the interpretations of Vatican II in the Roman Church today seem bent on preventing them from sprouting. But when they do, they will grow and eventually crack the relatively rigid vessels in which they were first planted. They will give rise to new forms of life-together for Christian faith based on new understandings of the relationship between the faith community and the human community which it serves.

As matters stand, however, the "people of God" model, despite its frequent appearance, does not really dominate the Vatican II ecclesiology in the sense of having become part of the metaphorical foundation of the document. None of the ecclesiological consequences one would expect to see, if George Lindbeck's commentary is correct,[30] has really taken root in the exposition. The church is at times considered as a whole people in which distinctions between "laity" and "clergy" are done away, but that is hardly the dominant note. Occasionally, especially in *Gaudium et Spes*, the radically historical perspective implied in the people of God image begins to come through. But again, the notion of the church as mystical body is more fundamental to the underlying ec-clesiology of these documents. Above all, the connection be-tween the sense of a people and the Holy Spirit at work both within and beyond the ecclesiastical institution is un-developed. Most passages, although not all, connect the Spirit primarily with the church as institutional structure.

Yet one has the sense here that there is a new ecclesiologi-cal vision waiting to break free of the old conceptions. The connection of the Spirit with the church, so amply attested in the New Testament and in the Vatican II documents, points ecclesiological reasoning beyond the institutional conception of the church and toward the many as yet untapped possibili-ties inherent in the people metaphor. This connection of Spirit with the church does not make the institution unnecessary, but it raises anew the question of the relation between the churches as visible bodies and the whole of God's involve-ment in human affairs.

4. Community as Decipherment of the Spirit

I have argued that a people of God ecclesiology strongly influences the work of Vatican II, but is not decisive for it. Yet especially in *Lumen Gentium* and *Gaudium et Spes* there is a new kind of ecclesiology in the making, pressing to escape the conceptual and institutional limits within which, even

today, it remains confined. Attempts in Rome to forget many
aspects of Vatican II, or to reinterpret some of its formulas
beyond recognition, suggest that many are aware of the potential of these documents. Ironic as it may be, Protestant
interpreters may be able to do more at present with this
Roman Catholic achievement than Catholic scholars themselves.

If there is a shortcoming in the Vatican II vision of a
people of God it lies in the failure of its documents to connect
that metaphor with the actual social reality of the people
themselves, with the *sensus fidelium* as it actually now exists.
There is a gap between the *conception* of a people in the
documents and the *actual* people represented, let us say, by
the crowd in St. Peter's Square. Of all the images or metaphors of the church, people of God lends itself most easily to
the perspective of sociological realism, to a sense of the fabric
of actual history. But *Lumen Gentium* and *Gaudium et Spes*
venture no more than a few tentative steps in this direction.
These documents do not wrestle with the actual, complex,
ambiguous, socio-religious reality found in this crowd and in
all the other gatherings of human beings found today in symbolically Christian space. It is time to try to link the scriptural
and traditional notion of a people of God to the question of an
actual people of God. To what extent and in what way can
such a people become concretely visible and active in human
affairs? Can we find the universal church, so powerfully sym-
bolized by Michelangelo's design for St. Peter's Basilica and
by Bernini's colonnades, in the tenuous fabric, the tentatively
shared understandings, and yet the worldwide connections, of
the crowd?

Scripture and tradition alike make clear that the assem-
bling of the people of God is a work of the Holy Spirit. It is not
by accident we begin the third article of the Apostles' Creed
with the words, "I believe in the Holy Spirit, the Holy Catholic Church, the Communion of Saints. . . ." The new ecclesiological understanding we seek involves more than a sociology
of the crowd, more than new strategies for participation by
the laity, more than greater sensitivity to the people's con-

cerns in the curia. It requires a new understanding of the relation between the Holy Spirit and the ecclesiastical institution, and with that a new grasp of the way ecclesiological metaphors either block, or open up, possibilities for understanding the Spirit's humanity-forming work.

Spirit, people, and church go together. Luke tells us how a crowd begins to become a people as the Spirit founds the new community of the apostolic church. In his account of the Day of Pentecost (Acts 2), we read that the coming of the Holy Spirit upon the apostles is, as it were, overheard by a crowd of Jewish pilgrims in the city for the Feast of Weeks. What happens to these pilgrims becomes the significant theological fact. Not only do they hear the Spirit speaking in the languages of the cultures and nations from which they come: their ability to understand the message as Peter interprets it poses a question for Israel's self-understanding, and ultimately a question about God's relationship to humanity.

Peter begins to speak to this issue in his remarkable sermon. The apostle's rhetorical strategy (as represented by Luke) is to connect the event going on before him with words from the prophecy of Joel. One is impressed both with the inclusiveness and the visionary character of the spiritual community the prophet envisions. The Spirit is poured out on "all flesh." Sons and daughters shall prophesy. Young men and old men shall see visions and dream dreams. The community transcends class: "menservants" and "maidservants" will receive the spirit and prophesy. Peter also identifies the community with a Davidic, that is messianic, interpretation of the recent events concerning Jesus of Nazareth, crucified and now raised up as Lord and Christ. Hearers are invited to repent, be baptized, and enter definitively into God's promise to the people of Israel by joining the apostolic community. A thousand souls do so, and begin to devote themselves to "the apostles' teaching and fellowship, the breaking of bread and the prayers." A new form of life-together quickly develops. It involves sharing of possessions, and help to those in need. Significantly, it also involves daily presence among those who assemble in the outer court of the Temple.

The remainder of the Book of Acts describes the remarkable ramifications of these events as Peter has interpreted
them. A lame man is brought into the Temple precincts in
violation of law and custom. Peter and others are arrested and
released. Each new event occasions further interpretation of
Scripture as the people's story. Infractions of the new faith
community's principles are punished. Officers are appointed
to look after widows. Slowly, and not without controversy, the
larger implications of the existence of this new community
begin to become plain. The work of the Spirit is seen to
involve Gentiles. Paul's conversion, his relations to the Jerusalem church, his preaching journeys and his writings all concern the implications of this move beyond the boundaries of
Judaism. The theology of justification by grace alone is designed precisely to build a bridge from Israel's traditions to
the Spirit's work among Jews and Gentiles alike. The Spirit is
"bearing witness with our spirit that we are children of
God . . ." (Rom. 8:16). And a few verses later, "The creation
waits with eager longing for the revealing of the sons of God"
(Rom. 8:19). Romans 9-11 then wrestles with the questions
any Jew would raise. How is this new community, in which
the very meaning of creation and history are embodied, related to Israel? How does the scriptural people of God
become the universal people of God? "For God has consigned
all men to disobedience, that he may have mercy upon all"
(Rom. 11:32).

What is being said in this array of texts? The coming of the
Spirit on the crowd of pilgrims, together with the interpretation of the event in Peter's sermon, says that the many languages and cultures represented by these visitors to the Holy
City can be vehicles for the Spirit not merely in Jerusalem but
also in the many diaspora lands. If Jews from other parts of
the empire can hear the Spirit's call in Jerusalem, they can
hear it also within the cultures they represent. This is what
happens for some when they hear the same gospel preached,
if in different words, by Paul in the course of his missionary
journeys. They quickly realize that the Spirit is speaking not
only to them but to Gentiles who share the same vernacular

culture. The language of the Spirit becomes the tie which binds them to believing Gentiles who are their neighbors. Paul's theology of justification by grace alone enters the picture as an explanation in revisionist rabbinic terms for what is happening. Gentiles are being empowered by the Spirit to hear and understand the message, and they are joining the people of God. Paul asks how this can be. In Galatians, Romans, and elsewhere, he calls on justification by grace alone to explain the salvation of Gentiles. Only when this is understood can Paul's Jewish listeners begin to realize that their own inclusion in the community of faith has the same ultimate theological basis as the inclusion of the Gentiles. All is grace. For Luke, the formation of the new community in Jesus Christ is the work of the Spirit whose people-forming power runs from Jerusalem to the ends of the earth.

What is the relevance of all this to our understanding of people of God image for the church's thinking today? It is that the people *metaphor* begins to have power only when it is connected with what can happen when *the actual people*, both gathered and scattered, are led by the Spirit to understand and embrace the gospel. That coming of the Spirit activates many languages and cultures to be its vehicles, and it directs those on whom it comes to look outward to its actions in the life of strangers, those "outside the camp." If we want to find the universal church, the place to look is not upward toward the baroque monuments above us but downward and outward in the attempt to grasp the meaning of the people-configuring work the Spirit is already doing. In this perspective, the gospel becomes a kind of decoding device. We can identify the Spirit's work by looking for those qualities in the life of human communities which are consistent with the conviction that Jesus is the Messiah come "in the flesh." In turn, the results of our attempts to "decipher"[31] the Spirit's worldly work play their role in ecclesiology. We will have found the "sense," the "lived logic" of a larger, trans-ecclesiastical peoplehood in the gospel under God.

St. Peter's Square, I have argued, is a place whose symbolism requires that questions such as these be asked. But it is not necessarily a place whose symbolism provides the answers. I will argue in chapter 4 that the Roman Church and other churches embody political metaphors which, carried over into theology, limit the possibilities for articulating the relation between God and the world and, hence, our ability to understand the Spirit's role in history. To carry the inquiry further we will need a new set of metaphors, a new kind of conceptual equipment for deciphering what happens as God's people begin to identify one another, especially as this goes on within existing cultural syntheses and social structures.

5. Sense and Signification: A New Ecclesiological Vision

What does it mean to say that a community, through its fabric of life, makes a certain kind of sense? The insight that this is so derives from hermeneutical, or interpretative, understandings of the human sciences. What do sociologists or anthropologists or social psychologists really study, and what do they really know? Some say they study the meanings which human communities generate and repeat in their patterns of interaction. Communal meanings are not only conveyed in language; they are also conveyed, and preserved, in typical configurations of interactive behavior. Such meanings may be enshrined in a group's formative stories and sagas in such a way that action in the society concerned is part of, or a continuation of, the story. Such meanings may also be embedded in the metaphorical structures of common speech. Human scientists who study these things often say that societies are like complex "texts." They are there to be "read." If that is so, we can understand at once what it means to say that a social group has the power to "signify." By what it is, it expresses in readable form the sense that it embodies.

Carry this idea over now into the field of theology. I will argue that the Holy Spirit, as energy field of God's reign, brings human beings into patterns of shared meaning. The Spirit comes to historical expression in gestalts or meaningful wholes which make sense.[32] A hermeneutical sociology enables us to decipher these patterns of interaction: to "read" the meanings which come to expression in them. To put the matter differently, Jesus Christ is present in the forms of life which the Holy Spirit engenders in history, and these forms of life can be read if we have the right deciphering equipment.

What is that equipment? Not a sociological theory. Not some means of observation or analysis applied from a safely neutral distance. I will seek to show that the means for deciphering the people-forming works of the Spirit in history is itself a community, the community called church. By the kind of community it is, by the ways in which it is involved in the life around it, a congregation can make the energy-field of the Spirit partially visible. It thus becomes a sign, sacrament, or instrument of humanity's unity and union with God. To put the matter in more traditional language, the church makes the "communion of saints" provisionally visible without claiming to be identified with that communion.

The church does not accomplish this signifying through its own wisdom and ingenuity, but as *Lumen Gentium* says, "by its relationship to Christ." Dietrich Bonhoeffer speaks of the church as "Jesus Christ taking the form of a community."[33] How does this happen? Chapter 3 will lay out the matter in detail. It is enough to say now that the church's relation to Jesus Christ must also be worked out in terms of a hermeneutical human science. The heart of the matter, as we shall see, is not Jesus' self-consciousness or even his teaching as such. It is rather the historical shape of his impact on the people and events of his time. It is the kind of re-forming or re-shaping of the social fabric which Christ's ministry brings about that should claim our attention.[34] The Johannine criterion for "testing the spirits, to see if they are of God" is that the authentic Spirit "proclaims that Christ has come in the flesh." I take that to mean not merely "incarnation" in some Greek metaphysical sense, but a shaping involvement of God in human social reality. That divine incursion left a definite, identifiable, mark in the matrix of history, a figure known by the name of the Messiah Jesus. If the church is to be a sign of the Spirit's people-forming work, it must identify itself persuasively with that form of life.

When I speak, then, of the sense of a people I mean two

things. First I mean the theological *idea* of a people of God:
the idea of the human race ordered as an expression of God's
will to dwell as Spirit in history, functioning in ecclesiological
reasoning. Second, I mean the sense this people *makes* in its
fabric of life when it becomes visible: what it conveys as a
lived text which signifies something to the world. These two
senses of the sense of a people need to coalesce in actual life.
The church's fabric of interaction needs to convey *as* lived text
the same meaning that we intend when we write theologically
about it. The church is that part of the human whole which
conveys *to* that whole *its* destiny as the space of God's reign.
The church is a community in which the whole of humanity
may see signified *its* calling to become a people of God. One
may say all this theologically, as I am doing here. But the
statement is not convincing unless it is also said in a fabric of
life together which signifies in concrete terms what the theological statement conveys conceptually.

The church can be a sign or sacrament in the sense intended by *Lumen Gentium* through its ability to gather a
company of people into a signifying texture of life. Bernini's
arms reach out and embrace an assembly of human beings
whose potential is enormous, but whose reality falls far short
of the potential. The crowd as it is tends to be an incoherent
and strikingly varied gathering, just as Christian congregations are in many parts of the world today. But one can
imagine, using the mind's eye, that the visible church manages to bring together a particularly strategic group of people
and manages to form them into a community whose nature
and activity speak. Then the church may become a sign, sacrament, or instrument of humanity *as* God's people. Essential to
those involved is some conceptualization of what this ecclesial
process is about. It is about the possibility that the whole of
humankind could be drawn into a common life fit to be the
dwelling place of God in the Spirit.

I believe that the proposed ecclesiology is close to what
might have come out of Vatican II if attention had been given
to the crowd outside the basilica where the "fathers" met, if
the people of God theme had then been allowed truly to

control rather than merely accompany the main line of argument in *Lumen Gentium*. But the possibility of such a development, now involving all the churches and not merely the Roman Catholic Church, is still before us. The churches hold open social space for the question of a people of God to be asked in a world which otherwise is unlikely to formulate such a notion. The churches, as they stand, are not able to answer that question because they are dysfunctional in the concrete forms of life from which their working categories come. But who is to say what possibilities may yet be realized in the expectant space between Bernini's outstretched stone limbs?

II

An Unraveling of Assumptions

Dysfunction and New Life

Ecclesiology, despite this discipline's esoteric reputation, is never pursued in a vacuum. It is always an attempt to understand ". . . the Holy Catholic Church, the Communion of Saints . . ." as a work of the Spirit in relation to the concrete conditions of some particular society or culture. The church is by definition a reality of history, not merely an eternal ideal. But how are the churches, as tangible institutions, related to what the Spirit is doing among the people they actually embrace as communicants and among those they never reach? Where and how does something called a "communion of saints" or "beloved community" actually appear on history's stage?

These questions grow harder to answer with each passing year. Today we are seeing so complete an unraveling of long-standing theological assumptions that classical approaches to ecclesiological reasoning no longer suffice. This is not to say that the old ecclesiologies have nothing to teach us. On the contrary, the more questions we ask today the more sympathy we have for the struggles of those who have gone before. But we now need a new way of framing the question: one which, among other things, takes account of human-science insights about what is going on in an increasingly mobile and interdependent world.

I have argued that the churches hold open social space in which the *question* of a beloved community of humankind can be asked. Yet, with their present structures and self-understandings, they are not able to account for the actual people-gathering work of the Holy Spirit in their midst and beyond. This is why I speak of the churches as "dysfunctional." It is not merely that as organized bodies they *mal*function, although that certainly happens. It is rather that their presuppositions prevent them from understanding, let alone manifesting, the reality of the people whose possibility in the Spirit their institutional existence implies.

There are many reasons for this dysfunctionality of ecclesiastical bodies. Most of them are inherent in the theological or religious situation of our time. The circumstances in which we live involve an unraveling of assumptions about the *relation* of churches as visible bodies to the spiritual community they are called to represent. One thinks at once of Augustine's formulations of this problem: a "city of God" called into being out of Rome's crumbling "city of man," an "invisible church" partly manifested in the "visible church." Today we sense that such solutions are satisfactory only if the churches have achieved a relatively stable social role in a relatively secure political situation. The church of Augustine's day, in spite of competition from gnostic and Manichean sects and in spite of barbarian invasions (for which some thought the Christians responsible), had attained a reasonably secure position in Roman society and, like Rome itself, had begun to think about its role in world history. Augustine interpreted this situation with pastoral realism and theological genius. In his eyes the church, "mixed body" that it was, could be confident in claiming to be the earthly expression of an invisible company of the saints. Today, however, it is hard to see the churches, divided and confused as they are, in any such light. The dysfunction we experience is not a matter of bad faith: it

is a symptom of the disintegration of a whole fabric of interacting assumptions concerning the relation of church institutions and their traditions to the spiritual realities they are
supposed to make visible.

To grasp all this clearly, we need a method which can
critically illuminate the churches' theological understandings
of their own social realities and roles. The scholar who can
help us most is the German historian and theologian Ernst
Troeltsch (1865-1923). Troeltsch struggled to describe the
churches' grasp of themselves as participants in theologically
understood dramas of society and history. He sought to come
to terms with the dilemmas of historical relativity. I will first
set my argument concerning the people of God within a Troeltschian perspective. Then I will examine more closely several
dimensions of what Troeltsch and his successors saw in the
modern world: increasing difficulty with the very idea as well
as the social embodiment of tradition, the emergence of radical pluralism in faith communities, and a crisis in theological
conceptualization. Finally, I will weigh the emergence in this
confused situation of new forms of ecclesial existence: the
base communities and other innovative expressions of common life in faith. I will ask whether these communities come
closer than the traditional churches do to giving visible expression to a global people of God.

1. Ernst Troeltsch: The Churches in Socio-Historical Perspective

Early in his career, Ernst Troeltsch began to see the gap
between the churches' classical self-understandings and the
actual human and social reality of the people in and around
them.[1] In *The Social Teaching of the Christian Churches*[2]
(1912, ET 1931) he argued that the historic expressions of
Christian faith, at least as he knew them, could not "master"
the social conditions of modernity. By this he meant that in
none of its known forms of life was Christianity likely to find
a coherent relationship with the emerging culture of modern
Europe, or, for that matter, with its offshoots in the Americas.

The key to understanding the real nature of the Christian reality in any age, Troeltsch thought, lay in understanding the churches' concrete communal embodiments: their relationships to their social, political, and intellectual contexts, their forms of awareness of these connections, their teachings concerning the purposes such involvements served.

In the entire history of Christendom, only two such syntheses of thought, practice, and social reality had been truly comprehensive, potent, and lasting. One was the medieval social-cultural ideal, typified by St. Thomas Aquinas and the cathedrals, and continuing today in many aspects of modern Roman Catholicism. The other was the form of Calvinist asceticism which, beginning in the sixteenth century, informed the rising bourgeoisie in Europe, Britain, and America, and whose aftertaste we now know as the "Protestant ethic." Troeltsch thought that both these syntheses, despite their continuing achievements, had by his time "spent their force."[3] If there were to be a new, and culturally fruitful articulation of Christian faith in his time, new thoughts would be necessary that had "not yet been thought."[4]

Perhaps they still have not been thought. Troeltsch set the terms of a question with which theologians and historians are still wrestling. Troeltsch's question arises whenever the question of the church's social being is brought not merely to theological but also to socio-historical awareness. Ecclesiology then becomes a critical discipline, which treats the Christian doctrine of the church not simply as the set of doctrinal assertions presupposed by polity or canon law, but rather as the question of the faith community's actual form of life in its social and historical setting.

Such critical questioning is clearly an Enlightenment product. But we must distinguish Troeltsch's realism in describing what he found in his sources from his philosophical views about the nature of the historical process. Troeltsch sets aside church-historical or history-of-doctrine perspectives in favor of a sociologically realistic approach to the churches' self-understandings in their worldly contexts. But Troeltsch's views of the nature of history as such rest on metaphysical

presuppositions about causation, about the interconnected-
ness of events, about the unlikelihood or impossibility of interventions from beyond the nexus of history, which (as we shall
see) contradict the usual logic of thought in faith communities
which believe themselves to be guardians of unique revelation. There is much we can learn from Troeltsch's socio-theo-
logical observations without accepting his naturalistic meta-
physic. Yet in the end the two may be connected. Despite
"postmodern" developments, we remain children of the Enlightenment in many ways. We assume, every time we read
a newspaper, that history is a seamless web of causal relationships. Christian revelation must then be either a special case
of miraculous intervention to be treated in a unique way, or
revelation must somehow be brought into a demythologized
context—ethical, existential, psychological, or otherwise—
that renders it understandable in the contemporary world.

My suspicion is that even believers in miraculous intervention do considerable demythologizing and remythologiz-
ing in actual practice. Certainly this is true in the language of
pastoral care and in the illustrative rhetoric of sermons.[5]
There is an important consequence. Persisting traditional expressions of Christian faith—architectural, institutional, liturgical—become populated by people who understand them in
new ways without quite realizing, or being willing to admit,
that something new has happened. Often the new thing is an
individualization or privatization of faith. As Troeltsch saw it,
by the opening of the twentieth century, if not earlier, both
Roman Catholic and the Protestant versions of the faith were
carrying on in forms of corporate life which were adaptations,
with somewhat different contents and social functions, of the
cultural and intellectual achievements of the past. Both
within and beyond the traditional structures there had arisen,
particularly among educated elites, the peculiar form of religious individualism which took its rise in various forms of
what Troeltsch confusingly calls "mysticism." Reformation
understandings of faith in which the soul was felt intimately
and directly related to God had become by Troeltsch's day
mere religious individualism: the sense that the singular per-

son alone is arbiter of belief and its consequences. People might still be drawn to the liturgy, or to great ecclesiastical events, but the meanings they felt would be individualized, unsharable, quite possibly unique. There could be as many interpretations of an event in St. Peter's Square as there were persons present.

I want to suggest an image for what has gone on here, a figure prompted by the geological term *pseudomorphosis*. This is a state of affairs in which erosion has washed out the original content of a mineral and a new and different substance has flowed into the old granular or crystalline structure. Just so, the churches look the same but their inner substance has changed.[6] Today this pseudomorphotic process has touched off a struggle between those who would maintain the old forms at all costs and those who take risks in hope for the appearance of something new. The more one thinks about this the more difficult it becomes simply to take sides. Individualism, autonomy, and self-determination may wash away the old content. But can these contemporary human predilections do much to determine the content which takes its place? And will the new content eventually mandate new outward forms? Troeltsch finds his own way of describing this process, (anticipating Edward Farley's attack on the "house of authority" in *Ecclesial Reflection*)[7]:

> Radical individualism will probably soon be an interlude between an old and a new civilization of constraint. This individualism may be compared with the process of taking the materials of a house which has been pulled down, sorting them out into the actual individual stones, out of which a new house will be built. What the new house will look like and the possibilities it will provide . . . no one can at present tell.[8]

In Troeltsch's view, this modern religious individualism has little or no capacity for generating stable collective expressions of its own. He writes that this type

> creates no community, since it possess[es] neither the sense of solidarity nor the faith in authority which this requires . . . It

lives in and on communities which have been brought into existence by other, ruder, energies; it tries to transform these groups from confessional unities into more organizations for administration, offering a home to very varying minds and energies.[9]

Having borrowed the visible structures of past syntheses without having comprehended what these earlier achievements really meant, modern religious privatism may eventually dispense with the decaying churches altogether. It will then become a diffused popular cultus of vaguely Christian tinge, vulnerable to exploitation by the whims of the moment or, worse, by official powers bent on using it for their own purposes. Troeltsch foresaw the "German Christians" who were ready in 1934 to be organized within the framework of the Nazi state:

> Richard Rothe and Hegel did not prophesy in vain that the Church would become merged in the State, that is, the complete autonomy of the religious "mind" directly united with the collective reason and its social organization.[10]

This total picture is astonishingly close to what numbers of contemporary observers now see happening to Christianity, at least in North America. But such observers tend not to heed the Troeltschian warnings. Robert Bellah has written extensively of the American "civil religion"[11] and has suggested that the churches, if they wish to survive, must provide spiritual services tailored to the many individual varieties of personal response to this generalized cultus. Thomas Luckmann painted a similar picture in *The Invisible Religion*:

> Religious themes originate in experiences in the "private sphere." They rest primarily on emotions and sentiments and are sufficiently unstable to make articulation difficult. They are highly "subjective"; that is, they are not defined in an obligatory fashion by primary institutions. They can be—and are—taken up, however, by what may be called secondary institutions which expressly cater to the needs of "autonomous" consumers.[12]

Still more recently, Bellah has developed a similar analysis in *Habits of the Heart*.[13] There are great collective themes running through North American religiosity: "republican" and "biblical" virtues, therapeutic and bureaucratic traits of character. But there is also a radical individualism, a spiritual aloneness memorably expressed by an interviewee named Sheila who claimed to be a member of a faith with one adherent, a religion appropriately named "Sheilaism."

Where can this state of affairs lead? Surely not to what Troeltsch called the "new completion," the sought-for new synthesis between tradition, society, and culture which would generate a new collective articulation of Christian faith. Must faith inevitably come to terms with religious consumerism? Must the churches be related to each other primarily as similar but not identical institutions operating in the same business: that of meeting, in return for financial support, whatever "religious" needs are out there in the market? Is Christianity simply one of many options for persons in a secular culture who seek interesting ways to spend their spare time? Troeltsch's picture is chillingly prophetic, for this is approximately what most people in the Western world, and especially in the media, simply take for granted about the nature of "religion" and its appeal. The customer is always right. Little is the attraction of any form of traditional dogma. What counts is whatever is in the head of the individual no matter how theologically idiosyncratic. The churches will thrive so long as they meet personal needs and so long as they offer a sufficiently entertaining program of religious "theater."

There are weaknesses and blind spots in Troeltsch's work, as well as contributions yet to be fully utilized by his successors. It is ironic, in the light of this writer's importance for ecclesiology, that he himself has little sensitivity to this subject. He understands Christian faith to have been, at its start, a romantic, non-cultic, religious individualism which took on organized form only when (to its detriment) it became a community focused on worship of the heavenly figure of the risen Christ.

The gospel of Jesus was a free personal piety, with a strong tendency toward profound intimacy and spiritual fellowship and communion, but without any tendency toward the organization of a cult, or toward the creation of a religious community. Only when faith in Jesus, the Risen and Exalted Lord, became the central point of worship in a new religious community did the necessity for organization arise.[14]

There is a second drawback, perhaps connected with the absence of an ecclesiology. Despite Troeltsch's historicism and sociological realism, he never moves from the churches' *teachings* about society, their theological *understandings* of the relationships they should have to the social order, to dispassionate analysis of their actual social reality. Hans Georg Drescher has put it this way:

Troeltsch limited his task in *The Social Teaching* to questions framed in terms of the history of dogma and he saw his work as complementary to Harnack's. . . . There is no contradiction here when one sees that Troeltsch, unlike Harnack, makes room in his account for the sociological self-construction of Christianity and for its social relations. Troeltsch knew that his methodological starting point should really lead him further, namely not only to an account of the history of social theories but to an examination of the historical reality itself. He comments that his powers were not adequate for this.[15]

It is crucial for us to find ways of reaching "the historical reality itself." Does Troeltsch, despite his modesty about his powers, offer any hints? Running through his later work, *Historismus und seine Probleme*,[16] is the well-known but largely unexploited idea of the "historical individual," Troeltsch's misleading term (certainly in English) for what otherwise might be called an historico-social synthesis. Troeltsch himself uses the word *Gestaltung*, meaning "configuring" or "shaping." Peter Hodgson, as we will see in chapter 6, interprets this term in the light of its Hegelian background. He sees both the possibilities and the limitations of Troeltsch's notion of "creative compromises in response to concrete historical situations."

Troeltsch sought an alternative to the linear teleology of the old salvation history model, but without losing the conviction that history has an orientation to the future and a structure that gives it meaning. Troeltsch's "teleology" envisioned a process of shaping ever-new cultural syntheses through creative compromises in response to concrete historical situations. Such syntheses are relative, fragmentary and ambiguous, and the work of creating them is an open and unending process. Setbacks and reversals occur as well as advances, and total annihilation or destruction remains a possibility. Troeltsch understood the act of shaping as in some sense the actualization of a particular moment of the divine ground of life, but he was never able to work out the idea of God in a satisfactory way.[17]

This idea deserves to be kept in mind. It is possible that the new and renewed Christian communities in some way make visible, or signify, worldly gestalts which anticipate the blessed community of the kingdom of God in the midst of history. It may be that the primary message of the gospel is that such provisional realizations of the end are possible. Any proposal based on Troeltsch's work must remember his honesty and realism, suspecting all the while that his idealistic, individualistic conceptual equipment may not have permitted him to go further than he did.

2. The Travail of Tradition

The social form of the community of faith shapes the taken-for-granted logic of that community's view of the world, and hence of its theological reasoning. A characteristic style of reasoning is handed down over the centuries as "tradition,"[18] the *paradosis* or handing on of the substance of faith. But many today are uncomfortable with the understanding of tradition being maintained by ecclesiastical bodies, sensing that such a constituting of reality can only live in protected and detached social worlds. Yet no adequate substitute for such traditional understanding, despite many attempts to articulate one, has as yet gained broad support. Meanwhile, something like a popular deconstruction of the classical Christian assumptions concerning scripture, dogma, and the teaching authority of the church is going on in our time.

What is tradition? It is not merely a given content: it is a content constantly determined and redetermined in the thinking through which the integrity of the community is maintained. It is this thoughtful transmission process which has now become problematic. In his recent book, *Ecclesial Reflection*,[19] Edward Farley offers an "archaeology" of the churches' thinking designed to uncover their basic institutional assumptions. The churches have maintained themselves through space and time with remarkable unanimity about sources and their interpretation. Both Roman Catholic and Protestant traditions see the church, in Farley's words, as a "house of authority," that is, an ordered community of interpretation continuous with that of the apostles. Within this "house" one finds certain distinct assumptions concerning scripture, the doctrinalization of the tradition in the "fathers" and the councils, and the ongoing teaching role of the institution. It is remarkable, indeed, how similar are the Protestant and Roman Catholic versions of the "house," how comparable their logic when seen in classical form. Each represents a continuing development within the church of forms of life and thought expressed in different ways at different times: all in the name of what Farley calls a "logic of triumph."

In the early period of its polemic against Judaism, Farley shows, the church needed a clear understanding of its claim to be "the New Israel" and found it in the assertion of identity between its own historical, institutional reality and the true Israel of God's intent. There also arose the need to define, transmit, and interpret the dogmas related to salvation, a task which required that the institutional guardian be vested, under carefully defined and controlled conditions, with a supra-dogmatic authority. And finally, the church's definition of salvation as involving the fate of the individual soul led it to seek institutional control of the sacraments needed in the salvation process. Without these steps, according to Farley, "salvation is turned over to the failures, sins, and fallibilities of human beings, or to the contingencies of nature and history."[20] In sum,

> the church not only passed through its own early charismatic and millenarian phase toward institutional stability; it found a way to sanctify that institution as a location of God's communication. The church's institutionality became part of the theological given, that which must be attended to as normative by those who would discover what is to be believed, taught, and practiced.[21]

Catholicism, in short, extended its early identification of God's will with the content of Scripture to apply to dogma and finally to the teaching office of the church itself, bringing this principle to its high water mark at the First Vatican Council (1870).

In a different form, the same logic emerged in Protestantism.[22] Protestants rejected the external features of the Roman Catholic institutionalization and their related theological themes and justifications, but still needed some institutional setting for the interpretation of Scripture and for the management of the means of grace. Moreover, the Protestant churches in general shared the theological convictions which emerged in second- and third-century Christianity concerning the divine origin and role of the ecclesiastical institution. As Farley puts it:

> Protestantism with its *heilsgeschichtlich* framework and its doctrines of election and glorification could not conceive of God acting salvifically in Christ and then letting the outcome be determined by human autonomy or historical contingency. Rather, God's work in Christ is followed by God's work at Pentecost and the creation of the new Israel. This salvific work continues in the inspiration of the apostles, the result being the New Testament Scriptures. God's special providence continues with the church in its early elaboration of trinitarian faith in the ecumenical councils. Further, in addition to providing objective conditions of salvation (justification), God creates

subjective and social conditions in the internal testimony of the Spirit and in the gift to the church of ministry and the means of grace (preaching and the sacraments).[23]

Protestantism, of course, avoided any doctrine of the church's necessary infallibility. The dialectic of the church visible and invisible, the concept of *ecclesia reformata et semper reformanda*, the notion of confessions as subordinate standards of faith, the doctrine that councils can err, and the principle of *sola scriptura* all bore upon this point. Even so, the Protestant churches did not see themselves as contingent and relative historical forms, but as required to be what they were by the demands of the gospel and of scriptural specifications about church order.[24] Aided by their own version of the Scripture principle, the Protestant churches could in practice claim divine sanction for their sacramental doctrines and practices, for their understandings of ordination, and for their polities.[25] The conviction that church assemblies could "discern and declare the very communication of God',[26] of course, rested on the confidence that such assemblies could rest their claims on Scripture. Farley calls this notion a "qualified or quasi-doctrine of infallibility."[27] In the words of the Second Helvetic Confession:

> The Church does not err. It does not err as long as its rests on the rock of Christ, and upon the foundation of the prophets and apostles. And it is no wonder if it errs, as often as it deserts him who alone is the truth.[28]

Here we have what Farley correctly considers "not a theoretical but a *de facto* claim for infallibility which came to preside over both Lutheran and Reformed Christendom and which grounded the confidence by which they excommunicated the heterodox."[29]

By the middle of the eighteenth century, this network of assumptions and claims—whether in the Roman Catholic or the Protestant format—had begun to break down, especially for educated North Americans and Europeans. Now in the late twentieth century, these assumptions and claims have become problematic both within church circles and in the general culture beyond. Three dimensions of this problematizing of tradition deserve mention here: the academic criticism and reformulation of tradition; the incongruity between new styles of community life and traditional styles of theological logic; and finally, the profound impact on tradition of its passage through the popularizing and politicizing of "civil religion."

First, it is clear that the crisis of tradition owes much to the development, as long ago as the early nineteenth century, of historical-critical method. Insofar as tradition has consisted, then or now, of assertions vulnerable in either form or content to criticism by scholars trained in modern methods of historical inquiry, it has gradually lost its force in the religious community. This has been particularly true where the reality sense of the "scientific" historian has spread to the community at large. Much of the constructive theological work of the nineteenth and early twentieth century (of which more later) was in fact devoted to attempts to restate the tradition in terms more amenable to post-Enlightenment consciousness. One is struck in examining these contributions, as well as others like them, that every time the received tradition is brought into line with some new philosophical or cultural reality sense it is distorted selectively in both emphasis and content. Of course there always have been ecclesiastical authorities ready to restate the tradition as "received," so that the work of revisionist theologians has had little impact on those content to remain faithful and orthodox members of the religious community. Theological criticism and reconstruction has until recently been a phenomenon of the university. Now, however, the functioning of traditional authority as such is being called radically into question.

One can see now, and this is the second dimension of the problem, that the "logic of triumph" is less and less practically functional in relation to the actual life of faith communities as these have grown and developed in the contemporary world. Modern sensibilities reject the rigidity and arbitrariness of traditional doctrinal deliverances, and observe that the traditional centers represent very regional, culturally restricted, organs of faith interpretation which are in fact in competition with other, less formal but practically potent centers of interpretative activity. Christian faith has now begun to take certain forms, to adopt certain patterns of reasoning, which have their home outside the official "house of authority." The very conception of community life underlying the old theo-logic is foreign to modern sensibility. It will soon need to be replaced by more contemporary ideas of how communities, with their traditions, persist over time.[30] Christian congregations and religious communities today have not only spiritual, or ecclesio-political difficulties with traditional centers of authority, but also an uncertainty about how to relate to the traditional content of faith in ways congruent with the sorts of communities they are.

It is easy, no doubt, for some to assume that such perceptions come mainly from theologians who have sold out to Enlightenment rationality. Traditional authority is under attack today in every sector of society. From the moment Max Weber proposed the notion of the "rationalization" of conduct, the common wisdom has been that decisions are taken today in order to fulfill freely chosen goals by the most efficient and effective means, not because things have always been done in a certain way. *Sapere aude*, "dare to think for yourself," said Immanuel Kant. And we do. Modern men and women are learning to consult their own minds and feelings and to reason in a means-ends calculus. They are no longer, as Bonhoeffer put it, under the "tutelage" of the church. This is not to say that traditions as such have ceased to function in our culture. Far from it. At the level of unconscious motivation, in the context of community norms, tradition and traditions remain powerful. Yet the sense of having thrown off the ecclesiastical and social heteronomies of the past is part of contemporary consciousness in the West, and will not easily go away.

But the critique of the house of authority and all that goes with it is also being mounted today from within the church by thinkers who have the well-being of the faith community, not defense of the Enlightenment, in mind. Farley argues that many features of the "scriptural principle," of the dogmatic elaboration of apostolic teaching, and of the teaching authority of the institution quite simply may never have been appropriate to the sort of faith community the New Testament church set out to be. One may ask, of course, if anyone today can know, apart from these very suspect sources, what that original intention was. In any case, scholars today critically interrogate the institutional settings and logics through which tradition has been transmitted, discovering that these channels have introduced serious anomalies and distortions.

There are questions of inclusiveness: how far were the contributions of women and perhaps others systematically suppressed? There are problems of evidence: how far were the early decisions about authority and tradition dependent on taking dogmatic propositions as if they were history? There are problems of consistency: how far did the distinctive form of the "scriptural principle" adopted by the early church correspond to its essence as a community? And there are problems of conceptualization: how far did the notion of tradition rest on particular theological understandings, let us say, of the churches' teaching as identical with the will and purpose of God, or of "salvation history" as a logic dependent on a monarchical metaphor of the divine? Today these inner anomalies, these fateful choices by the early church of principles of institutional continuity inappropriate to its nature, must at last be confronted. The new situation of the churches does not create these difficulties, but it does expose them by framing the question in ways we can no longer avoid.

Finally, and this is the third point, one cannot forget the changes wrought by tradition's passage through the general public consciousness of the West. In this respect, continental Europe, Britain, and North America offer substantially different experiences. But in all three cases, Christianity, in both explicit and subliminal forms, has played an important role in the general store of attitudes and ideas underlying speech and action. Indeed, it is probably true to say, despite the secular-

ization of these societies, and despite the radical decline of
biblical knowledge both in the churches and in culture, that
Christian tradition continues to infuse its dreams and themes
into art, music, and various other forms of popular culture.
This is particularly true in North America. It is why Martin
Luther King, Jr. discovered the Bible to be so powerful a
rhetorical ally both inside the church and beyond. People still
think in biblical images, speak in its language, feel in its forms,
perhaps without knowing what they are doing. A biblical
ethos continues to exist, and indeed to survive the decline of
the churches which originally sponsored it in the culture. This
is certainly true in much contemporary American literature,
where not only archetypal biblical scenes and narratives have
their influence but writers make use of genres such as the
jeremiad, the saga, the parable and the apocalypse. Likewise,
music and lyrics reflecting biblical imagery and communicating with prophetic power has migrated from houses of worship to concert halls and opera houses. The Bible has become
an element in American culture transcending its original settings and patterns of interpretation.[31]

Enough of these echoes persist to mislead secular opinion
makers, media personalities, and even certain television
evangelists, into thinking they are correctly stating the tenets
of Christian faith when they are not. Christian ideas and
images—of a kind—may have reached a broader general cir-
culation today than at any time in the past. That neither
theologians nor church authorities approve of the form these
ideas and images take in their cultural dispersion does not
change the basic truth that there remains a certain Christian
content in today's varieties of "civil religion."[32]

In North America, for example, the political use of culturally dispersed elements of Christian tradition by forces on the
right is simply a part of the religious situation. It is not hard
to discern what happens to traditional content in such a situation. The original direction, thrust, and internal logic of the
tradition become unrecognizable as disconnected fragments
of it adhere to, or are taken over by, essentially alien interests.
This means that it is extremely difficult for historically knowl-

edgeable and theologically responsible interpretations of the tradition to get a hearing. Everyone, according to his or her political interests, already "knows" what the tradition says. Or, to put the same point in different terms, the dispersed and distorted tradition becomes "irreformable."[33] Nothing the organized faith community can do will change the public perception of what the tradition is and means. The community of faith may well discover that its own members gain more knowledge of their religious heritage from films, popular novels, and the evening news than they do from the religious community's own teaching. But this also means that the tradition is bound to be interpreted in multiple, sometimes mutually incompatible, ways. The problems of pluralism and contextuality are thus bound to emerge.

3. Pluralism and Contextuality

As theologians struggle with the problems of tradition in the house of authority, life in the myriad cultures, faith communities, families, and persons represented in St. Peter's Square does not stand still. The seeming deconstruction of, or loss of confidence in, the ecclesio-logic of religious establishments has been simultaneous with a multiplication of different expressions of the faith in religious communities and situations of many sorts, whose common factor seems to be that they are culturally marginal to the sort of venue in which the traditional "logic of triumph" typically finds its home.

What is going on here? Two concepts have become salient in recent discussion: the notions of *pluralism* and of *contextuality*. These ideas need clarification if we are to have any frame of reference at all for what must, initially, be a matter of attentive listening before it becomes a question of analysis or criticism. It remains to be seen whether what is particular and local is for that reason more likely to be authentic.

Pluralism of one sort or another has always been a characteristic of Christian community life. Why does it seem suddenly so important now? After all, the New Testament itself is a collection of documents from different contexts displaying important differences of presupposition, perception, rhetorical method, and theological perspective. What is new today is not the fact of pluralism, but rather the theological significance attached to it. Edward Hobbs, in an important article "Pluralism as an Issue,"[34] suggests that while the reality to which the word "pluralism" refers has been with us for millennia, the *concept* of pluralism is of recent vintage. The appearance of a concept means that it has become important to mark the reality, if not to advocate it, at least to insist that it be taken into account. Hobbs distinguishes the new sense of "pluralism" from two older notions: "indifferentism" and "toleration." The first means that differences of religious belief and practice are considered unimportant. The second, that we may permit what we do not necessarily endorse or approve. In contrast to both these understandings, the word pluralism now says that something important has happened to society such that the perennial multiplicity of languages and communities of faith has become salient, and thus claims attention.

What is the basis of this claim? Some are saying that it is a moral claim. Philip Hefner has written that in our world, "each of the parts requires and demands acknowledgment and the opportunity *to be itself* on terms that are commensurate with its integrity."[35] Our planet has become a "multicultural liberated global village."[36] The easy communications we enjoy appear to have intensified the themes of individuality and group identification. At a time when notions of "planet earth" and of the whole human race as a "global village" have become vivid to our imaginations, we are also coming to realize that humanity is many communities, self-identified and discerned on the basis of many different rationales, each "requiring and demanding" the right to exist on its own terms. And we feel the moral pressure in these demands.

The emergence of pluralism as a factor to be reckoned with is a cultural and political as well as a moral event. Until the recent past, the dominant groups in society have always been able to define reality so as to "mask" the public identity of the poor, of women, or of marginalized ethnic groups. The dominant groups "defined the nature of reality so as to make their own political resolution to be the equivalent of the "natural order'." But our planetary society, now as never before, is composed of groups and individuals who "possess their own integrity, identity, and experience which requires that they be acknowledged in their own right."[37]

This new recognition of pluralism has made "contextuality" a theme to be reckoned with. If one can no longer take for granted that the expression of faith traditions in traditional ecclesiastical contexts is simply normative, then one must ask how other interactions between tradition and society are to be regarded. One must ask how such relationships are forged. And the copious evidence of pluralism and contextuality throughout Scripture and church history begins to be seen in a new light. It is not surprising, then, that ecumenical dialoguers have encountered this new vision of pluralism and wondered what to do about it.

Depending upon the situation, the struggle for integrity in faith may take a variety of forms, so much so that one community's life-or-death issue may be of little concern to others. For faith communities in Western Europe the questions to be addressed in confessing the faith are liable to be very like the questions of their contemporaries both inside the church and out, couched in the despairing terms of a piety "after the death of God," and hence addressed to the processes of secularization and pluralization in society generally. For congregations in Eastern Europe, until very recently, confessing the faith meant clarifying the line *between* them and their contemporaries, hence restating the traditional faith against outside pressures. It is too soon to know how developments of the last two years will change this situation. In Latin America, the life-or-death issue is that of justice in the society as a whole. In North America, it is difficult to discern what issue is central to the integrity of Christian witness. The problem of witness may lie precisely in the multitude of problems, and in the difficulty faithful persons find in addressing such issues without lapsing into "single issue politics," or into the religious individualism which Robert Bellah has identified in *Habits of the Heart.* One might go on. And these broad differences of perspective hardly begin to get at the specific nuances, questions of indigenization, challenges to local witness, and the like which distinguish the question of confession in each particular situation from that obtaining in every other situation.

In terms of an analysis of the "logic" that inheres in different ecclesial forms of life, pluralism and contextuality raise a whole new set of issues. It is not merely the outward appearance or coloration of the gospel that is different in different contexts. Situation seems in large measure to determine what the faith-community believes the gospel message *is.* An underlying family resemblance may exist between the forms of the gospel preached, say, in a West German Lutheran congregation, a Roman Catholic parish in Nicaragua, a conservative Baptist church in Texas, or a Russian Orthodox parish in St. Petersburg. But there will be great differences in the ways the gospel is expressed: the center of the message will be located at different points, and the networks of inference and implication from that center worked out in different ways.

Is there "one gospel for the whole world?"[38] We need to know how radical the reality of pluralism is, how total the dependence of faith articulations upon context, including the unique context of each individual. On the one hand, one may hold to the view that tradition and faith are one despite their many forms. On this showing, all that is needed is skill in adapting the *depositum fidei* to the conditions that obtain in any given case. At the other extreme, one may conclude that we are faced with what amounts to an irreducible diversity of modes of Christian faith and life. If so, there may be no "one gospel for the whole world" or at least none that can be articulated as a unity.

Perhaps the truth lies somewhere in between. Still the intellectual and spiritual challenge is formidable. The church faces life-or-death issues, issues around which cluster questions of basic integrity, and faithfulness to the gospel. But the issues in different parts of the world are not the same. In the West the "crisis of cognitive claims" continues to be very real.

But in Latin America the issue is between the Christianity of the rich and the Christianity of the poor. And what about South Africa, Eastern Europe, or Asia? It is not merely a question of adaptation or application of the gospel to circumstances, but rather fundamental differences of perspective, divergent ways of conceiving what the gospel is about. When pluralism reaches a certain point, contextuality begins to become more important than tradition, more important than any ideal or essential unity the faith may possess. How far along this path is it legitimate to go? What theological method, in touch with tradition yet open and creative, might be adequate for making sense of this new situation?

4. The Crisis of Conceptualization

Let us briefly review the argument to this point. On the one hand, the notion of "tradition" is in trouble. The house of authority with its traditional logic of triumph—all that Bernini says architecturally and much that is implied in scores of Protestant church bureaucracies—is dysfunctional with reference to the gospel's setting in the present human situation. On the other hand, the faith is now being articulated and lived in a multitude of apparently incompatible forms, some deeply communal and morally engaged, some radically privatistic, each bearing witness to an apparently different version of the gospel.

In such a situation it is no wonder that the churches are experiencing a third dimension of perplexity, a seeming loss of coherence, indeed of reality sense, in theological reflection. The fact of disarray in the professional theological community is obvious enough. There is little or no accord in the Christian world now about the objectives, materials, or methods of theological discourse. The great modern schools of constructive theology—neo-Thomism, neo-orthodoxy, and others—seem played out. They have been replaced by myriad regional or individual theological initiatives, none of which has yet captured and reordered the theological enterprise as a whole. Moreover, constructive theological work—and there is a surprising amount of it—seems alienated from, and in some cases distrusted by, communities of believers. It is not clear even that theological work which claims a relationship to some specific community is in fact known and embraced by most members of the community in question. There is a distance between "Black theology" and the reality of the "Black church." So too for feminist theologies, Hispanic theologies, and even for the various Third World theologies of liberation.

What has gone wrong? The collapse of methodological and systematic coherence in reflection has been more acute in Protestantism than in Roman Catholicism, but no part of the church has escaped. It is well known, for example, that somewhere about the mid-sixties the dominantly Barthian "dialectical theology," known in its North American, mainly Niebuhrian forms as "neo-orthodoxy," ceased for many to be persuasive. Langdon Gilkey in a celebrated *Christian Century* article[39] described the sensation as one of feeling the solid ground on which he thought he had been standing turn to shifting floes of ice. This is not to say that Barth, Tillich, Bultmann, the Niebuhrs, and others have had no intellectual children and grandchildren. There remain many teaching today who are basically neo-orthodox, if only because little else with staying power has come along. A continuing neo-orthodoxy of the left follows Troeltsch, Bonhoeffer, Lehmann, and Reist. A growing right-wing neo-orthodoxy, mainly followed by "evangelicals" in search of something more faithful than literalism, has rediscovered Karl Barth. But the neo-orthodox school as a whole has lost the preeminence it once had. It shares attention today with a multitude of other initiatives, some already mentioned, some yet to be described.

Roman Catholic thought enjoys, if that be the word, a stabilizing factor and agenda-focusing mechanism which Protestantism does not: the teaching *magisterium* which defines formal doctrinal teaching as opposed to the *theologoumena* of the professors. One therefore feels less disoriented by a multitude of individual voices, and readier to put the work of particular teachers in their place. Besides, Roman Catholics have not succumbed quite as Protestants have to the "star system." It is not so clear, for example, that the relative eclipse of a Rahner or a Schillebeeckx would mean loss of their essential insights. These have already been woven into the thinking of others, well known or not. A whole new generation of Roman Catholic writers has emerged, writers who build carefully both on tradition and on the work of their immediate predecessors in a way that individualistic Protestant authors writing episodic essays still need to learn.

Perhaps one may generalize about the entire post-World War II generation of theologians, Protestant and Roman Catholic alike. They have failed adequately to clarify the relation between faith and history, between doctrine and lived experience. With respect to the Protestants, the critique by Van A. Harvey in *The Historian and the Believer*[40] was and continues to be devastating. And what Harvey demonstrated conceptually was felt by many experientially. As a recent dissertation by William Silva[41] has shown, neo-orthodoxy never caught on in the parish. The old chasm that this school was intended to bridge, between the old orthodoxy and the experience of modern human beings, between the "evangelical" and "liberal" interpretations of the faith, remains very much in place so far as the church is concerned. The dialectics and subtleties of Barth and Rahner were too much for either pulpit or pew.

One consequence of all this has been the emergence of a type called by Van Harvey "the alienated theologian,"[42] the theological scholar who has few roots in the community of faith, who writes mainly for his or her colleagues in the academy. Even when the intended result has been different, many a thinker has ended up this way, finding that the requirements of honesty in dealing with evidence and clarity in following arguments made it all but impossible to produce materials of use in the community of faith. As a result, the conceptual construal of Christian faith today has lost the sense of solidity and integrity it once had. The theological faculties no longer make clear to the church what it means to be Christian. Rather, they tend to produce work which unsettles the faith community, provoking misunderstanding, resentment, and alienation in return.

Graduating seminarians of every background, and those

who induct them into church leadership, feel keenly this cultural gap between classroom and parish. What continues to be taught in theological faculties and seminaries fits poorly the disordered reality of today's Christian life-in-faith, which is not in fact what any of the traditional theologies presuppose it to be. Yet for theological reflection to take place at all there needs to be some stable community of faith, worship, and witness to function as a reality-base. Today one may find the appearance of such theologically articulated community, but seldom the reality.

Each of the classical traditions of theological discourse has tacitly presupposed some community of believers whom those who have the theological vocation serve. This has surely been true of the great historic confessional bodies: Roman Catholic, Orthodox, Calvinist, Lutheran. But it has been true as well of the different schools of thought. Existentialists and process thinkers, for example, have at least thought they were addressing modern human beings of a particular kind, say anxious members of the bourgeoisie, or scientists unhappy with the totalitarian claims of positivism. But it is not clear that these connections between schools of thought and identifiable groups now exist. It is hard to find the historic confessions alive in distinctive and coherent communities (the Orthodox in some places may be the exception). And the human types supposedly addressed by existentialist, process, and other schools are remarkably elusive. They may exist in one decade, or in one culture, but not in another.

Today the theological situation is both worse and better. Worse, because the shifting ice floes sensed in 1965 by Langdon Gilkey and others are now being swept out to sea and melted altogether by the storms of deconstructionism. Better, because the radical relativism of our time opens the door for a reaffirmation of the value of faith communities gathered again around the full riches of their traditions.

Deconstruction radically questions the relationship between discourse and reality. What hold, if any, can that which we say have upon something called truth? In the hands of a philosopher like Michel Foucault, our whole way of seeing the world, our whole conception of factuality, is radically historicized. Knowing is related to the discursive practices which are in power in any given time or situation, and these change radically from one moment in history to the next. As the feminist theologian Sharon Welch puts it, "the distinction between true and false is shown to be contingent, shifting, and beyond our grasp and conscious control."[43] What passes for knowledge is related to ways of putting the world together, which is largely determined by those in power at a given time. One can speak of a "political economy of truth."[44]

Indeed, the coherence of what we mean by "humanity" itself is now at risk. The different "human sciences," which should have some grasp of this "human" reality, today represent a complex and incoherent set of constructs[45] representing the power of the professorate and of those who fund and administer the universities in which they teach and the grants they receive for research. Human science is part of the Western establishment, and for Foucault, it has fastened a series of interpretations (psychological, sociological, anthropological) on human beings which fail to grasp a large part of what human experience is about. We are witnessing today, Foucault asserts, a protest against this academic imperialism in the form of "an insurrection of subjugated knowledges."[46] Human beings are summoning the courage to insist that others must do more than put them in categories. Others must come to know, so far as that is possible, what it *is* to be a Central American *campesino*, an asylum inmate, or a member of the suppressed democratic opposition in China. The human sciences need to relativize their theories and assume listening postures.

The theologian can take a certain comfort from all this unrest. Epistemological modesty and a posture of listening are already part of his or her program. Perhaps the unraveling of theological systems has not been a sign of the collapse of that discipline at all. Perhaps it has been an early warning to sensitive people of something happening across the whole range of human knowledge. Perhaps the unique task of theology today is to give voice to all the "subjugated knowledges" that truly represent the human condition and that up to now have been largely excluded from consideration in the academic arena.

But this agenda can be read in at least two ways. On the one hand are those who say that the most important "subjugated knowledge" in modern Western culture is that of classical Christian faith itself. It is this faith, some say, which can both welcome the excluded and downtrodden, and, in a world of relativism, help human beings put their lives together around shared values. A valued tradition fully lived can then be free of the need to defend itself against reality definitions alleged to be held by all genuinely modern human beings. In this view, the Enlightenment vision of the world no longer has pride of place. The faith tradition can be the criterion of reality within which one lives, moves, and has one's being. This is approximately the position now being maintained by an increasing company of neo-traditionalists: Hans Frei, George Lindbeck, Thomas Oden, Stanley Hauerwas, William Willimon, and others.[47] It is a position which rejoins the theologian to the community of faith. Yet perhaps it does so at the risk of encouraging a new sectarianism or even fideism, in which the theologian would work without significant links to the wider range of human consciousness and human concerns.

The other reading of our situation now is that which seeks to construct a "public theology," an interpretation of faith which can pass muster in terms of widely held criteria of valid knowledge and argument. For the public theologians, writers such as Gordon Kaufman[48] and David Tracy,[49] theology has the duty to be part of what Richard Rorty calls "the conversation of humankind."[50] A public theology seeks to remind the culture at large of questions of origin and meaning. It seeks the public good. It seeks conversation with other faiths, viewing all faiths as related to each other by analogy. Traditions are not seen merely as the inheritance of particular faith communities but rather, in David Tracy's phrase, as available to all in the forms of religious "classics." The risk here, obviously, is that theological work becomes merely the dialogue of those who read the great books. It is not certain that many are listening. Faith communities, which should provide theology its social base, receive little immanent critique or support from the thinkers they nurture and send forth.

One aim of this book is to write an ecclesiology that can learn from both these relatively new, yet in another sense very old, theological programs. In fact, I argue that the question of the church can offer these viewpoints a unique common arena for dialogue. The ecclesiological question today concerns the effort of traditional yet often dysfunctional communities to recover the meaning of their traditions. To their surprise, they may find these traditions being enacted, sometimes more authentically, in the public world. Hence they must be the church even as they re-imagine the very nature of the church. The challenge is to conceive of traditioned forms of life, not as sectarian groups sharing no life beyond their own, but as gatherings which, because of the content of the tradition by which they live, can give voice to the many ways of knowing the work of the Spirit—some of them still subjugated—in the "public" world around them. If such groups become seemingly "sectarian," it is to gain the coherence of heart and mind needed for a genuinely ecumenical task. They may live by tradition, but that tradition compels them to turn outward, to listen, to include. We must now ask how far this is happening in certain new forms of Christian life that are beginning to emerge in the midst of the old.

5. *The Search for New Forms of Life*

Perhaps it is an illusion of historical distance to suppose that Christian life as actually lived has ever been coherent with received ecclesiastical assumptions and expectations. But the impression persists that past epochs saw greater wholeness and stability in the relation between formal theological affirmations and the lived stream of faith experience. Surely a century and more ago it would have been easier to find communities that followed what could be identified as a Reformed, Lutheran, Anglican, or Roman Catholic way of life. But today one can read the old theological manuals, survey the old moral admonitions, without quite knowing what it must have been to build a daily life on their terms. We cannot grasp what it must have meant to live in an era in which Christian life together was lived in the way the books say it should have been. We cannot recover the sense of what it must have been to exist in Calvin's Geneva, or in Counter-Reformation Rome. We no longer know how to link the life of faith with thought in the old ways. The churches maintain their continuity as institutions, but their members' sense of the meaning of the faith as a coherent form of life has undergone a sea-change which makes many traditional theological formulas, and some new ones as well, indecipherable.

The Enlightenment may have been responsible for some of this. But more likely one should credit the advent of a mass culture in which church members absorb their understandings of faith more from reflections of it in the media than from their own congregations' faint-hearted (and often amateurish) educational efforts. Capitulation to such a culture has meant a combination of theological amnesia with trivialization of ethical reflection. Contemporary traditions of public discourse—the commonly shared vocabularies and usages of government, the media, and so on—are ignorant of or unable to fathom the languages of confessional practice, if they do not simply identify such language and practice with its worst examples in the electronic evangelists. The churches, too, must employ these debased vocabularies, for they have no other basis on which to communicate with their thoroughly acculturated members.

If this is a correct perception of our present situation, what follows? Alasdair MacIntyre, in *After Virtue*,[51] makes strikingly similar observations with a hypothetical parable of catastrophe in the history of science. Suppose, writes MacIntyre, that through some sort of philistine uprising the whole establishment of natural science were destroyed: laboratories sacked, equipment smashed, schools closed, faculties scattered. A generation or so later we begin to have some inkling of what we have lost, but all we can lay hands on is a few volumes, a few journals, the edges of their pages scorched.

Could we, from these written works alone, quickly recover the sense of what it *was* to be scientific theorists and investigators? Could we recreate the lived sense of the community of science? Could we discover quickly again what it *was*, in terms both of understanding and practical skills, actually to work in a laboratory? MacIntyre's answer is that we could not do any of these things authentically. Not without the continuity of the living practice of the profession and of the tradition of the community of inquiry. So it is with the relationship today between theological literature and the life of faith. It is impossible to recover from the literature what life totally shaped by that literature's vision must have been like. The passage of time has meant loss of the reality. Only the words remain. Traditional *institutions* of faith with their characteristic styles of expression have largely lost the ability to mediate the shared *substance* of faith to the contemporary world.

At the end of his book, MacIntyre calls attention to an earlier time in which a religio-political institution similarly began to lose touch with, to dissipate, its inner spiritual substance. He points with caution to parallels between our era and that of the decline of the Roman Empire into the Dark Ages. The ancient *imperium*, which had replaced its pagan cultus with Christianity at the time of Constantine and within whose precincts the very idea and practice of "virtue" had grown up, began to be perceived by discerning citizens as institutionally no longer adequate to the task of maintaining all that "virtue" had meant. The official organs, with their ways of thinking and acting, began to be seen by some as no longer able to grasp what the classical, and now the Christian, ideal had been about. Corruption within, barbarian invasions from without, all wreaked their havoc. The whole Roman system, which still looked much the same from the outside, had become empty and dysfunctional inside. It needed to be revitalized by new forms of life that *remembered* as they innovated. MacIntyre puts it this way:

> A crucial turning point in that earlier history occurred when men and women of good will turned aside from the task of

shoring up the Roman imperium and ceased to identify the continuation of civility and moral community with the maintenance of that imperium. What they set themselves to achieve instead—often not recognizing fully what they were doing—was the construction of new forms of community within which moral life could be sustained so that both morality and civility might survive the coming ages of barbarism and darkness. If my account of our moral condition is correct, we ought also to conclude that for some time now we too have reached that turning point. What matters at this stage is the construction of local forms of community through which civility and the intellectual and moral life can be sustained through the new dark ages which are already upon us. And if the tradition of the virtues was able to survive the horrors of the last dark ages, we are not entirely without grounds for hope. This time, however, the barbarians are not waiting beyond the frontiers. They have already been governing us for quite some time. And it is our lack of consciousness of this that constitutes part of our predicament. We are waiting not for a Godot, but for another—doubtless very different—St. Benedict.[52]

This oft-quoted passage is still worth remembering. Despite its aristocratic overtone, it is saying that some Roman citizens, in the midst of change and decay, had the discernment and enterprise to maintain the classical republican and Christian ideals in social forms which could nurture them until an age dawned—presumably the high middle ages—which would appreciate them anew.[53] The barbarians come off poorly in MacIntyre's picture, yet what these barbarians' sixteenth-century German, Swiss, and Dutch descendants made of Christian faith was just as important for the future as what St. Benedict made of it, if not more so. The Reformation, Roland Bainton used to say, was the indigenization of an originally Mediterranean faith in northern Europe. The Protestant progeny of the sixth-century invaders of Rome, learning from what the monasteries preserved, made their own signal contributions to ecclesiological understanding.

But what about St. Benedict himself? Could he have imagined, as he drew up the rule for his new order on Monte

Cassino, that he was not only reinterpreting an established but dysfunctional tradition, not only nurturing a new spirituality, but also giving classical and lasting form to a new logic of belief in a new form of life? That he was providing social space for insights and impulses present among persons and communities in the Roman Church of his day but not previously able to find expression in that Church's late and beleaguered Constantinian compromise? In communities bound to a rule of life the Christian faith of the late Roman Empire found a live embodiment which enabled this faith both to renew its identity and to find new, and unexpected, relevance to its times.

Historians say that what Benedict accomplished in founding his Order was to combine a sense of order, proportion, and decency from the Roman *res-publica* with the aspiration to mirror the simplicity, the holy poverty, and the purposefulness of the early church in Jerusalem. He put these things together in a freshly conceived ecclesial form with a new logic of common life at its core. There had been monasteries before, but Benedict studied what had been learned in them, added ideas of his own, and codified the whole in a form that could be replicated elsewhere. What resulted were unexpected, but potent, expressions of Christian faith centered on a spiritual discipline within and exerting immense political, social, and cultural influence on the human worlds around them.

The Benedictine Rule, of course, was not the only new logic of Christian life together to make an impact on its times and beyond. Other movements did comparable things—the Franciscans, the monks of Cluny, the Jesuits, the *Devotio Moderna* founded by the monks of the Brethren of the Common Life under Gerhard Groote. In the words of Margaret Miles, the last-mentioned "quickly became a lay movement, inspiring gatherings of hundreds of groups of people in the Netherlands and eventually reaching into southern Europe."[54] Miles has called these the base communities of the fifteenth century.[55] They were motivated by the idea that life in the world, and not only in the monastery, could be a spiri-

tual discipline. Members were expected to continue their ac-
customed lives, but now in a way powerfully informed by
communal study, discussion of Scripture, and prayer.

Movements like these are appearing again today. They
are, for the most part, not products of theological cogitation or
strategizing, let alone of analyses such as MacIntyre's. They
are, rather, eruptions of spiritual energy in their various situations which only subsequently give rise to theological reflection. Iona and Taizé have been with us for more than a
generation. The "base communities" in Latin America and
elsewhere spring to mind, and likewise that now almost forgotten American phenomenon, the "underground church."[56]
The network of sanctuary churches, while it lasted, offered
another model involving, for the most part, established congregations. There are, of course, many other centers of spiritual and communal renewal.

Many contemporary renewal communities are expressions of larger theological movements which need to be understood in their own right. Feminist theology, racial/ethnic
theologies in North America and elsewhere, the varying liberation theologies of Latin America, Africa, and Asia—all find
their expressions in actual communities of believers. The bet-
ter-known communities of renewal and those connected with
particular theological ideologies are not the only ones that
should count in this recital. New communal expressions of life
within familiar congregational forms today deserve to be
numbered among the witnesses to reforming spiritual energy.
In fact, these less visible expressions are by far the most
numerous and may, in the end, be the most important. Seldom
today does what actually happens in such seemingly conventional gatherings of believers actually conform to established
ecclesiastical norms. Each such congregation becomes a
unique culture, or sub-culture, in its own right. The new field
of "congregational studies"[57] demonstrates that one needs
categories from cultural anthropology or ethnography, rather
than from traditional ecclesiology, to understand adequately
the fresh forms of life that are springing up, in the first and
second worlds as well as in the third and fourth.

These innovative Christian communities across the globe have important testimony to bear because they are often closer to the situations in which the future of humanity may possibly be beginning to appear. These gatherings are remarkably comprehensive. At various times and places they embrace priests and laypersons, women and men, Protestants and Roman Catholics, believers and unbelievers, adherents of other religions and of no religion, and no doubt categories unimagined. They are able to discern, and cooperate with, the workings of the Spirit both within and beyond the formal boundaries of "church membership" or communion. They are able at certain moments and in various ways to make a new human reality visible to the world. They provide their own kinds of social space in which unexpected things can happen. They are like seismic data-gathering points which detect changes in the spiritual terrain by being in touch with events below the surface, with socially subjugated experiences and forms of knowledge in which the human future is taking form.

But it is not enough simply to view all this romantically or ideologically. What is new, what is exciting, may or may not faithfully express the gospel in its context. One tends to approach the contention between Cardinal Ratzinger of the Congregation for the Doctrine of the Faith in Rome (formerly called the Holy Office and before that the Inquisition), and the host of ecclesiastical innovators his Congregation has called to account, simply by taking sides. But this takes too lightly the question of the unity and catholicity of the people of God. The new faith communities in and of themselves seldom create difficulties for the ecclesiastical authorities. Theological interpretations of them that challenge traditional ecclesiological assumptions do. An example of such challenge, and of the prelatical response, may been seen in the controversy between Cardinal Ratzinger and Friar Leonardo Boff.[58] Boff is only to a limited degree the instigator of spiritual ferment among the poor in today's Brazil, but he is a major theological interpreter of it. Boff's books, which circulate worldwide, imply a theological claim to apostolicity and catholicity for the base communities and their vision of the church which runs counter to the tradition as understood in Rome. If not by the methods of Cardinal Ratzinger, how *shall* the church determine what is faithful and authentic and what is not? Clearly we need some new means of interpreting the life of Christian communities which come together in innovative ways around issues of human well-being and destiny in today's world. The next chapter begins a search for the needed way into this subject. Taking a clue from Boff, we will call the formation of these new communities "ecclesiogenesis:" the literal recreating of the universal church in each place where they live and grow. We will then look for a way of studying the formation of such communities adequate to their nature and intention. Because what goes on in these gatherings is a shared "reading" of the Spirit's people-shaping work in the world, we will need a "hermeneutic" or principle of interpretation to guide us. Making clear what that means is the task of the next chapter.

Toward a Hermeneutic for Ecclesiogenesis

If the analysis just offered is even partly accurate, the churches will need to think new thoughts about how they do their thinking. The social realities of faith within and around the churches today do not correspond to the expectations implicit in these bodies' formal structures. We have seen some of the reasons why. Tradition does not shape faith community the way it once did. Pluralism is rampant. Theological conceptualities are in disarray. In short, classical confessional norms for judging the authenticity of church life are more and more dysfunctional in today's world. Yet all this is happening just at the moment when new kinds of socially engaged congregations, base communities, religious orders, liberation organizations, and issue-focused associations are bursting forth with fresh spiritual energy for the church and for the human community. How are we to "test the spirits" in such a fluid situation? How are the churches to rethink their nature and calling? How are we to begin to reframe the very idea of a church universal?

1. A Perspective for Ecclesiology: Discernment and Vision

This chapter proposes a perspective for ecclesiology in this situation. My hypothesis is this: by their relation to Jesus Christ, Christian communities of faith are lived decipherments and expressive embodiments of the people-configuring work of the Holy Spirit in the social and cultural worlds in which the churches live. Congregations discern Spirit-formed social realities in the world and bring them into a christological frame of reference which makes them visible. Congregations thereby articulate the human communities around them *as* spaces in which the Spirit's people-gathering power is active. By proclaiming the gospel, celebrating the liturgy, and acting prophetically they signify that God is continually forming communities of people to be agents of justice, peace, and freedom. Christian congregations are not to be identified with the people of God. Rather they discern its signs and seek to express these signs sacramentally.

In order to do this, congregations bring together myriad elements of shared human life. Church members bring with them specific genetic inheritances, cultural idiosyncracies, traits of character, educational backgrounds, habits of language, economic involvements, family ties, occupational perspectives, and so on. Through their networks of relationship with others they represent still wider ranges of human experience. All these things are ingredients for the church community's construal or metaphorical construction of the world. A faith community cannot be adequately understood solely by consulting its formal polity. It can only be understood as a gathering of persons who bring with them all the kinds of life substance mentioned and more, a community which aims at configuring all this so as to represent the identity of Jesus Christ and thereby to articulate the shapes of God's presence in the world through the work of the Holy Spirit.

In practice, of course, it may be difficult if not impossible to find the Spirit's people-shaping work. The effort to discern and signify the reality of a people of God often finds the world of human action to be ambiguous, murky, or worse. Our best efforts may be short-circuited by misperception. Yet traces of a people-forming Spirit are sometimes discovered in seemingly unpromising situations of personal, economic, cultural or political life. This can happen when events are found to have some inherent reconciling power, or when participation in them, often entirely outside the bounds of the congregation, can be seen as an act of witness to the reign of God.

The churches' ties with the American civil rights movement during the 1960s are a case in point. The effort to achieve equality for Blacks was at first largely based in the Black churches, but it soon came to involve many other groups and social forces: unions, universities, the legal profession, and so on. White congregations were often indifferent or antagonistic, but white denominational leadership and the liberal wing of the white clergy not only rallied to the cause, but also found in it a sense, all but lost now for a generation or more, of God's active involvement in human life. One could readily understand the people of God to be those at any given time who worked together in the movement to be instruments of God's justice for humankind. Many congregations discerned here a larger people-forming work of the Spirit. None could identify themselves with this work; it was much larger than they. But some could and did find ways to manifest its deeper meaning sacramentally.

Thus it made sense for many Christian bodies to identify with and draw strength from the March on Washington of August 28, 1963. For many, the crowd in front of the Lincoln Memorial when Martin Luther King, Jr., delivered his "I have a dream" speech itself seemed itself to have "the soul of a church."[1] To this day those who were there remember not only the celebrated address, but also the sense of spiritual communion among the many political, social, and religious agendas represented in the crowd. Many commentators called attention to the power which lay in the convergence of these forces: civil rights organizations, labor unions, political action groups, veterans' groups, local synagogues and congregations, national denominations, government workers, dele-

gations from overseas, and more. A strange courtesy and for-
bearance animated this throng through hours of waiting for
the program to begin. Temporary and highly diverse "neighborhoods" coalesced on the sidewalks and lawns, companions
breaking bread, conversing quietly, sharing expectations.
Here was a threshold moment: like that in St. Peter's Square,
but still more inclusive. A multitude of attitudes, agendas,
cultural assumptions, economic and political interests, and
forms of faith or unfaith were transformed for a few hours
into vehicles for something more than the simple sum of what
they were as they came. These forces were momentarily re-
grouped into a new pattern of meaning. Many churches identified themselves with that new meaning. They found in it the
work of the Holy Spirit, and included the story of the day, at
least for a while, in their own stories of faith.[2]

I argue that this is a paradigm for *ecclesiogenesis*. The
formation of churches always involves some sort of discernment of the Spirit's work in the world and an attempt to
manifest that work in visible forms of life. With sufficient
vision, the churches may come to see that the Spirit's people-
forming work is larger and more inclusive than anything they
can possibly represent with their own resources. Hence
becoming the church does not mean making exclusive claims.
It means prophetic decipherment on the one hand, and lived
signification on the other. I maintain that this is essentially an
exegetical or interpretative process which leads to the building and constant re-forming of the visible church in the midst
of the world.

Such an interpretative process needs to be governed by a
hermeneutic or pattern of principled reflection concerning its
meaning. A "hermeneutic for ecclesiogenesis" is thus a coherently thought-through understanding of what is going on
when believers form a community which interprets the world
as the space of God's reign. Such a hermeneutic seeks to
understand the process through which the congregation *itself*
becomes a readable sign of the Spirit's work. The congregation reads the signs and symbols generated by the Spirit's
energizing presence. It then appropriates these signs and

symbols—makes them its own—so as to become itself a living sacrament or sign. But what makes the signs of the world "readable?" What happens when they are appropriated so as to form a church? And what is the proper method for studying these moves? Is it some hermeneutical form of the sociology of religion, or is it ecclesiology in the fully theological sense of the term?

2. A Phenomenology of Spirit

I have been using the word "spirit" (small "s"), as well as the related but distinct terms "Spirit" and "Holy Spirit," in descriptions of the way a world-involved people of God comes to be deciphered and made visible in particular faith communities. What justifies this terminology? How do these words function in my argument? Social reality is "readable" in the manner sketched above because it is an objectification of "spirit" (small "s") in the sense of shared human intention and meaning. Intention and meaning take concrete form in the structures of society and the achievements of culture, as well as in less permanent expressions. Given the right clues, these expressions, linguistic and otherwise, can be "read." I will argue that a reading of human "spirit" in the light of Christ can discern "Holy Spirit," and that a doctrinal construction of what is involved here can yield a concept: *"the* Holy Spirit."[3]

On the way to this worldly objectification of spirit is the unending dialogue among life possibilities which constitutes the realm of spirit as such. Spirit grows from consciousness to self-consciousness through encounter with others. It finds symbolic means of expression from the simplest to the most complex. It generates metaphor and language and narrative and history and philosophy. Spirit is not something ghostly or other-worldly or even idealistic. It is the substance of human life together seen as inherently, by its very nature, an expressive medium. By speaking of human being-in-time as "spirit" we are saying that it is alive, it is meaningful.

I am contending that congregations are lived readings of

this human life process. I want to say more about human spirit now, leaving Holy Spirit for the next section of the chapter. Human spirit is lived sense in the social world. It is important for our analysis to have a vivid idea of how the different elements of human sociality participate in something that can be called by this term. How can the social world be understood as intrinsically a field of interacting intentions and meanings?

Let me now begin to draw a map of the conceptual field we are entering. The social world as space of enspirited interaction has both synchronic (meaning what is the case at any given moment) and diachronic (tracing the movement of persons and institutions over time) perspectives. At any given point in time, society exists as a vocabulary of possible shared significations. Sense-bearing gestures, symbols, metaphors, rules of syntax, parables, narratives, liturgies, conceptualities, the social order itself seen as text like, are all pre-given to potential social actors. These elements are ready to be set in motion as persons engage them in action or speech. The actual making of sense in the spirit and the gathering of human communities around resulting meanings is, then, a process of activity through time. In social interaction we selectively activate the possibilities of meaning at hand in the available sociocultural vocabulary, in the process creating new vocabulary for those who come after us. These two elements, the synchronic and the diachronic, are separable only in analysis. In actual life they go together. We will look at the ways in which human initiative and interaction engages works of spirit already existing and generates further configurations of sense or spirit in each succeeding moment of human consciousness.

What is the nature of the energy which powers this process? Many answers have been given. In interpreting Hegel's *Phenomenology of Spirit*, Alexandre Kojève identifies the force behind the dialectic as "desire."[4] Spinoza spoke of a life-force, the *conatus*, which urges organisms to persevere in being.[5] Possibly the most persuasive contemporary formulation of how such energy works in social process can be found in the work of Paul Ricoeur. This philosopher has written what in its most basic intent is a spiritual phenomenology of the human will. Ricoeur speaks of our "effort to exist and desire to be," and of our "appropriation" of the signs and symbols we encounter or generate along the way.[6] We come to know our lives hermeneutically: that is, we read the sense-bearing products of those life efforts which express our existential desires. We will see that Ricoeur develops this position with special reference to narrative or story, a connection which will be helpful when we seek to show that living in faith is living a commonly held narrative. The appropriation of signs which Ricoeur sees in the life of the individual makes sense also for the life of congregations looking for signs of Holy Spirit in human spirit. At this point in the argument however, my focus is on spirit as human phenomenon. How does it come about that the social world is intrinsically a space for the outworking of spirit as the ensemble of enacted human intentions?

I will argue that our "effort to exist and desire to be" may be expressed as a lived dialectic between *power* and *imagination*. The shared assumptions, the symbolic forms, the social institutions, the classical texts resulting from this dialectic in turn mediate a kind of *presence*. They make present in the social order certain shared interpretations of what that order means, and of what interpretation of reality it therefore conveys.[7] These interpretations will generally include expressions or formulas of theological import, formulas which point to what the community believes to be the encompassing reality in which the social process is set. A community's total store of symbolic resources—expressed as custom and law, literature, architecture and all the rest—serve together to make present a sense of the ultimate conditions and goals of its shared discourse. In this analysis of spirit the three realities—power, imagination, and presence—interact. No one of them can be defined apart from each of the others.

By *power* I mean the capacity to direct my energies so as to influence the conditions of my own life or the lives of others. One must ask, of course, from where the impulse to bring energy to bear comes in the first place: to act rather than to remain inactive. Otherwise the origins and goals of human action as such remain a mystery. Why, we ask, does history move? This much we know: the effective application of energy always involves the use of imagination. I must rehearse in my mind *how* I may use my capacities effectively in relation to centers of initiative and resistance over against me. My ability to use energy effectively may be considerable, or it may be very small. To have power is to stand in a configuration of circumstances such that I have capacity and scope for some sort of effective, that is situation-altering, action. Power thus is not the same thing as force. Power is always defined in relation to some imaginative construal of the action world as a place for doing what I can do, however great or little that may be. Thus power is a felt capacity, and the felt capacity arises not only from an awareness of being endowed with resources, but from a certain reading of the situation as amenable to the organized use of these resources. A social actor with little command of raw force may exercise great power given the imaginative construal of the situation which makes the most of the capacities available. Power, in short, is the ordering of life energy within an understanding of the social world that invites meaningful action, within a way of seeing which portrays my situation as offering meaningful possibilities. Such meaningful action, in concert with or in opposition to other human beings, is an ingredient in the historical-cultural dialectic of spirit.

The nature of *imagination* comes to light as we mentally envision and rehearse possible ways of exercising power, or of dealing creatively with the fact that our literal capacity for action is limited. I imaginatively consider possible interventions in, or responses to, some situation in which I have a certain sense of my capacity, or lack of it, to bring influence to bear. Such deliberation generally proceeds with some symbolic or narrative construction of the action world. It begins with rudimentary hypotheses about the world and other selves. It reflects not only my sense of my physical surroundings, but also my construal of the capacities and intentions of my fellow human beings. I perceive others as beings who imaginatively construe *me* in return, and who have a greater or lesser power to act upon me or in response to me. Eventually such deliberation becomes an acted-out interpretation of society's panoply of symbol, metaphor, and narrative, of the signifying fabric which makes society what it is. This process of imagined and then enacted intervention is repeated many times over by individuals who depend on already existing social patterns and who by their activities, help to create new ones. A society's stock of narrative literature—from epic poems to novels to newspaper accounts—is basically a storehouse of possibilities ready to be simply reenacted, or given imaginative variation, or continued into novel episodes or new chapters in response to situations utterly unforseen by earlier actors in the narrative.

The dialectic of power and imagination is the field of human spirit. On a large scale this dialectical process eventually precipitates certain more or less stable forms: a given civilization's worlds of business, politics, academic life, artistic endeavor, and so on. Taken together these worlds constitute a fabric consisting both of culture (art, music, literature, rituals, customs) and of the economic and political arrangements which make culture materially possible. In any given case society and culture objectify the supply of shared meanings which social actors draw as they seek each day to "make sense" to one another. It is as "objective spirit" that social reality is readable for congregations of believers who seek to discern, and then to signify, a more profound sense of God's configuring work in the historical process. I will discuss the significance of such objective spirit as "presence," and indeed as "real presence," in chapter 4.

3. Meaning-Bearing Elements in the Social World

It will be useful now for purposes of analysis to disassemble these processes of the objectification of spirit into some of their meaning-bearing elements. As played out in actual events, the production of socially shared meanings is enormously complex. Its aspects intricately interact. But it is probably possible to distinguish, no doubt rather artificially, a series of levels of the power-imagination-presence dialectic from the dawn of consciousness itself to the generation and maintenance of the whole social organism. And at each level, as in the whole, ontogeny probably recapitulates phylogeny: the genesis of individual consciousness recapitulates the genesis of the social organism. One can look at the total sociocultural process as an intricately articulated arena for the emergence of spirit, or shared sense, or intersubjectively maintained meaning.

Short of Hegel's phenomenology, there exists no "unified field theory" of the social genesis of spirit. I will not try to offer one here. There is no single route into the tangled underbrush of human social awareness. Instead, one chooses an approach corresponding to what one wishes to know. If one is interested in the origins of selfhood in society one may perhaps read George Herbert Mead. If one is interested in the roots of signification one reads Thomas Sebeok, Roland Barthes, or Umberto Eco. If the preoccupation is signs and the generation of knowledge in a community of interpreters, one goes to Charles Sanders Pierce. If one is concerned about the grammar of language games and their relation to "forms of life" one consults Ludwig Wittgenstein. If one needs help with the meaning of metaphor one engages Paul Ricoeur or the writings of George Lakoff and Mark Johnson. If the topic is texts and social phenomena as text-like, again the source is Paul Ricoeur.

These writers are my chief guides in the paragraphs that follow. From their works I lift up five ways into the dynamic phenomenon of human sociality as a field of spirit. These perspectives are arranged roughly in a series of levels or dimensions of increasing complexity. But they do not represent discrete provinces of meaning. Each dimension or perspective is present throughout the whole fabric of human interaction. Together they may come close to canvassing the elements which should be included in any "thick description"[8] of human social reality.

(a) Gesture and the Social Self

The dialectic of spirit arises, as George Herbert Mead showed in *Mind, Self, and Society*[9], at the very threshold of consciousness. Mind emerges in an intersubjective process. One becomes a self through participation in social interchange: first rudimentary and then more complex. Before there can be selves in communication, we must account for the emergence of selves with meanings to communicate in the first place. The key term in Mead's account is "significant gesture." The self is given to itself, that is, it becomes self-conscious, through observation of the response other persons give to the self's gestures. I discover the meaning of my gesture by seeing what it means to another person. My initiative, say in pointing to or grasping something, taps into the patterns of imagination which already exist in society as I see how other people respond. I come to know what I "meant" in the symbolic currency of my society because I discover what the other self interpreted the gesture to mean. The self comes into being through communicative processes.

This begins to happen at the most primordial level. Each newborn re-experiences the genesis of social meanings. The infant's flailing of arms and legs, the child's cries, are exercises of innate capacity that explore the world by acquainting the infant with resisting objects and the responses of persons. This exploration leads to an initial construal of the world in the infant's imagination. Further initiatives encounter more reactions which build up for the child a fuller picture of the world. What begins as raw undifferentiated energy begins to be tagged with various sorts of inner meaning reflecting what the child observes in others. Innate capacity is refined through imagination to become a greater or lesser ability to exercise power.

In Mead's view, thought is the internal language of such exploratory and finally meaningful gestures. By the time gestures become consciously signifying, the objects which the gestures involve or to which they point have become signs. Inevitably, the reference of these signs becomes in part socially shared. The genesis of signification thus brings us to the next level or dimension of sociality as spirit.

(b) Signification and Language

A symbolic-linguistic field now emerges in which elements and objects of the world take on meaning in relation to human intentions. The society establishes a pattern of broadly agreed sign values for such elements or objects. For grasping the meaning and implications of signification at this level I turn to the philosopher Charles Sanders Pierce. Pierce envisioned communities as conversations involving complex interchanges of signs. The formation of such a sign world is the first step toward what a community eventually takes to be "common sense," toward what it eventually understands as logic. Without the development of stable systems of signs, communities cannot exist.[10]

Signs refers to objects, or objects function as signs, in such a way that socially generated and maintained interpretations of the world are available to the community of interpreters. A sign may resemble the object designated (as in the case of a map); or it may have conventional meaning (a stop sign), or it may refer to a general category or class of things (words in a language). There may be signs which designate the relationships between other signs. The study of signs teaches us that all knowing is communal and inherently open-ended. What we know is tentative and fallible. Knowledge is refined in a communal give and take.

The French writer Roland Barthes has shown how far this conversion of the action world into a realm of signification can go. He has studied popular culture: clothing styles, posters, sporting events. He has also studied the semiotic conventions to be found in literary texts, and in urban settings of various kinds. The Parisian cityscape, in its details and as a whole, sends many messages that its inhabitants take for granted. Without these messages, the Parisians could hardly function as social beings.[11] A person who walks on a Parisian street wearing cowboy boots is then sending a message of his (or her) own.

Language is a special, privileged, and highly elaborated

system of signs which have become conventional and shared. Language permits human beings to move beyond gestures and objects as elements of signification to expressions— sounds and words—exclusively dedicated to the signifying function. This step makes possible experimentation with combinations of signs and the development of signs which express the relationship between other signs. Above all, language is a sign system which enables us to express what is fictional, to signify what is in fact not the case but which can become the case in the world of imagination. And an imaginative world sustained only by language can sometimes literally come to power; a utopian vision may fuel a revolution and be tried out in the "real world." Again, we are speaking of one aspect of the genesis of spirit.

(c) Grammar, Syntax, and Logic

Languages and cultures evolve customs for putting signs or signifying actions together. We call these customs rules of grammar or syntax. The combination of signs into messages, like the combination of words into sentences or physical movements into meaningful actions, requires certain implicit rules or codes which make possible the construction of complex messages. "Grammar" in this sense is not in the first instance to be found in grammar books. It is, as Ludwig Wittgenstein says, embedded in "usage," in the way signs or signifying actions customarily go together (*syn-taxis*) in a given human setting or situation.[12]

The native speakers of a language, the birthright members of a culture, are able to speak or act "correctly," usually without being able to articulate the "rules" their speech or actions embody. If the rules need to be stated, they have to be extracted by trained observers from a large number of instances. The native speaker or actor does not need such help. He or she can utter an infinite number of correct sentences with ever new content, or carry out an infinite number of socially understandable actions, all the time evincing the culture's rules for the combination of signs without being able to state what they are.

These rules of thought and action, spoken or unspoken,

together constitute what Wittgenstein called "forms of life."
One cannot use language outside of the particular language
game played within a given human setting. Language governed by such rules comes close to constituting what we mean
by sociality. A given society has a linguistically sustained
sense of reality itself. Sub-cultures within a larger society
have their own versions of this reality sense. Forms of life,
then, carry with them rules for thinking about the world as an
arena for human action which, for participants in that world,
quite simply represents the way things are. Yet such visions of
the world are enormously varied in different cultural settings.
What seems immutable to a French *philosophe* in 1789 may
not seem so to a German romantic poet in 1821. What is
logical to a captain of industry in 1890 may not follow for a
union leader in 1947. And the differences named lie within
the context of Western society. The differences are greater
between the West and the East, between the "first world"
and the "third." Logic itself, some say, is a notation for describing the socially maintained syntax of signs and expressions, and therefore the form of world coherence that obtains
in a given human community at a particular time or place.
Again, I am describing an aspect of objective spirit.

(d) Metaphor, Concept, and Symbol

Very soon certain signs begin to take on special importance because they violate these syntactical codes, or do interesting and unexpected things with them. Fresh combinations
of signs enable the confrontation of otherwise disparate
realms of discourse to create new meanings. Juxtapositions
which bear such creative power we call metaphors. Language
acquires a metaphorical structure that eventually gives rise to
concepts, which in turn are represented by symbols.

Paul Ricoeur, in *The Rule of Metaphor*, argues that our
sense of reality itself is based upon the juxtaposition of disparate signs to generate new kinds of meaning.[13] Ricoeur's theory of metaphor is important to an unpacking of the process
of objective spirit. This philosopher has helped us see that
metaphor is more than a trope consisting of deviant naming

("the moon was a ghostly galleon . . . "). It is, in fact, a form of "impertinent predication," a form of *discourse* which says something that could not have been said before. Metaphor is a kind of "seeing as" which suggests a new way of relating imagination to power, a new way of orienting oneself to the world.

Once this is understood, it begins to be clear that a metaphorical process has been at work through all the levels of signification discussed here, from the origins of language and action in significant gesture to the most advanced achievements of culture. Signification itself can be understood as a metaphorical process. To say "jazz is a blind drummer" is to be present at an origin of meaning which incorporates and extends the reach of all the gestures and signs that hover about the primordial power of imaginative expression which the jazz idiom represents.

The power of metaphor in ordinary language, once fully understood, is striking. George Lakoff and Mark Johnson show in *Metaphors We Live By* how metaphors dominate basic concepts in our language and hence in our life world, where they control the ways in which power and disempowerment are imaginatively construed.[14] Examples make the point. It is clear, for example that in English and many other Western languages "argument" is metaphorically understood as a kind of warfare. "Your claims are indefensible," we say. Or, "He attacked every weak point in my argument." Or, "His criticisms were right on target."[15] Or consider the reach in Western imagination of the metaphor of the marketplace. From barter in the village square to world economic order to the notion of a "marketplace of ideas," this trope occupies a dominant position in our contemporary social imagination.

One receives a hint of the extent of this dominance by trying to imagine the metaphorical structure of our world view as other than it is. Suppose, Lakoff and Johnson suggest, we lived in a society in which argument is not a form of warfare but a kind of dance.[16] Participants then would not be combatants but performers. Their goal would be not to wipe each other out but to interact in an aesthetically pleasing way.

In such a society, the military metaphor for argument would not be available; it would not be part of the stock of metaphorical possibilities. With just this one change, our life world would become radically different. Or suppose that the world of human interaction were not thought of as a marketplace, but as a context for the exchange of gifts, a realm of mutual generosity. Again, certain meanings common to our civilization would not be available, while others would come into play.

A very wide range of expressions belonging to specific semiotic domains or provinces of meaning show their rootage in metaphors, primitive at first yet eventually enormously ramified. Even the most abstract concepts, including notions both scientific and theological, are ultimately metaphorically based. Take, for example, the physical sense of "mass." It is grounded in the sense of bulk or weight, but has reached a very abstract and precise meaning through mathematical and, therefore, symbolic refinement that could not have taken place in the way it has were it not for the metaphorical ground. The same could be said of the concept spirit. It goes back to a metaphorical identification of life with "wind" or "breath," but has been elaborated to refer to the form of God's presence in the historical process which we call Spirit or Holy Spirit. Without the metaphorical work underlying them, certain thoughts could not be thought at all, much less brought to such conceptual elaboration.

(e) Texts

Using all the just-analyzed elements of expression, each society and culture constructs and maintains its characteristic texts. These often take narrative form. The stories or epics or poetry or liturgies of a culture are intelligible because they are expressed not only in grammatically correct sentences but also represent a recognizable grammar of actions and ideas which exemplify the culture's metaphorical construction of reality. These texts are most varied in genre and social function. Only some achieve classical status: that is, only a few are recognized by the society or culture in question as in some respect normative or disclosive of the culture's highest values or transcendental grounds. Thus in ancient Greece the Iliad of Homer apparently had this status, in Judaism the Hebrew Scriptures; in Christianity the New Testament; in German romanticism Goethe; in America the Bible, the Declaration of Independence, the Constitution, or the works of Mark Twain.

But a given society also produces a rich profusion of texts which are constitutive but not classical. Memoranda, shopping lists, reports, brochures, and the like help to constitute the society as a realm of discourse. Some of these documents will hark back in one way or another to the culture's classics, although in modern times such references and echoes grow fainter and less frequent. The important point is that there is bound to be some relationship between the society as realm of discourse and the styles of activity that the society regards as meaningful, understandable, or sane. Indeed some philosophers, following Paul Ricoeur, are now saying that societies *themselves* may be understood "on the model of the text."[17] That is, they are text-like in that they consist of interconnected networks of signifying elements and actions. Societies, in short, are tapestries which follow rules of grammar and exemplify metaphorical constructs. Hence, as patterns of human interaction, they can be read.

We now begin to see how the study of culture can be a "hermeneutical" science. If what the human scientist studies is, in effect, a "text," or if it is for heuristic purposes text-like, then human science cannot be content with functional or structuralist or material approaches to culture. The student of society and culture needs to decode what any given tract of human expression and action is saying. The meaning of action goes beyond what social actors intend or have in mind in what they say or do. The panoply of action is like the combination of sentences in a poem or in a novel. Action—analyzed in terms of the gestures, signs, grammatical codes, ruling metaphors, and now the rules of syntax involved in text construction—takes on a meaning in its own right which can be ascertained. A culture text is neither simply what the original actors had in mind nor what the observer reads into it. It is what it is. It is this fact, Paul Ricoeur thinks, that gives the human sciences their "objectivity." They interpret the meanings which social realities convey by existing as text-like realities in the world.

(f) Synthesis: Making Sense

Taken together, these levels of analysis can function to constitute what Clifford Geertz calls "thick description," a method which rests on the notion that the cultural fabric of society is drenched with sense, or as we could also say, is a realm of spirit. In this thickly described realm of socially maintained sense, the activities of persons and institutions generate meanings that both turn the social world into what Jürgen Habermas calls a realm of "communicative action,"[18] and also add to the stock of sense available to social actors yet unborn.

We have also come as close as we can to what Hegel meant by objective spirit. "Objective" because it exists in tangible social and cultural forms; "spirit" because it consists of embodied forms of sense which can be read and interpreted. And yet here lies the danger of which Ricoeur warns: that objective spirit becomes embodied in political "totalizations" that represent forms of imagination which have definitively come to power. However laudable such a system's claim to foster a realm of reason and freedom may be, it may also become a principality or power menacing to human well-being. The great instruments of such totalization, Ricoeur says, are the state and the institutional church.[19] Hence the need for the prophetic or critical spirit, and the requirement that institutions be open to reform.

It is important, thus, to link objective spirit to what I have called "presence." The power of a given metaphorical-social system to represent what we take as "reality" is related to the accuracy of its underlying observations and the persuasiveness of its arguments. It also is tied to forms of imagination that have come to power in a given social context. Presence is a form of socially enacted power which has won a definitive victory in the human perspective of a given time or place.

Presence is something like the total life vision of ancient Rome at the height of its influence, or the combined vision of the American "founding fathers," or the view of the world from the higher reaches of the Vatican curia. It is an interpretation of the world so seemingly obvious and close at hand as to be entirely unproblematic for those who live within it. Here lies a reality of which the churches must be critically aware as they try to understand themselves in their socio-cultural settings.

4. Churches in the World of Social Meanings

What happens when churches arise within this meaning-making process? Churches are sub-cultures within the larger social process. In simplest terms, they exist by selectively appropriating signifying elements from the cultures that surround them. Just as an individual appropriates the signs generated by his or her passage through the social world in an "effort to exist and desire to be" (Ricoeur), so a congregation, living a story which embodies its own identity, takes on certain signifying elements of the society and culture around it. Forms of governance, works of art and architecture, perspectives related to class race and gender, newspaper stories used as sermon illustrations: these are the sorts of things that are appropriated into the fabric of ecclesial existence. Such elements of sociality will in turn will be composed of ingredients of the kind analyzed in the preceding pages. They will be texts or text-like combinations of primordial gesture, sign, syntax, and metaphor, parable, narrative. They will be elements of society and culture.

By being appropriated, these elements will inevitably be in some degree transformed in meaning. If a particular denomination or congregation is only "the Republican Party at prayer," the change will be slight. If another Christian body is radically critical of society to the point of subversion, the change will be much greater. But in either case the faith community involved is living in society and appropriating elements of it which signify the *sense* of its passage through it.

The sense acted out in that passage will naturally reflect the congregation's or denomination's understanding of the biblical story and its idea of how and where that story is being continued in the social world. The story may be understood as confined to the religious community concerned. Or it may, as this book argues, be discerned to be going on in the larger human world, wherever configurations of human spirit are momentarily identifiable as the work of Holy Spirit establishing the conditions of God's reign.

When these things happen, appropriated social meanings are transsignified. They are organized around new *foci* of meaning. They are thereby enabled to convey the identity of Jesus Christ. The church bodies in which such trans-significations take place *themselves* become signs or parables within the social orders they inhabit. They join their societies' stock of meaning-bearing elements, to be respected or mocked, comprehended or misunderstood, as the case may be. Something like this must be the meaning of the sentence of *Lumen Gentium* discussed in chapter 1. "By her relationship with Christ, the Church is a kind of sacrament or sign of intimate union with God, and of the unity of all humankind." What is true of the sacraments is thus true of the worshipping, witnessing, gathering itself. Ordinary social substance is taken up "from a common to a sacred use" without ceasing to look and feel—and in fact be—what it has been before. Transsignification occurs in the forms of human life together without making these forms unrecognizable.

The most obvious example of such transsignification of culture is the parable, which combines elements of common life into new configurations that now perform metaphorically. They enable the hearer, as Paul Ricoeur says, to see the possibility of a different way of being, of living in a "world in front of the text,"[20] without leaving this present world. John Dominic Crossan adds that parables function not only metaphorically but subversively. Over against the tendency of socially maintained meanings to turn into myths which portray the world as a realm of opposites—clean versus unclean, civilized versus savage, raw versus cooked, we versus they—

parables subvert the myths imposed on us by powerful establishments, break their power over our lives.[21] They also open
us to the possibilities of the life in the Spirit. Above all, the
parables see through the constellations of power (in Paul's
words, "principalities and powers") which maintain certain
imaginative constructions of life in being. So it is with the
story of Jesus, a parable writ large. And so it is with each
congregation or base community: each is called to be a kind
of lived parable, a kind of metaphorical transformation of the
social world in which it lives. It makes present a representation of the world as the realm of God's ruling. It thereby
enacts within the world something that is ultimately true
about the world but not evident without the word of faith as
hermeneutical key.[22]

The most powerful instruments of this transformation of
worldly meanings are no doubt the biblical narratives which
communities of faith bring interactively into their situations.
Every congregation continues the biblical story through its
own stories. These contemporary extensions of the biblical
style and plot in the congregation's own history become the
carriers of the faith community's identity. Such continuations
of the biblical story highlight significant events which have
had a certain transforming and binding power for those who
participated in them. The congregation's constitutive narrative inscribes a sequence of meaning through the field of
signs, usage codes, root metaphors, and texts of a given culture. It is the genre of lived text among all the others which
comprehends the phenomenon of change over time, accounting for the perception that this individual, this congregation,
this ethnic group, this nation, though it may change in important respects, maintains its essential identity.

Above all, such narratives recount stories of faith. While
faith as personal existential disposition is not wholly accessible to language, faith may be represented in stories which, in
effect, describe dramatic trials of truth, which embody the
question of ultimate loyalty, ultimate concern. The litany of
acts of faith described in the eleventh chapter of the Epistle
to the Hebrews is a case in point. By faith Abraham . . ., by

faith Isaac . . ., by faith Moses . . ., by faith Rahab . . ., to the point that we are "surrounded by a cloud of witnesses." Such narratives represent struggles with the claims of final Power—the ultimate Power with which we have to deal—as these claims are conceived to be present in the human action field. They are community-constituting answers to the question "Who is God?"

We need to pursue these insights still further. We must ask what it means in practice to "decipher" configurations of human spirit christologically, and thereby to approach them as points of meeting, however fragmentary, between Holy Spirit and human experience. Just as Paul Ricoeur sought to understand not merely philosophical formulas but also "the fullness of language," so we must find ways of grasping the many forms of grace-filled reality which Holy Spirit generates in its encounter with human spirit. Sociality is the medium in which the gift is given. It is therefore a primary datum for theological reflection, not just a consequence of practical reasoning. "The holy catholic church" is not merely a gathering of like-minded people. It is one of the gifts of the Spirit which, according to the creeds, we "believe in."[23] No mere principle, no mere invisible idealization or theological surmise is confessed here, but an actual historical reality. How is such a historical reality possible? How does the holy catholic church of the creeds "subsist" in the institutions we know? How is the gift of grace in the form of sociality to be discerned there?

5. Decision-Making in the Congregation: Practical Reasoning

One answer is that the gift is to be discerned in the actual decision-making processes by which a community of faith conducts its affairs so as to maintain its identity as sacrament and sign of the kingdom. At the close of his book *Christ and Culture*,[24] H. Richard Niebuhr wrote an epilogue, "A Concluding Unscientific Postscript," in which he made clear that no amount of doctrinal or cultural analysis, however insightful, can foresee the actual decisions by which a faith community is carried forward through time. The lives of individuals and their communities are lived in an historical process in which every decision is made in the midst of culture's relativities, in objective uncertainty about their true motives and about the outcome. There is no direct way to move from the community's story up to a given moment to certainty about the actual decisions it must make if it is to continue authentically to exist. The continuation of the story always rests on the lonely acts of faith of individuals whose decisions nevertheless need to take the existence of others into account and whose moves in concert with others make the faith community what it will be.

> We raise our existential questions individually, doubtless, and we do not forget our personal, individual selves. But the existentialist question is not individualistic; it arises in its most passionate form not in our solitariness but in our fellowship. It is the existential question of social men who have no selfhood apart from their relation to other human selves.[25]

The church arises and continues in existence as faithful persons make the choices which determine their relationships to all the other human beings they meet. It may be, of course, that looking back on these decisions we will find a pattern. They may look like the latest pages in the story of Calvinism, or Lutheranism. There may be evident what Jonathan Edwards,[26] and after him Edward Farley,[27] called a *habitus*, a theologically reflective disposition to shape life in faith in a certain way. But such is the existential, risky, character of decision in a field of relative values that one can never, in advance, simply translate one's confessional tradition into clear directions for action. One never knows enough. One never knows what will happen in the next day, or hour, or minute. One may know something about Calvinism, but one never knows what the next episode in the history of Calvinism will be or whether, by one's choices, one will be part of it.

Still, there are reasoning processes involved in such decision-making and acting. A congregation faced with issues needing resolution will engage in a process of deliberation or practical consideration. At some point, a decision will emerge: whether by vote, by "sense of the meeting," or in some other way. It is not always self-evident how groups move from an initial shared "interpretation of the situation" to a shared conclusion. At a certain point a decision seems to take form. All or most of the relevant factors are perceived by a majority to be in place. The conclusion appears as a precipitate of the deliberative process. Suddenly it is there, needing only a formal action to catch it in words. This does not mean that existential uncertainty disappears. It is only that a certain decision seems right *for now*. For this moment, the deed is done.

Clearly, this process is not a purely logical or syllogistic one. Presuppositions, images, symbols, and feelings all play large roles. Above all, as we have seen, a given community is likely to share a certain pattern of social imagination within which there is an interpretation of power. The group tacitly understands where power is located, what assumptions motivate its use, and how it is likely be exercised. Such understanding forms within a certain parabolic, narrative, or other construal of the life world. This process of practical reasoning is well worth study, and indeed has attracted the attention of philosophers over the centuries. Aristotle believed that the wisdom of the scholar is built upon the *phronesis* or practical reasoning of the wise person, or of the community exercising practical wisdom. In order to devote him or herself to theoretical matters, the sage must possess, or presuppose, "practical knowledge."[28] This insight also goes back to the ancient Roman concept of the *sensus communis*: which Hans-Georg Gadamer defines as "the sense of the right and general good that is to be found in all men, moreover, a sense that is acquired through living in the community and is determined by its structures and aims."[29]

Interestingly enough, the notion of *phronesis* is plainly visible in the rhetoric of Paul. Many of Paul's references to a collective "mind" employ the Greek noun *nous* as in references to "the mind of the Spirit" (Rom. 8:27), "the mind of the Lord" (Rom. 11:34), and "the mind of Christ" (1 Cor. 2:16), but one especially important instance employs a verb related to the noun *phronesis*. This occurs at Phil. 2:5: "Have this mind among yourselves which you have in Christ Jesus." The Greek is *touto phroneite*. The context has to do with shared decision-making in the Philippian church. Paul ties this *phronesis* to the christological hymn of Phil. 2:5-11. The Philippian congregation is implored to conform its practical reasoning to this particular interpretation of Jesus' ministry. Yet the existential element of radical uncertainty is not absent. Paul also advises the Philippians that in his absence they are on their own. "Work out your own salvation with fear and trembling" (2:12b). This is not, as subsequent commentators have sometimes feared, a lapse into what later became Pelagianism. The "working out" of salvation is *phronesis*, practical reasoning in the community of faith.

The patterns which in fact emerge from any particular case of communal deliberation call for explanation. *Some* tradition of interpretation, whether that of Phil. 2:5-11 or otherwise, generally lies embedded in the systems of signs and symbols that make up a congregation's social life world. The pages ahead will seek to analyze this phenomenon further. For now, let us say that interpretations of the meaning of Christian faith are implicit in the way congregations or base communities put their worlds together. These interpretations may or may not correspond to any of the great confessional traditions. If they do, they represent those aspects of these traditions which have found their way into the taken-for-granted systems of meaning that make the world of action coherent for the people concerned. In any process of discussion or deliberation, whether in a congregational meeting or in an individual soul, some courses of action will unaccountably recommend themselves more than others. Some possibilities will "make sense." People will be able to envision themselves more easily doing this rather than doing that. Because the symbolic shape of the life world is largely below the level of conscious awareness, and especially if the tradition embedded in that unobtrusive symbolic shape tends to reinforce risk-taking and personal responsibility, decisions will still be existential acts of faith, not risk-free processes of inference from conscious premises to conscious conclusions. Those who make such decisions act in the hope that, when the results are in, their life worlds, and with them their communal and personal identities, will still be intact.

Narratives of faith capture in retrospect, and make available for purposes of interpreting the world, events which in the actual experience were often deeply ambiguous, uncertain, and risky. Yet the social worlds in which these acts of faith took place, the traditioned communities that lay behind the faithful actors, already predisposed them to make some choices more readily than others. So it is today. Never do socially embedded predispositions eliminate risk. Never do they make it inevitable that the next chapter in the story of faith will be this rather than that. But the socially projected patterns of faithful behavior enable the character of faith to be objectively read. If one wishes to talk *about* faith, the only authentic way to do so is to tell the community-forming and communion-maintaining *story*. If one wishes to be *in* faith, the only way is to join those who riskily try to write the next chapters in the story themselves.

This position has important implications. I am saying that although faith decisions are made in existential uncertainty, the meaning of faith does not lie in my inward and inaccessible feelings or dispositions. The meaning of faith lies in certain traditions of shared understandings. These may run from Abraham to Exodus to resurrection and beyond. Faith's meaning also resides in some continuing tradition of shared behavior arrived at in the practical reasoning process. Theological concepts, indeed, as we will see, depend for their intelligibility on their anchorage in a public historical tradition, such as the life of Israel or the experience of the church. These histories, with the narratives and parables in which they are told, become part of the "grammar" of each theological idea.[30]

I think of the churches' transsignification of social reality as creating a heightened version of what I have already called presence. This is meant as a challenge to deconstructionists for whom nothing is made present by human expression in any of its forms. The activities of believers may come to constitute more or less stable communities in the world which deserve more than sociological analysis, more, even, than sociological analysis informed by a "hermeneutic of everyday life." I have already related the word *presence* to interpretations of reality so sustained, stable, and pervasive that for those who participate in them they *are* reality pure and simple. But the notion of presence is also a way into understanding what the Christian tradition has meant by *parousia* (the word presence in Greek), or the coming to power anew in our social imagination of a messianic vision of reality referred to traditionally as the "second coming of Christ." It is also a way into what has been meant by "real presence" in the sacramental sense. The churches mediate a presence in the midst of the social world which has its own coherence as the portrayal of a Person. This presence is composed of the symbolic materials of the world around it reconfigured and thereby transformed—like the many-colored pebbles in a mosaic—in such a way as recognizably to represent Jesus of Nazareth as the Messiah. Human spirit taken into this Messianic reconfiguration tells a new story, that of a people of God as the worldly instrument or expression of Holy Spirit.

IV

Real Presence

On the Meaning and Possibilities of Doctrine

As lived parables, churches tell stories of the otherwise invisible company of those whose lives give hope to humankind. Faith communities seek to discern places where human spirit bears witness to Holy Spirit and to signify this possibility in their form of life. They can do this partly because they themselves employ a variety of expressive forms: Scripture, liturgy, hymns, codes of canon law, patterns of justice-seeking activity. But, above all, churches make present the reality of the people of God by what they *are* as communities. They have a kind of sacramental character. They give Jesus Christ, with the people who represent him in the world, a form of presence often called "real."

But what is the force of that word real? What sort of reality is meant? Among the churches' means of expression are formulas which are propositional or referential in form. They seem to make truth claims. They purport to speak of realities behind the appearances. Above all they speak of God. Loosely, we call all such formulas "doctrines," although strictly speaking doctrines are only those theological statements which have creedal, conciliar, or some other kind of ecclesiastical authority. Other utterances are only what the Europeans call *theologoumena*, the opinions of theologians. I will use the word doctrine here to mean any theological proposition regarded by a faith community as belonging to orthodox belief. And such belief has nearly always been assumed to have to do with what is the case, with what is true, with what, for example, is real about "real presence." To speak, as I have done, of Holy Spirit, or even of *"the* Holy Spirit," is to venture into the doctrinal arena. It is time now to say what I mean.

This is no easy question. It is at the point of doctrine and the kind of truth that doctrines purport to convey that much of the difficulty felt by churches in the modern world arises. Rival claims to truth have given rise to religious wars and continue to do so. Wolfhart Pannenberg graphically demonstrates in *The Church*[1] that during the centuries of strife between rival Christian factions in seventeenth-century Europe each claimed truth for its doctrinal formulas and believed that, if its propositions were true, seemingly contrary, or even somewhat differing, statements must simply be false. These rivalries left thoughtful persons weary and ready for something better. The Enlightenment of the eighteenth century sought to affirm a universal human reason. Many theologians sought to restate Christian faith in ways compatible with such generally held truths.

With the rise of nineteenth-century natural science, of course, the question of theological truth claims took a new form. Now the question concerned such claims' compatibility with theoretically plausible and carefully reasoned conclusions about the world based on experimental evidence. Christian doctrines seemed to involve a kind of knowledge different from that attainable by science and, in some cases, to contradict scientific findings. Natural science, however shaky its own philosophical base, became the public paradigm for knowledge as such. Secular forms of knowing even took on moral tone; anyone who reasoned otherwise, was thought to be either ignorant or dishonest. By 1965, Van A. Harvey could write a book titled *The Historian and the Believer*,[2] which spoke of a modern "morality of knowledge" reflecting the practice of academically reputable scholars. The paradigm case was none other than Ernst Troeltsch. The different Christian bodies, their own traditional doctrinal disputes largely unresolved, came up against a secular reality consensus which led to wars of religion in a new form. These wars were not merely of the sort fought at the "Scopes Trial" between biblical views of the world literally construed and the postulates of natural science concerning the origin and nature of the universe. They were also between "liberal" and "evangelical" factions in the church and between rival fundamentalisms within Christian faith and beyond.

Chapter 2 described the present fragmentation of opinion among academic theologians. One of the most difficult questions today concerns precisely this matter of doctrinal propositions' relationship to reality. Do we believe that doctrines express objective "truth" in any viable or defensible sense of the word? Edward Farley in *Ecclesial Man* speaks of the theological community's "nasty suspicion about itself."[3] "Could it be that there are no realities at all behind the language of this historical faith?"[4] Many who regard themselves as "believers" do not really believe in a correspondence between doctrinal propositions and any intelligible notion of "what is the case" in the world. Yet it is useless to talk about churches without accounting for the reference of the reality propositions on which their lives have historically been based. If doctrines are not descriptions of reality, what are they? Some, Farley included, today would say that the answer to this question lies in exploring the *communal function* of doctrines and doctrine-like propositions.

1. Searching for the Real:
A Turn Toward the Life World

It is hard to say whether it is a comfort or a further challenge for theologians to find themselves in the same bed with philosophers for whom the connection between language and reality has come loose in ways just as serious as for the theologians themselves. A seeming deconstruction (described in chapter 2) of the long-assumed correspondence between doctrinal formulas and a reality they are thought to describe parallels the collapse of assurance among certain contemporary philosophers that there are universal categories for human reasoning in *any* field of inquiry—ecclesiological, scientific, sociological, or otherwise. Many writers, in what has come to be called the "postmodern" mode, question whether there *are* foundations for human knowledge which can claim be trusted as valid under all circumstances. It begins to seem that knowing is as relative to culture and context as any other human activity. Human discourse in all its forms—literary, scientific, even mathematical—ceases to have any certain or reliable contact with an underlying unchanging reality. Everything is story, and every story is ultimately fiction even if for the time being it is useful or lived-out fiction.

Such questions are spreading. Philosophers of human science increasingly doubt the cognitive validity of major theoretical constructs in such disciplines as anthropology, sociology, and psychology. Such constructs may be heuristically valuable, but they do not describe what *is*. The philosophers' preferred solution is very much like that of the theologians: to get closer to the data themselves, to become immersed in the textures of life as lived. Calvin Schrag, in *Radical Reflection and the Origin of the Human Sciences*, calls for a "hermeneutic of everyday life that exhibits a new posture of understanding and an expanded notion of reason."[5] Needed, Schrag says, is "an interrogation of the originative senses of fact and value as they emerge within the fabric of human affairs".[6]. His call for a hermeneutic of everyday life echoes Edmund Husserl's attack, in the 1930s, on positivist, objectifying science in *The Crisis of the European Sciences*.[7] Schrag writes:

In succumbing to the ideal of an objective, mathematized, universal science of man and the world, philosophy and science alike have dissociated themselves from that praxis in the life-world in which practical interests, taken-for-granted knowledge, and ordinary language already register their significations.[8]

One can read these words as epitomizing a conviction that has become increasingly widespread in the intellectual world. The great theoretical syntheses in the human sciences stand at an increasing distance from the fields of common human life which they are supposed to illuminate. As has been noted before, this point has been made repeatedly by Michel Foucault with his claim that we confront "an insurrection of subjugated knowledges"[9] which neither psychology nor sociology nor anthropology in their academic forms can grasp. As if in response, the *Annales*[10] school of French historiography seeks to understand the very texture, say, of life in medieval villages, as Emmanuel LeRoy Ladurie does in his *Montaillou*,[11] a study of an Albigensian village in southern France from 1318 to 1325. With methods such as these, we may hope for a conversation in which theology addresses the meaning-laden reality field which underlies both the human sciences and its own forms of reflection.

We are learning, moreover, that the *seeming* universality and reality reference of categories is often the result of their being maintained by powerful institutions or, as I have said, through forms of imagination which have come to power so as to create and maintain an apparent presence. This is as true of theological concepts maintained by churches as it is of political and scientific categories maintained by establishments of other kinds. Sharon Welch[12] has argued that the connection of alleged universals with power centers, in which such categories are formulated and maintained for ideological or self-securing reasons, makes them inapplicable to local forms of life, unable in principle to grasp the fabric of life together as it is experienced at particular times and in particular places. And yet it is just in these particular times and places, rather than in speculation about universals, that the question of truth is most authentically raised for our time. Above all, this is the case for language about God.

> The truth of God-language and of all theological claims is
> measured not by their correspondence to something eternal
> but by the fulfillment of its claims in history, by the actual
> creation of communities of peace, justice, and equality.[13]

This statement appears to relinquish all claims to correspondence between theological claims and eternal truth as we
have known them and at the same time to make a far-reaching claim of another sort. The *truth* of theological discourse—
including ecclesiological discourse—is tested instead in its
embodiment, that is, in *praxis*. What is being said? That theological propositions are pragmatic: that their truth inheres in
the forms of life which express their meaning in the "real
world?" Or that such propositions are transcendental: that
they state the conditions under which forms of life representing them are possible? Or that God language is eschatological,
that humanity is always on the way to fulfilling its claim but
will not arrive within the limits of history? Whatever interpretation we favor, it is clear that inherited theological and ecclesiological formulas need to pass through re-embodiment in
forms of life expressive of their meaning for our time before
we will once again know whether they are true, and, if so,
what their truth is. Whatever form the argument takes, theories of this type are saying, in effect, that truth is an attribute
of the faith community in what we have called the ecclesiogenetic process. Truth has to do with the practical reasoning,
the *phronesis*, needed to maintain the community's identity
and integrity through time. It is an attribute in the first instance of the community, rather than of propositions about
reality which may arise in the course of the community's
thinking.

It follows from these insights, both in their theological and
in their philosophical forms, that doctrine is true in a second-
ary or derived way. It is true when it figures symbolically in
the practical reasoning of a community which is true. Doctrine
is not true, nor, of course, is it false either, when it stands
alone in propositional form, claiming some kind of universal
validity and reality reference. But if doctrine arises in the
community's practical reasoning it will be bound to reflect the

forms of language, symbols, metaphors, and texts which constitute this community as an arena of discourse in the first
place.

We are confronted with a version of the sociology of
knowledge. The project of seeking the truth of doctrines in
faith communities' actual forms of life brings theology directly
into touch with the human sciences. Many issues arise when
this is done, among them the threat of reductionism, or the
collapse of theology into sociology of religion. Yet without
using historical, sociological, anthropological, or socio-linguis-
tic methods, we have no way of getting at the shared life of
faith so as to find the reality meant in real presence. The art
is to avoid letting human science dominate theology or theology dominate human science. There needs to be a conversation between them. Eventually this conversation must reach
the point of asking whether there is a final or ultimate reality
behind the social reality we see, and whether this theological
question can be posed differently for having been in touch
with human science perspectives.

We need to weigh these questions, first by projecting
them experimentally upon two actual periods of the history of
doctrine, and then by asking whether the results of our inquiry can be appropriated in contemporary theological self-
understanding. In the next section, accordingly, we will look
at the doctrine of the church, seen in the context of different
sociologically derived projections of the relation between God
and the world, in Augustine, Calvin, and their followers. Following that we will examine the proposed theological ap-
propiation of this perspective in the work of George Lindbeck.

2. Ecclesial and Social Roots of Doctrinal Conceptualization

In the actual shaping of doctrines, churches necessarily
have recourse to images, symbols, and metaphors already at
work in their lived interpretations of the world. In particular,
communities of faith inevitably borrow available metaphors
of the nature of the *polis*—monarchical, democratic, organic,

populist and the like. These in turn tend strongly to influence, and even to dominate, the way churches imagine and conceive their own forms of life. And because ecclesiastical polities have such metaphorical power over our ways of thinking, ecclesiology becomes central to regulative reflection about God's relationships to the world. This applies particularly, as we will see, to conceptualizations of the work of the Holy Spirit.

How has this process worked out in the traditional Catholic and Protestant ecclesiologies? I will argue that ideas concerning God's relation to the world arising within these communities have reflected a variety of monarchical and hierarchical conceptions present in the social orders of the time, and that these conceptualizations have in turn shaped a variety of other formulations. In "catholic" settings, for example, theologians have tended to see God as related to the world in a great chain of being whose pyramidal form is replicated in the structure of the institutional church from the hierarchy of prelates at the apex to the people in their total socio-cultural reality at the base. In Protestant contexts, by contrast, God tends to be pictured as far above the world and in no way immanent in its structures or forms of life. The realm of human action, far from being suffused with divinity, is pictured as a field of competing interests regulated from afar by God's commandments, but also following its own inherent economic or political principles.[14]

Let us look at each of these worlds of perception more closely. For Catholics, God "s ordering and redeeming power is thought to suffuse the body politic almost as an electric charge, a divine energy. The people and their social institutions are understood to be related to God through their incorporation into the grace-suffused system of the ecclesio-social body. One is incorporated into this body by being a member of the community, by being in communion with the holy persons and institutions which represent it from the symbolic summit of power down to its least significant yet characteristic expressions. The body politic depends upon its personal head, and represents the life and charisma of that person in every aspect of its being. The "universal church" then is quite concrete: it is the sum of those who stand in communion with a supreme pontiff.

Where does this set of metaphors come from? It has its origin in the political metaphors of the patristic era. Defenders of the Constantinian establishment, such as Eusebius, see in the Roman emperor a rule on earth corresponding to the divine sovereignty of the God of Christian faith. Thomas Parker writes:

> A veritable chorus emerges, one God, one Caesar, one church, one faith, one universal community, one peace, one order embracing all, even though it is expressed in two cities and two ends—the divine superior to the human. Augustus is Christianized as the political and Christ romanized as the spiritual image of the divine monarchy.[15]

Augustine draws on this picture, generalizing and universalizing it. In the *City of God*, the great North African bishop thinks in organic, communitarian terms reflecting his experience of the polity of the Roman Empire, but his imagination goes further. He sees the church as part of a world-historical drama. The Christian story concerns not just a particular culture or nation but the totality of humanity. Unlike Eusebius, who follows the classical tradition going back to Plato and Aristotle—philosophers for whom civil pieties always presupposed some natural human community already defined by common territory, language, customs and the like—Augustine reaches a *theological* notion of humankind as a whole, a city of man reflecting the reach of the Roman Empire but yet in principle transcending it. The human city is a community of concupiscence and self-love which in principle includes all human beings irrespective of ethnic or political affiliation. The city of man, thinks Augustine, for all its expansion throughout the earth and for all its diversity in this place and that, is a single community. But with the coming of Christ, this human family is caught up in a drama of salvation, from creation to fall to redemption to consummation. With the emergence of the church, this human whole comes to be configured visibly in such a way as to represent God's saving purposes in history. In the midst of the human city there begins to appear, through the agency of the church, a city of God. Church and city of God are not identical, but without the church there is no way of imagining or knowing God's ultimate purpose for the human community as a whole.

Augustine's city imagery rests on his unquestioned assumption that Rome is the appropriate model for universality; it is the obvious image in the world of his time. The church of Augustine's day has already taken on an ecclesiastical polity modeled on that of the Roman Empire, and the same political ideal shapes the saint's vision of the holy city which the church visibly, if imperfectly, represents. Rome, Augustine sees, has subdued the whole world, has brought it into a single society or republic under law, and has bestowed upon it a widespread and enduring peace. In the same way, he explains, God will join the saints together in a single society in earth and heaven: a society that will "rest and see, see and love, love and praise for this is to be the end without end of all our living, that Kingdom without end, the real goal of our present life."[16]

Augustine's understandings of "election" and of the distinction between the "invisible" and "visible" church fit into this general conception. The identity of the elected ones is known for sure only to God. They are both within and beyond the borders of the visible church. The church on earth is a mixed company, a *corpus permixtum* Augustine called it. It contains both wheat and chaff. The church is imperfect and God is free. Therefore the church can never be *identified* with the community of the elect. There is an "invisible church" representing those whom God has truly called. The "visible church" functions in this world to make the elect at least presumptively visible.

Similar conceptions of election and of the church visible and invisible are found in Aquinas and in the deliverances of the Council of Trent, from which they pass into modern Roman Catholic ecclesiology, including that outlined in

Lumen Gentium. The invisible reality, as opposed to the institutional representation, of God's redeeming work comes to be
thought of as an idealization of the ecclesiastical polity, the
"mystical body" thought to dwell in and with the visible
institution. The relation of the mystical body to the visible
body is then understood on the analogy of the relation between divine and human natures in Christ. The visible
Church in its total social reality is the place where the mystical body tangibly dwells. Here the mystery is being constantly
revealed. The mystical body "subsists in"[17] the ecclesiastical
polity, but it is always something more. It remains mystery:
the church in its true reality stands behind the reality that
appears. In this model it is impossible, ontologically inconceivable one could say, to believe that God would entirely aban-
don the church, for it is present in the world as the humanity
of Christ is present: irrevocably and finally. The mystery may
be veiled, indistinct. But it cannot go away.

With Protestantism one enters a different world, yet one
with many ties to the Catholic order it supplants. Reformation
ecclesiologies, particularly those of the Calvinist type, arise
from a different political metaphor. Society is no longer a
pyramid or organic whole through which the charisma of the
ruler is suffused. It is rather a field of competing interests—
individual, economic, political, religious—whose claims need
to be adjudicated. This regulation is achieved through civil
statutes which are understood to reflect, and protect, citizens'
adherence to the law of God taught in and through the
church. Even for the redeemed the law has its instructional,
monitory value. God is still a monarch, but one now situated
above and beyond the field of battle as both lawgiver and
redeemer for human persons and institutions. One is related
to God as an individual is related to a sovereign. One is in
favor or out of it, treated as just or held at a distance. The
community is organized both in the ecclesiastical and civil
spheres as a polity designed to regulate differing economic,
political, and personal forces. Success in competitive endeav-
ors may or may not be indicative of the individual's standing
before God. The competitive field of human society is, as it

were, the stage on which quite another drama is played out, the drama of salvation. In such a polity the universal church is not conceived as one great mystical body with which one must be in organic connection in order to be saved. It is rather, as Calvin said, "a multitude gathered from all nations; it is divided and dispersed in separate places, but agrees on the one truth of divine doctrine, and is bound by the truth of the same religion."[18] It follows that the universal church, unlike the local church, has no single visible form. Rather it exists, or subsists, in many forms. Calvin's classic, and polemic, definition of the church's essence refers mainly to local congregations. "Wherever we see the word of God purely preached and heard and the sacraments administered according to Christ's institution, there, it is not to be doubted, a Church of God exists."[19]

Yet the imperfection of the visible ecclesia, combined with the freedom of God to call those whom God will in the Spirit, must be dealt with in this model too. But now, instead of an idealization of institutional patterns resulting in a notion of mystical body or invisible church, one finds an extension of the motif of individuation. The reality of what God is doing comes to expression in election, by which particular persons are chosen for regeneration and salvation. One has been graciously chosen before the foundation of the world or one has not. The true church is in principle invisible. It is the company of the elect. It is the task of the institutional ecclesiopolity to make the elect, the saints, somehow visible. If a person responds to the preaching of the gospel by being part of the church's visible communion, that creates a presumption that she or he has been marked from the foundations of the world as a member of the elect community. However, this cannot be known for sure. In this sense the church is an imperfect but indispensable instrument for deciphering the outlines of God's redemptive work in history. The visible church and the company of the elect do not coincide. The number of the elect is less than that of the visible membership of the church and extends to an unknown extent beyond the church. In this model it is possible for the visible church to fall away from grace entirely. If it does, God will find new ways for God's will to prevail in the world.

In Calvin's picture there is greater emphasis than in Augustine on God's "eternal decrees," more attention to election's logical consequence that those not elected must be chosen for "reprobation," and a further development of the themes of visible and invisible church which stress that these are not to be understood as two separate communities but as two ways of speaking about the one church. The most important gain in Calvin, however, is a more developed understanding of the work of the Holy Spirit. The Spirit shapes and guides the life of faith. It also illumines the reading of Scripture so that the words become vehicles of revelation through which God accommodates God's purposes to our understanding. With these formulations we have foundations for the experiential understanding of faith which arises several generations later. The Spirit illumines the reading of Scripture, but Scripture in turn illumines the meaning of what the Spirit is doing in us.

In later Calvinism, especially where the church's reality definitions are challenged by Arminian or incipiently secular alternatives, the emotional conversion experience functions as hermeneutical key for decipherment of God's intentions. To have had such an experience strongly suggests that one is a member of the company of the elect. Jonathan Edwards seems to have built his notable but controversial ministry in Northhampton, Massachusetts, on this assumption. As one commentator on his life has said, by allowing only the "converted" access to the communion table, he sought "to make the saints visible again."[20] Under the pressure of alternative conceptions of life already manifest in the Connecticut Valley of the mid-eighteenth century, Edwards in effect sought to collapse the distinction between visibility and invisibility in the church. Yet his congregation, which eventually voted to remove him from his position as pastor, well illustrated that distinction's descriptive relevance.

The notion of the church as in some sense a visible sign of what God has done and is doing among human beings, yet not to be identified with that divine work which is ultimately a mystery to us, is thus deeply embedded in the tradition. But the way in which this is worked out theologically is so dependent on the available political metaphors of each time and place that one wonders how it is possible to think of either the church or its doctrines as mediating something real beyond the reality with which sociology is able to deal. The sociological analysis of the origins of theological conceptions is illuminating. But that analysis needs to be integrated in some way into the practice of theology itself. That, in effect, is what George Lindbeck has tried to do. In the light of the analysis of ecclesiological types just offered, how persuasive is his attempt?

3. Doctrine: Real Presences and Regulative Ideas

George Lindbeck's book *The Nature of Doctrine: Religion and Theology in a Postliberal Age*[21] deals with doctrinal language in a way which reflects the search for reality—in both its philosophical and theological forms—in the language and practice of the community of faith. Hence Lindbeck also wrestles with the question of theology and the human sciences. Drawing in particular on Wittgenstein and Geertz among the thinkers introduced in chapter 3, he writes:

> It has become customary in a considerable body of anthropological, sociological, and philosophical literature . . . to emphasize neither the cognitive nor the experiential-expressive aspects of religion; rather, emphasis in placed on those respects in which religions resemble languages together with their correlative forms of life and thus are similar to cultures (insofar as these are understood semiotically as reality and value systems—that is, as idioms for the constructing of reality and the living of life). The function of church doctrines that becomes most prominent in this perspective is their use, not as expressive symbols or as truth claims, but as communally authoritative rules of discourse, attitude, and action.[22]

If doctrines are rules, then presumably their function is to articulate the encoding or decoding instructions which are implicit in the religious community's characteristic way of construing the world. Lindbeck refers to his proposal as a "cultural-linguistic" approach. He calls the implied view of doctrine a "regulative" or rule theory.

Much of the force of Lindbeck's presentation derives from the contrast his argument portrays between his cultural-linguistic theory and the two other positions mentioned, the "cognitive" and the "experiential-expressive."[23] Cognitive approaches are those which continue to claim that doctrines embody knowledge of reality, that they somehow describe what is the case. One finds this position in Protestant fundamentalism, and also in certain Roman Catholic theologians. The experiential-expressive viewpoint, most often attributed to Schleiermacher, argues that doctrines are cognitive renderings of religious experience. One finds this approach, Lindbeck notes, in college professors of religious studies, who find it very persuasive to students who would otherwise have little to do with issues of faith and certainly steer clear of churches and their creeds. The cultural-linguistic theory contrasts with both of these views in claiming that adherence to religious faith is somewhat like learning a language or entering a new culture. One simply learns to symbolize the universe in a new way. The cultural and linguistic resources of a given religious position are what make it possible to experience the world in a certain sense. The symbols come first and then the experience, not the other way around.

Lindbeck has been attacked for the apologetic framing of his own position in contrast to those of others. One assailant is Brian Gerrish, who argues that if Schleiermacher is taken as an instance of experiential-expressivism, the subjectivism Lindbeck attributes to this view falsely represents the true position.[24] It is probably fair to say that many modern representatives of the viewpoints Lindbeck holds to be in contrast with his own find ways to accommodate at least some of the insights found in the cultural-linguistic approach.[25] Still, *The Nature of Doctrine* is an important statement, not least because it connects modern human-science theories of religion and society, such as that introduced in the preceding section of this chapter, with theological discussions of confessional language, and connects both with the problems of ecumenical dialogue.

Lindbeck argues that doctrines function as "rules" for the community's thought and action. But we have already seen that there is an intrinsic relationship between the actual social reality of the faith community and its doctrinal expressions. What eventually becomes doctrine must already be somehow present *in nuce* in the community as a form of life. How then can doctrines function as "rules"? The word implies that doctrines have an authority which is not merely a reflection of community norms. One can say, of course, that doctrines are simply normative crystallizations of the community's metaphorical view of the world: convenient compendia, so to speak, of the existing reality sense. But Lindbeck seems to mean more than this. *How*, exactly, do doctrines function as rules? What is the reality which gives them authority?

The ancient notion of the *regula fidei* gives legitimacy to the question, but work needs to be done today to clarify what is meant. The ancient formulas of faith seem to have been connected with both liturgy and loyalty. Many of the ancient "symbols" were, or began as, baptismal confessions spoken by the new Christian as he or she was immersed in the pool. The creeds also functioned as talismans of orthodoxy. Their adoption signified loyalty to imperial authority in a nominally Christian realm. The creeds also functioned to map the field open to speculation, to set limits for the work of theologians. In addition to playing these traditional roles in new ways, doctrine today needs to be much more connected with the total symbolic fabric and practice of the faith community. But, given what we know now of the relation between doctrines and practical reasoning in the congregation, Lindbeck has not yet shown *how* doctrines function in a truly regulative mode. It is not clear how one moves *from* doctrines *to* practical prescriptions for life together rather than the other way around. Has Lindbeck done more than baptize a version of the sociology of knowledge?

Part of the problem is that most doctrines, including some

Lindbeck uses as examples, are not regulative but propositional in grammatical form. They appear to refer to realities beyond this world, and have undoubtedly been so understood by the great majority of Christian theologians and believers from the origins of the church until now. How are we to account for this? My tentative answer stems from the notion that the community of faith *itself* mediates a form of real presence to which doctrines directly or indirectly point. The community does this by signifying the reality of the people of God, which is the place of God's "dwelling" in the universe (Rev. 21:3). I will develop this idea further, but we must come to it by several preliminary steps.

The critic George Steiner, in a book (fascinatingly for our purposes) titled *Real Presences*,[26] claims that art, music, and literature, rightly understood, have a reality-mediating or "underwriting" function which resembles what we are claiming for the community of faith. Only for Steiner it is less a mediation *of* presence and more a wager *on* presence as a "necessary possibility," a possibility always there, a possibility on which the book never closes. He suggests,

> that any coherent understanding of what language is and how language performs, that any coherent account of the capacity of human speech to communicate meaning and feeling is, in the final analysis, underwritten by the assumption of God's presence. I will put forward the argument that the experience of aesthetic meaning in particular, that of literature, of the arts, of musical form, infers the necessary possibility of this "real presence."[27]

And he continues,

> This wager . . . predicates the presence of a realness, of a "substantiation" (the theological reach of this word is obvious) within language and form. It supposes a passage, beyond the fictive or the purely pragmatic, from meaning to meaningfulness. The conjecture is that "God" is, not because our grammar is outworn; but that grammar lives on and generates worlds because there is the wager on God.[28]

That grammar can generate worlds means that we must reckon on the possibility that the universe is embraced—encompassed about—by transcending meaning. This meaning, we would say, completes and "underwrites" the sense we encounter in language, music, and art. Is there justification for saying that the notion of a sacramental transsignification of the meaning-bearing elements of sociality that signal the reality of a people of God requires us likewise to reckon on the possibility of God's reality, and indeed to decide to stake our lives on this wager—in the objective uncertainty of a life lived by faith? I think so. But the evidence of God we have in mind is not confined to art, music, and literature. It is all of that plus the common everyday sense of our social world transfigured as the Christ-bearing mosaic of persons in the faith community.

Such a picture makes the most sense if we believe with Northrop Frye that art, music, and literature are already suffused by "the great code,"[29] a vast coherent structure of meaning centered on the Bible. Then we could claim that the faith community possesses, indeed itself embodies, the hermeneutical decoding device for grasping what art, music, and literature, are fundamentally about, for discerning the ultimate wager they require us to make for the sake of understanding and existential appropriation. But Frye's and Steiner's visions are both too confined to worlds of conscious symbolic representation. I am more interested in the way human communities may encode the biblical message in their ways of living. I am also concerned about the paradoxical similarity of Steiner's position to that of Jacques Derrida who, after severing virtually all connection between language and reality, all sense of presence, seems to replace the whole with "writing" or "scrip-ture', which he calls "the divine milieu." Hodgson throws light on this proposal. Why writing?

> Derrida provides a clue by pointing out that the first writing was "hieroglyphic" or "sacred inscription." Derridean deconstruction, at least, invests writing with a kind of sacrality, since it understands writing to be a self-referential interplay of

signs, an endless milieu of significations that refers to nothing
other than itself, the condition of possibility for consciousness
and the object of consciousness, an unending play of differences in which the "ever-never-changing-same" eternally
recurs in a *coincidentia oppositorum*, an "abiding passage."[30]

I believe that Steiner means more than this, but I am not
sure that he makes his point. The churches have indeed been
great patrons of art, music, and literature, but they must
gather into sense a still greater field of meaning: the field
constituted by all the signifying interactions that make up the
human community as a whole. This gathering deciphers and
bodies forth the "sense" that inheres in the otherwise
crooked,[31] tangled, and senseless exchanges of humanity itself, the sense that the earth's population is one people under
God, a people constituting in its consciousness the articulation
of God's unfolding presence in the historical process. In the
nearly limitless field of human discourse, art, music, and literature play a powerful but hardly dominating role. And the art,
music, and literature of the West are only part of the story.
There are other, non-Western, expressions of the people's
sense which also enter into the Church's sacramentality of
transsignification.

Instead of thinking of works of music, art, and literature—
all of them examples of high culture unfortunately connected
for many in our society with the sensibility of elites—let us
think of the texts, narrative, poetic, and otherwise, generated
in situations in which can be discerned signs of the forming of
humanity as one people under God. These signs demonstrate
that demons are being cast out, that the Messiah has come in
the flesh. Think of all these instances, evanescent though they
may be, as the library of a real world, not merely the literary
or artistic worlds, a library of possibilities there for congregations to decode and signify by embodiment. The congregation,
with its thinkers and seers, then functions like the critical,
appreciative and participating audience for artistic creation in
Steiner's book. It finds, in the sense made by all these instances of redemption and reconciliation in the social order,

both under Christian auspices and beyond, grounds for at least a "wager" that such patterns of meaning are "underwritten" by the reality of God, the ultimate author of the sense which can be made of things.

But what *sort* of reality sense is implied in such underwriting? The task is to see *how* certain formulas become regulative for the community while pointing to the community's transcendental grounds. I will carry Lindbeck's notion of doctrines as rules one step further. Let us try the following. doctrines seek to put in words the nature of the ultimate arena of discourse, say God's presence in the world through the gathering and shaping power of the Spirit, to which some particular feature of the faith community's immanent discourse or pattern of activity in principle points. Here I am drawing on the philosophical notion of *appresentation*[32]: the idea that we may be able to see enough of a reality to know what it is as a whole, inferring the "appresented" aspects of the reality we cannot directly apprehend. As a particular Euclidean theorem presupposes or appresents the entire, theoretically infinite, system of understanding of which it is an instance, so some image or metaphor within the immanent language of the faith community makes present or instantiates an infinite conversation of which it, too, is an instance. One can think of many figures which function this way: metaphors of fatherhood and motherhood, of creativity, betrayal, reconciliation and consummation. Above all, are instances of the transfiguration of human spirit by Holy Spirit. Doctrines offer a means whereby the infinite conversation to which such notions point (as Steiner sees meanings in literature infinitely "underwritten") can be immanently understood. They articulate the larger meanings which are the context of the community's intrinsic, immanent, forms of sense.

This understanding draws on Kant's notions of the regulative idea and of transcendental propositions.[33] In the Kantian perspective a regulative idea or principle presides over a manifold of interconnected particulars which make sense together because they are ruled by that larger complex of meaning.[34] Kant argued that we always reason *as if* our field of discourse has an inherent unity and wholeness implied by the specific terms of our argument but not accessible as an object in itself. In "rational psychology" for example, our arguments presuppose that we are dealing with a reality called the "self" inside which or in relation to which psychological faculties such as memory and will function. Although no one can point out a self as an empirical object, one cannot conduct a psychological argument without implicitly or explicitly making use of this idea. In fact the idea rules the discourse: hence it is called a "regulative principle." Likewise in "rational cosmology" our arguments presuppose the idea of something called the world or the "universe" within which all observable phenomena and relationships fit coherently. Although one cannot point to a "world," one cannot reason cosmologically without presupposing it. And finally "rational theology" functions *as if* the sum of all appearances, the sensible world itself, had a simple, highest, and all-sufficient ground beyond itself, a self-subsistent, original, creative reason we call "God." Again, this "God" is a "regulative principle." These regulative principles, for Kant, are all "transcendental ideas." That is, they are rational constructs which point beyond the limits to which reason is confined by its need to be tied to our "intuition" of data presented empirically. "Transcendental ideas" point to the conditions of possibility for something we already know from experience is the case. In Kant's *Critique of Pure Reason*, for example, transcendental ideas indicate what must be the case if there is to be such a thing as Newtonian mechanics. In his *Critique of Practical Reason* they take the form of "postulates"—God, freedom, and immortality—which underwrite, or provide conditions of possibility and rational coherence, for the demands of the moral law.

The logical question for the argument of this book is whether the notion of a covenantal communion of humankind as space of God's presence in the universe and in history can function analogously to Kant's "regulative principles" or "postulates" of moral reasoning. Clearly such a communion is not literally to be met with in experience. But I am urging the churches to organize their thinking, and to live, in the light of a coherence supplied by "the sense of a people" of God as a transcendental ecclesiological idea. For me, of course, such an idea is not a construct of "pure reason." It rather partakes of rich and complex metaphorization by selectively taking up into itself the symbolic products of human life. Such a hypothesis is not purely Kantian, but rather, as Paul Ricoeur says, a kind of "post-Hegelian" Kantianism. It makes use not merely of "transcendental ideas" but of the progressive unfolding of the metaphorical content of historical experience. As such, I have already proposed that it begins to take on some of the properties of Husserl's and Alfred Schutz's notion *appresentation*, particularly as that idea is appropriated by Edward Farley.

Examples may help bring all this down to earth. If I do a theorem in geometry or a problem in calculus, my work consists of expressions and operations which make sense together. But they make this sense because together they constitute one expression of a greater whole: in this case the whole body of geometrical axioms and proofs. The particular mathematical operation I have carried out makes the sense it does because it presupposes, and in a sense points to, the whole network of assumptions and definitions in which my particular moves play a role. Just so, Christian communities of faith make sense when they become visible expressions of a larger logic: the logic of God ruling in and through God's people. The sense of a people, then, is the universal grammar of human relationships under God, which faith communities make present by the way they live and by what they do. This is not simply a matter of *pars pro toto*. The whole grammar is present in each relationship, each act. It is the bearer of real presence.

Consider a second, rather different, illustration. A hologram conveys a three-dimensional image with startling clarity and realism, yet the objects imaged are really "there" only as a particular organization of refractions of laser light. If the hologram is broken into many small pieces, the whole image is still, indistinctly but identifiably, visible in each one. Each such fragmentary image presupposes the whole, points to it, while representing it in fainter, sketchier form. The whole image is now visible *only* in these fragments: together they *appresent* it. So it is that the people of God may be represented, however faintly, in the churches and congregations which "belong" to it, each of which manifests a practical logic, a minimal recognizable configuration or sense, that presupposes and points to the larger, fuller sense. The whole figure is there in each local community, but it is not there in all its fullness until somehow the broken shards are put back together.

We are saying, then, that doctrinal language functions in a faith community to refer to the total logical context or conceptual frame of reference in which the community's working language and lived meanings are set. On the one hand, doctrinal formulas *reflect* the community: they are conceptual crystallizations of familial, social, cultural, political images already there. But on the other hand, they *test* the community's patterns of expression (Barth's *wissenschaftliche Prüfung*) by articulating their relationships to the wider worlds of meaning to which they belong: wider worlds such as the total history of Christian thought with both its biblical grounding and its myriad interactions with culture, or the "conversation" (itself an extended metaphor) between God and the universe.

Do doctrines tell truths? Do they function propositionally? I think we want to say that faith communities tell truths by what they are, and that doctrines have a regulative function in that truth telling. Apart from the communities in which they function, that is as bare propositions fending for themselves, doctrines do not tell truths. But as regulators of the community's truth telling, doctrines must have some relationship to truth which needs to be further defined. They cannot regulate truth telling without having some form of participation in a truth process.

Faith thus leaves a trail of figurative meanings that can be traced. But can we honor the cognitive claims that are produced along the way? Doctrines function as encoding the *essential logic* of the community. If there is a *logos*, a syntax, a grammar, in all this process, then doctrines try to articulate it. They are products of the process by which the community becomes conscious of its own lived logic, and hence function together as a guidance mechanism which ensures continuation of the community's identity. Doctrines "read" the ultimate significance of the ecclesiogenetic process and characterize it in language which often has propositional form.

It follows that doctrines *do* make reality claims: they show the *whole* (Bellah's "felt whole", but more) which is represented fragmentarily by the faith community concerned. In the argument of this book, that whole is God's rule in history through the growing reality of God's people. God language is that language among the different forms of expression the community uses which refers to the totality of what the community shows or signifies by its presence in history. If this claim can be upheld, we are restating in a different way the limit which Wittgenstein set for the functioning of language games and the "forms of life" they serve. Wittgenstein argued that a form of life may "show" a transcendental ground which it cannot referentially "say." I am arguing that as used by the community, doctrinal language is not literally referential, but it does point to and describe the community's showing, or signifying of the larger reality to which it belongs. The truth lies in what the community's life sacramentally makes present. Its language-in-use puts words to that truth.

But now I must say more about this "larger reality." I have spoken of the invisible communion of those persons in whose lives human spirit has been taken up into Holy Spirit. I have said that this communion of saints is a dwelling place of God, even an embodiment of God's humanity in time and space. This is language which has a certain appeal in the postmodern world. Yet it does not do away entirely with the difficulties with which we have just been wrestling. What way of understanding such words can justify their use?

4. Spirit, World, Church: Toward a New Formulation

The creeds agree in locating the church in the "third article" dealing with the work of the Spirit and, hence, ultimately in the context of the dynamic role of the Trinity in human history. What, after all, do we mean when we say, "I believe in the Holy Spirit, the Holy Catholic Church, the communion of saints, the forgiveness of sins, and the life everlasting?" My line of argument seeks a fresh understanding of the *function* of doctrine as regulative for the churches' practical reasoning; it also calls for a rethinking of the *meaning* of certain theological formulas as well, particularly some which deal with the relation between God and the world.

What is meant by speaking of God—both in Godself and in relation to the cosmos—as "triune?" That is not easy to say. Writers such as Karl Rahner, Cyril Richardson, Thomas Parker, Eberhard Jüngel, and most recently Peter Hodgson and Michael Welker, are saying that the classical trinitarian formulas, which we owe to the early councils and to thinkers such as Augustine and Thomas Aquinas, leave much to be desired in themselves and yet offer possibilities still to be unfolded for today's world.[35] The heart of the problem, Parker argues, lies in what the Fathers and later theologians tried to do. They sought to reconcile God's monarchy, conceived in the political metaphors described above, with God's "economy" or dynamic process of salvation through history. On the one hand, God is sovereign, standing at the top of a hierarchy of being, or aloof as divine lawgiver. This is a metaphor for God developed in the political context of monarchical Israel, or of imperial Rome, or in a different yet equally static way in the budding commercial civilizations of Reformation Europe. Yet Scripture also envisions a God dynamically implicated in the twists and turns of human history: a God who wills to dwell among human beings through the ministry of a people and to be present as holy will in that people's law and way of life. Such metaphors of divine engagement and involvement were eventually reflected in what was later called the "economic" Trinity: God actively present in creation and history especially through the working of the Holy Spirit.

Would that the latter conception of divine presence had been consistently worked out early in the church's life. But far greater attention was devoted by the fathers to the immanent Trinity: the three "persons" in one hypostasis or substance, conceived in their complex internal relations elaborately described in a variety of terminologies and nuances. All that was made necessary by the apparent need to fit the economy into conceptions of divine monarchy. If, however, we now can transcend these monarchical metaphors for God, the doctrine of the Trinity can be liberated to support and deepen the conception of a people of God that, in this book, underlies a new vision of and for the church.

Parker persuasively argues that, shorn of the political need to accommodate metaphors of monarchy, the Trinity represents "a radical identification of the economy, the historical process of creation and redemption through Word and Spirit, with the very life of God."[36] This result demands careful attention. Parker goes on to say, what is claimed is that the economy of God is a revelation of God as well as the salvation of creatures. Behind the process is not another, different, alien ground of being, absolute and alone, simple and single, about whom we can only keep silence, but the one whose mystery of being transcends our ability to express it *exactly because it is the mystery of the economy, as mystery which assumes our humanity and is lived out in the community of faith.*[37] Such a vision, I claim, would be the sort of regulative or transcendental idea generated by a church which saw itself as signifying an inclusive community of the Spirit—marked by justice, peace, creativity, and care for the planet—in which God is coming to real presence as the one who loves in freedom.[38] It is hardly imaginable in a church for which monarchical metaphors still dominate. The fact is, however, that this sort of trinitarian vision is found mainly in the work of theologians, such as the present writer, who envision such a church and wish for its realization.

A few examples will indicate the range of writers who are saying something like this. As early as 1956, in a talk which became the title essay of *The Humanity of God,* Karl Barth spoke of the limits of his and others' early emphasis on God as "wholly other."

> But did it not appear to escape us by quite a distance that the
> *deity* of the *living* God—and we certainly wanted to deal with

him—found its meaning and its power only in the context of
His history and His dialogue with *man*, and thus his *togetherness* with man? Indeed—and this is the point back of which
we cannot go—it is a matter of *God's* sovereign togetherness
with man, a togetherness grounded in Him and determined,
delimited, and ordered through Him alone. Only in this way
and in this context can it take place and be recognized. It is a
matter, however, of God's *togetherness* with man. Who God
is and what He is in His deity, He proves and reveals not in
a vacuum as a divine being-for-Himself, but precisely and
authentically in the fact that He exists, speaks, and acts as
partner of man, though of course as the absolutely superior
partner. He who does *that* is the living God. And the freedom
in which He does *that* is His deity. It is the deity which as such
also has the character of humanity. . . . It is precisely God's
deity which, rightly understood, includes his *humanity*.[39]

One has to say that, if Barth had ever brought his doctrine
of the Holy Spirit out of the shadow of "christological concentration," he might have been led to develop these thoughts
more fully. There are other voices which argue in the same
direction, if in diverse conceptualities and idioms. Karl
Rahner in *The Doctrine of the Trinity*[40] identifies the economic with the immanent trinity, calling for a reformulation
which brings the Trinity more fully into the historical process
of salvation. Jürgen Moltmann, in *The Crucified God*,[41] sees
the cross not simply as an event external to God but, together
with the resurrection, as an event *in* the life of God. Eberhard
Jüngel in *The Doctrine of the Trinity*,[42] a book written with
special reference to Barth, argues the same case: "God's
being is in coming. As the one who is coming, God turns being
toward salvation. Thus God is the mystery of the world."[43]

Most recently, Peter Hodgson and Michael Welker have
made statements which deserve fuller treatment. Hodgson's
God in History develops the tradition of trinitarian thinking,
which for him culminates in Hegel, in the direction of a "shaping" or "configuring" involvement with the human world
which is the form of God's presence in history. He writes,

I think that, properly understood, the trinity introduces process and historicality into God, and my purpose is to show that God and history are correlative themes: the only God we know is a God who is in history and who takes history into God.[44]

Hodgson goes on to say,

The world is precisely *not* God, and because it is not-God it is a moment within the divine life. The extraordinary thing about God is that God overreaches and incorporates what is not-God within God. God is the identity of God and not-God, the event that takes place between God and the world. Thereby God is a God whose being is in process, and what is not-God has the possibility of being saved from its annihilating nothingness.[45]

He continues,

God's loving, suffering, transformative embrace of the world is an inclusive embrace, but like everything else in the world it does not appear everywhere all at once but in distinctive shapes, patterns, configurations. In fact, as I suggested earlier, it appears in the world liminally, at the margin of dominant world-formations, requiring for its discernment "hard labor." It also appears in a plurality of forms, none of which can legitimately claim finality or exclusive validity; all such claims are parochial and arbitrary because all are tinged with the contingency and relativity of history. But distinctive religious traditions and communities have experienced God's redemptive, suffering presence in the world in distinctive ways, and they have a right, indeed an obligation, to make it known, to proclaim it.[46]

Michael Welker has been at work for some time in a different, yet related way. He has published an important article on the Spirit,[47] with more detail promised in a book soon to come. Welker seeks to clarify the relation between the Holy Spirit and the holy catholic church of the creeds.

Welker's idea is that the Spirit instigates a "force-field" of Christ's "resonance," and that through the forgiveness of sins the many perspectives on Jesus Christ are permitted to come together in the church. He traces references to the Spirit (*ruah*) in Hebrew Scripture, noting that the one on whom the Spirit falls (Jud. 3:7ff., 6:34, 11:29) "restores solidarity, loyalty, and capacity for common action among the people."[48] More, in the Isaianic traditions, precisely those later read in Christian Scripture as messianic, we find a close connection between bestowal of the Spirit and justice for the poor, the "lowly of the land" (Isa. 11:1ff.) The same connection is found in Isa. 42: 1,3 and 61:1ff; "justice receives its dynamic power from the practice of mercy."[49] Such doing of acts of mercy is an expression of the forgiveness of sins. But, Welker asks, if acts of mercy are needed do we not look first today for tax-supported welfare and social engineering for the poor and oppressed? Do we not still believe in secular utopian philosophies? What room is left for understanding what it means to say that the Spirit is poured out "from heaven" on all flesh? Welker here offers a novel view of "heaven." "Heaven is . . . conceived as a complex of powers and uncontrollable forces, as the realm that is not amenable to human measurement or arbitrary manipulation, but at the same time decisively determines life on this earth."[50] Just as natural events such as earthquakes and windstorms are unpredictable, so are the social movements

> unleashed by the charismatic leaders on whom God's spirit comes. As in the case of wind, one wonders in vain why the movement could not be predicted. Why could not the people be led together previously? How long will the solidarity last? Why does unity of spirit dissolve again?[51]

"Heaven" answers this question for the biblical writers. Have we anything better?

> Heaven . . . brings and maintains together forces which on earth are dispersed in space and time. That is, when improba-

ble, inconceivable concentrations of powers and forces come about on earth, the biblical traditions regard what is going on as an activity "from heaven."[52]

This, Welker thinks, is what Luke, interpreting the prophet Joel, seeks to express in his account of the day of Pentecost. The Spirit "enables men and women, old and young, even slaves of both sexes, to unlock the future which God intends—and to do so with each other and for each other."[53] Pentecost means that God's intentions and actions are being made "accessible to all human beings." The fact that the Spirit is poured out from heaven means that human beings, "generate a trusting familiarity with the world, that they never achieve in their normal, finite, concrete perspectives."[54] The result is that

> what is unthinkable in the concrete earthly perspectives of individual human beings, and of societies and cultural circles which are marked off against each other, actually happens here with regard to "the mighty works of God." Successful universal understanding and enrichment, with simultaneous preservation of the multiplicity and variegated nature of life as it is really lived in its concreteness and as it takes on culturally diverse character, is achieved.[55]

Each human being on whom the Spirit has been poured out now stands in a "force field" in which he or she is filled with "the fullness of God" (Eph. 3:19). This creates a realm of "poly-concreteness" (cf. 1 Corinthians 12) in which the Spirit generates a "multifaceted, reciprocally strengthened and strengthening process of cooperation. Abstractions and the reduction to general principles cannot do justice to the pluralistic concreteness."[56] To find conceptual expression for all this "one would have to develop in the human sciences the ability to think in terms of field structures, and one would have to render that kind of thinking plausible."[57]

The New Testament clearly identifies this Holy Spirit as the Spirit of Christ (Romans 8, John 14:26, 1 John 4:1–3). But this personhood has its personalizing power by creating a social sphere which has a kind of "resonance." This is the word Welker uses to characterize webs of relationship through which we become persons and which are only partially dependent upon our own activity. A domain of resonance necessarily involves a multiplicity of perspectives. Just as my own "public person" involves all the different perspectives from which others regard me, so Christ's person in history is the totality of the perspectives through which he is known. The Holy Spirit, then,

> is the multiform *unity* of perspectives on Jesus Christ, a unity in which we participate and which we help to constitute. The Holy Spirit is thus *Christ's domain of resonance*. The Spirit is the public person who corresponds to the individual Jesus Christ.[58]

Welker goes on to say that "the forgiveness of sins is the process that creates the requisite condition for the unity of human beings with God where those conditions do not exist."[59] It is hard to identify those who are born of the Spirit. But this we know: they live from the forgiveness of sins. They are a heterogeneous lot,

> with a multiformity which characterizes life as it is really lived. They reflect the powers of the heavenly fullness in a way that must appear simply incomprehensible, indeed, chaotically lively, to those who are wedded to the world's homogenizing power-codes. . . . But precisely in this condition, they become the vital force-field that the third article of the Apostles' Creed sketches in just a few words.[60]

Welker's vision comes close to what I have described as the energy field of the people of God. He even goes so far as to suggest a need for human-science conceptualization of what this might mean. Where I have spoken in terms of a hermeneutical human science in terms of which worldly forms of witness to the Spirit's action can be christologically deciphered, Welker speaks of a sharing of resonance. Beginning with the doctrine of the Holy Spirit, Welker seems to join hands with my argument, which sets out, using a different set of metaphors, from the question of the church. If the resonance of the Spirit's global energy field is that of Jesus Christ, then in Christ the visible churches may be able to find the proper frequency in order to tune it in and make it audible as witness to the human race.

Clearly, if the church today is to rethink the relationships between God and the world, that will need to be done by reopening the case of the economic Trinity and asking just what is meant by saying that God is implicated, indeed comes to fullness of being, in the process of redemption and reconciliation through history. The literature just reviewed clearly moves in this direction. My own argument has sought to show that ecclesiology is an important key to this matter, and particularly so an ecclesiology of the people of God understood as primary arena and instrument of God's presence in the world as Spirit.

I argued in the previous section that one of the main obstacles preventing Christian theologians from grasping the meaning of God's worldly action as gathering, articulating, and energizing Spirit has arisen from an imprisonment of the concept of God within political metaphors of the relationship between power and community generated in Mediterranean and European culture and carried over into ecclesiology. We have already seen that a metaphor which sees monarchy as the apex of a social pyramid charged with the monarch's divinely bestowed charism lies behind ecclesiologies of the catholic type, while a metaphor of society as a field of competing interests and energies in which God is a transcendent and often withdrawn moral referee lies behind ecclesiologies of the protestant type. It is not that ecclesiology *per se* controls conceptions of the Trinity or notions of the relation between God and the world. It is rather that the church, reflecting its social context, tends tacitly to encourage the maintenance of a certain metaphorical construal of the world in which a doctrine of God is then worked out. The church's understandings of God's presence in the world have seldom been able to escape these metaphorical frames of reference. The result has been a developmental impoverishment particularly of those doctrines which the fathers located in the third article of the creed: Holy Spirit, holy catholic church, communion of saints, and even, as we now have seen, the forgiveness of sins.

If older ecclesiological metaphors have blocked otherwise promising theological developments, the present discomfiture of hierarchical and monarchical models is indeed a hopeful sign. The evident dysfunctionality of traditional ecclesial forms of life, the collapse of what Edward Farley describes as a "logic of triumph" (which sees only from the perspective of victors) now opens the way for a new understanding of Spirit and church of the sort appearing in much contemporary theological writing. These tendencies should be mutually reinforcing. I intend this study of the sense of a people to be seen in this context. This people is the instrument of God's coming to be in history, the venue of God's progress toward a form of being in space and time. The churches are communities which in many different ways bear witness to this historical process by acting as lived significations of it. These signifying communities, in turn, produce regulative theological constructs which account transcendentally for the ultimate conditions of such spirit-filled forms of life, for the "necessary possibility" of God.

5. Traditions Newly Understood: The Approach to Ecumenism

The notion that the church is in some sense a visible sign of what God has done and is doing among human beings, yet not to be identified with that divine work, is deeply embedded in Christian tradition. The vision just offered, of the church as signifier of the people-gathering work of the Holy Spirit, has affinities with ideas of the past, yet it also takes a new turn. Remember that for Augustine and Calvin the elect have been chosen as individuals before the foundation of the world. Their identities, and therefore their exact number, are already determined. There are certain differences, of course, in the way the two theologians work out the consequences. Augustine's city of God metaphor conveys a more corporate notion of the elect community than Calvin's language does, while Calvin's rhetoric concerning the divine decrees gives reprobation dramatic overtones absent in Augustine. For both, however, the visible church exists to bring persons to live out the consequences of their election, and thereby let the world know of God's gracious work.

But Augustine and Calvin lived in "Constantinian" circumstances. The visible church at least nominally included most members of society. Not all of these persons demonstrated fruits of the Spirit. It was thus natural to think of the number of the elect in the churches as smaller than their total membership. God of course could choose whom God willed, but given the classical theologians' low awareness of societies and cultures beyond their own, they had little to say about the possibility of a larger, far-flung chosen community, a people whose existence the churches might signify but never fully comprehend. But the situation of the church in the late twentieth century calls for a revision of this outlook. The church is now a minority in most human cultures. It becomes possible to imagine that the company of the elect is larger than the membership of the churches, or less closely connected with these bodies than we had thought. We can suppose that there are many chosen by God as vessels of the Holy Spirit whom the churches' deciphering efforts have thus far failed to identify. The gospel as preached by churches today may indeed be unrecognizable to many who belong among God's people. There may well be many outside the churches to whom "God has given welcome" even if we have not.

Most of us have long since abandoned the idea that the elect community consists of a fixed number of persons chosen before the foundation of the world. The people of God, as understood in these pages, consists of all those persons and communities of persons who *at any given moment* are instruments of God's Holy Spirit and who therefore give the world hope. The task of making such a company of humanity even provisionally visible calls on the churches continuously to practice the sort of discerning practical reasoning already described. The Spirit guides the interpretation of Scripture so that through it we may decipher some part of what the Spirit is doing both in the faith community and beyond it. Doctrine is no longer a series of formulations which purport to describe what is, but a set of regulative (and therefore reformable) ideas for the community's *phronesis* or practical deliberation about how, in each new moment, it will live out a "real presence."

Karl Barth made an enabling move when he affirmed in the *Church Dogmatics*, that God's election of humanity shows that God is the One who loves in freedom. Jesus Christ is both the electing God and the elected man in one. God's act of election is not only a predestining *of* human beings but a determination of God *for* human beings. The election of grace, accomplished in Jesus Christ, is simultaneously the election of God's community, the calling into being of God's people. Barth's account of the election of the individual comes *after* his description of the election of the community. As a member of this community the individual bears its witness to the world.[61] Those of Reformed background, as I am, are freed by these Barthian formulations from having to understand election as a decree concerning certain individuals handed down before the beginning of time. We are liberated to think instead of the gathering, configuring work of God as the Holy Spirit instigating new forms of life throughout the human community, a work to which Jesus Christ, the elect one, is the hermeneutical key. The notion of a christologically based ecclesial "deciphering" of the Spirit's work in the world permits a revised understanding of "visibility" and "invisibility" in the church. The visible community now *signifies* (even if only faintly, as in a fragment of a hologram) the invisible gathering work of the Spirit. The church still has the role of "making the saints visible." But it does so in a way different from that which Jonathan Edwards imagined. Now the church becomes a sign or sacrament of God's gathering of the human race. That is true whether this gathering goes on within the church or beyond its visible boundaries.

I am arguing, then, that we need to begin from a new point of departure: the sense of a universal people of God as a genuine spiritual community in the process of coming to be on the stage of history which the churches are called sacramentally to signify. I have also sought to show that the intellectual and practical conditions may be at hand for working out an ecclesiology based on this basis. Much greater sophistication exists today than ever before about the way social realities function, about the way they shape peoples' construals of the world. These new concepts let us speak of human gatherings as fields of symbolic action in which Spirit comes to expression in human lives and human works as they are enabled by grace to signify God's purposes. In this way it is possible to grasp the Spirit's work in human community building in ways that transcend given polities and their metaphors, while affirming that the Spirit always needs some concrete form of life for its expression. We are on the brink of understanding, not how members of the church belong to the institution, but rather how the different institutions belong to a larger community in the Spirit which is the expression, as Joseph Haroutunian said, of "God with us."[62]

The next step is now obvious. The churches cannot signify the gathering of God's people in the power of the Spirit if they continue to act separately and alone. Division in the life of the church threatens to efface the image, to invalidate the communal sacrament. On the one hand, real presence is the gift of the Spirit to each particular community of faith in its special circumstances. Therefore particular traditions, always revised to meet new conditions of life, remain indispensable. But if theological formulas are tied to the practical reasoning of particular communities of faith they are not in themselves universal. No single community of faith, out of its own resources, can formulate a gospel for the whole world. Only in an ongoing dialogue among the churches is an approach to universality possible, and then it is of a very different kind from that envisioned either by centers of ecclesiastical power or in the rationality of the Enlightenment. In a sense the one gospel lies in the fact of the dialogue itself. It can be stated as a set of regulative and transcendental propositions arising in the ecumenical conversation. It follows that participation in such dialogue, and in shared action flowing from it, is of the essence of being church in today's world.

The next chapter looks at some aspects of the theological work now going on in the World Council of Churches and other agencies. It asks whether the vision just outlined might illuminate that conversation or contribute to it. Could the sense of a people called out by the Holy Spirit lead to wider shared understanding among the churches?

V

Reframing the Notion of Catholicity

Vincent of Lérins, a fifth-century abbot, left us a classic formula for identifying authentic Christian teaching. The true doctrine, he wrote, is that which is believed "everywhere, at all times, and by all."[1] In today's church, this canon would be hard to apply. If any doctrinal formula were to survive Vincent's criterion now it would be one expressed at a very high level of abstraction and generality. And generalities tend to blind us to particular circumstances, where the real issues of faith and freedom are being fought out. How then is the identity of the Christian faith to be ascertained today in a way both inclusive in its reach and relevant to each local situation in which the churches struggle to hear the message and act on it?

The Christian faith's sense of universality, the church's quality of inclusiveness of "all sorts and conditions" of humanity, has been expressed in the ancient notion of catholicity. This term, used in various ways, has always referred *both* to the wholeness of the church *and* to the quality which a particular faith community has when it is representative of that wholeness. I will argue in this chapter that the understanding of "catholicity" today needs to be broadened and made much more dynamic if it is to address the issues described in these pages. In particular it needs to be defined dialogically. The terms used in classical discussions of the subject become moments in an ongoing encounter between different faith expressions. The different churches should find confidence in the dialogue itself, rather than in any static qualities they may possess on their own, that they participate in a universal communion in the Spirit of Jesus Christ. Accordingly, after first defining some issues more fully, this chapter will look at instances of the sort of dialogue I mean. The work of the Commission on Faith and Order of the World Council of Churches is a case in point. We will see the notion of catholicity taking on broadened meaning in three arenas of current Faith and Order discussion. First, there is the writing of ecumenical documents such as *Baptism, Eucharist, and Ministry*[2] (BEM) that, in effect, create new expressions of tradition in ways which seek to be responsible to all the participating communions, not merely to any one communion. Then there is the development of "intercontextual method." This seeks to bring new faith communities, representing emerging human issues, into dialogue on an equal basis with older Christian bodies. Third, there is the development of terminology through which the churches can understand their relationship to the wider whole. The terms "sign," "sacrament," and "instrument" are derived from *Lumen Gentium* but taken up into a wider circle of ecumenical debate. Finally, the threads are pulled together and related to the overarching sense of a people of God coming to being on the stage of history.

1. Placing the Term in Context

The church, according to the Nicene (Constantinopolitan) Creed is "one, holy, catholic, and apostolic." The four terms need to be taken together. Each contributes to the others' meaning. What is catholic is, by definition, also one, holy, and apostolic. But the term catholic by itself highlights the dimensions of wholeness or comprehensiveness in the church. It means, following Ignatius of Antioch, the general or universal church, as opposed to a particular body of Christians. Augustine introduces the metaphor of Rome's sway over all the civilized world. For him the word catholic becomes part of a proper name: the Catholic Church. After the edict of Theodosius in A.D. 380, it becomes the only legally permitted religion of the empire. Vincent of Lérins wrote, "For that is truly and in the strictest sense "catholic' which, as the name itself and the reason of the thing declare, comprehends all universally."[3] A modern writer makes the same point differently: catholicity means that "in Christ people of all times, of all races, of all places, of all cultures and conditions are brought into a living fellowship."[4]

It has always been difficult to translate this theme into practical terms. What is to be the tangible criterion of catholicity? The different confessional groups have each tended to envision the whole church in terms which place themselves at the center, terms which portray the particular communion in question as exemplary of catholicity's *essence*, even if other communions participate in that essence in lesser degree. From each such standpoint the whole *oikoumene* is envisioned in a particular way with corresponding terminology. The terms involved may or may not be inherently generous toward other communions. Thus the Roman Catholic claim has historically stressed jurisdiction: to be catholic is to be in communion with the Roman pontiff. Other doctrinal, liturgical, and practical requirements naturally follow. The Lutheran claim has stressed pure doctrine: to be part of the church's wholeness is to rest one's faith on the central truth of justification by grace alone. The Reformed claim has been similar, with a stress on an ordered church life based on Scripture interpreted as the Word of God by the power of the Spirit. Eastern Orthodoxy has focused on the continuity of tradition and on the integrity of the people in their historic culture gathered around their bishops. And so on.

Not one of these too-compressed descriptions, of course,

will satisfy those being described. The point is merely that the wholeness or universality of Christian faith has always been defined from the point of view of those doing the defining. This is true even of some of the new expressions of the faith in liberation groups and base communities. They too have projected visions of the *oikoumene*, the whole household of faith. These visions are of course different from the traditional ones in that they focus on supposed solidarity among the poor, the universality of the liberation struggle, and in some cases the general applicability of the economic or political theory on which the struggle is based. The conundrum is that there has in the past been no way to talk about the universality of Christian faith without using terms that come from some particular source, thus implicitly denying the universality these terms are intended to convey. What we now know of the relation between doctrines and the communities that hold them does nothing to mitigate this ironic situation.

Finding a more adequate, relatively unparochial, formulation for the notion of catholicity is not an optional task. It is demanded by the basic nature of the faith. The frame of reference for Christian faith has always (despite momentary eclipses of understanding) been the whole of humankind. Humanity here is not merely the potential audience for the message. The conviction that humanity is essentially one is a *presupposition* of the message and of the community which gathers around it. Humanity as such, not merely those on the membership roll, has been reconciled in Christ. Included in this reconciliation is not merely humanity in the theological sense, as defined in the biblical epic of salvation, but also humanity as a reality with independent secular meanings, as in the Enlightenment notion of "the rights of man" or the more contemporary formulations of "human nature" in the various human sciences. The meaning of catholicity for today needs to be worked out in the interplay between these theological and worldly meanings of the human. The churches must manifest a sense of this larger scope of reconciliation, both in their self-understanding and in their forms of life. For this reason I will argue in these pages that the meaning of

catholicity must now be extricated from all purely institutional and inner-churchly translations and working criteria. It
needs now to be defined in terms of whole human context in
which the gospel is preached.

But this is not easy today. The preceding chapters have
indicated the complexity of our situation. We now know that
tradition is the accumulated product of many historical and
political circumstances, that it often represents the viewpoint
of the victors in ecclesiastical controversy, and that it is deeply
ambiguous in its cumulative meaning. Moreover we live in an
age of pluralism. There exist myriad regional, cultural, issue-
oriented, and personal hermeneutics of the gospel message.
Countless communities of interpretation have appeared,
focused on such issues as inclusiveness in the community of
women and men, or of justice for the marginalized and poor.
These gatherings represent "regional hermeneutics" of gos-
pel-and-situation, often articulated with impressive integrity
and care. A revisioning of the church as universal communion
will only be accomplished by taking the testimonies of these
issue-focused communities into account.

No single conceptuality capable of mastering all this vitality and variety has as yet gained widespread assent. Perhaps
that is fortunate. The success of any particular concept of
global Christian identity, including the one proposed in this
book, would inevitably represent the triumph of some one
way of thinking over others. I argue that truth lies in the
conversation among different ways of signifying the transcending reality of a people of God. That fact confers extraordinary importance on the dialogues that have been going on
in the ecumenical movement. These conversations, while they
have not been focused on the term catholicity as such, have in
effect greatly broadened the working contexts of catholicity
and have begun to give that reality a new definition. A focus
on the recent work of the Commission on Faith and Order of
the World Council of Churches will illustrate what I mean
and give content to this broadening notion of catholicity.
Seemingly little known to many academic theologians, Faith
and Order has carried on a series of world-level dialogues

resulting in numerous publications from the 1920s to the present. The current program lifts up three issues: the reception process of the 1982 document *Baptism, Eucharist, and Ministry*, a study on the apostolic faith (notably the Nicaeo-Constantinopolitan Creed of A.D. 381) and its expression in the contemporary world, and a study now titled "The Unity of the Church and the Renewal of Human Community."[5] An inquiry into the doctrine of the church as such has been approved for the years immediately ahead.

The story of these studies is too long to tell in detail. My effort here is to see them in the light of the question of catholicity as just defined, and hence as standing at the center of the effort to understand what Christian faith is as global community in the contemporary world. It is my contention that this enterprise, long thought to be the special preserve of traditional dogmaticians interested only in effecting the institutional merger of essentially pre-modern church structures, in fact is dealing with issues directly in the center of the contemporary theological situation. It is important for ecumenism's detractors on both the right and the left to understand this, but perhaps even more important for this perspective to be grasped by those who participate in Faith and Order itself. These conversations are ultimately about the quality and meaning of human community on earth. They are a contribution to the effort to see the churches as signs of a people through which God, in the power of the Spirit, is gathering the human race to its destiny. The dialogues of Faith and Order can be described not only as moments in the history of Christian doctrine but also as language events that belong to a particular stage in the history of the human drama. Their importance, to use Hegel's phrase, could be "world historical."

2. *The Emergence of Ecumenical Tradition*

I once described the work of Faith and Order as "building fragile bridges of words between worlds."[6] I still think that is apt. The words which are drafted into ecumenical documents constitute bridge formulas which have a very distinct function of their own. They enable followers of different Christian traditions to articulate the Tradition (upper case "T") they hold in common. There is an apparent irony here. Tradition is by definition something very old which the churches in principle respect and revere. But it is all but impossible to recover it as such. Remembering what has been said about "the travail of tradition"—its connection with dominating and alienating "houses of authority" (Edward Farley) and its ambiguity except as interpreted by such authorities (David Tracy)—there are few classical formulas which can simply be quoted for this purpose. The "ecumenical" creeds of the early centuries probably can be, but even they have been altered from time to time to suit the viewpoint of particular regions and communities. Beyond that the notion of *the* Tradition is more idealization than it is a set of formulas to which the churches can actually agree. Hence when *the* Tradition is articulated in ecumenical formulas it is, paradoxically, usually in new language written for the occasion.

The first question to the churches which accompanied the publication of *Baptism, Eucharist, and Ministry* said it clearly: "the [Faith and Order] Commission would be pleased to know . . . the extent to which your church can recognize in this text the faith of the Church through the ages."[7] Even if the full meanings of ancient formulas cannot be reconstituted to the satisfaction of all, the basic *patterns* of the past can be articulated in new ways. A new expression of the tradition can be such that the apostolic witness is recognizable *in* it. This, in fact, is the way tradition has always been transmitted into new situations. Now, for the first time, it is being done by the churches acting together.

How is this possible? In essence, the Faith and Order process is enabling representatives of the major Christian bodies to develop new expressions of tradition which reflect the demands and opportunities of the ecumenical context itself. Ecumenism is a context of faith in its own right, and it requires the same creative use of the classical "syntax" to say new things as doctrinal construction does in any new setting.

It is not simply a matter of stitching together into a new quilt pieces of what the different communions have been saying all along. Nor is this work only a matter of artful political compromise among competing perspectives, although elements of that are present too. Faith and Order seeks to extend a common understanding of the faith into areas not before explored, *and this requires fresh language which constitutes new tradition in continuity with the old.*

Where success of this sort has been achieved, one must credit a carefully cultivated atmosphere of good faith and confidence in the enterprise, as well as an enormous amount of hard work over decades. Simply for representatives of the different confessions and communions to get to know and trust one another has made a difference. The growth of an ecumenical language tradition into which new participants are periodically initiated has been indispensable. But none of this accounts for the underlying fact that divergent doctrinal expressions of the faith thought for centuries to be at odds are no longer seen as church dividing. It is no longer believed that if doctrinal formulas use different language and even seem to say different things that only one can be "true" and all the others must be "false." One can formulate new tradition which embraces the values of both.

I have looked at this question already in my discussion of George Lindbeck's *The Nature of Doctrine.* It became apparent there that a cultural-linguistic theory allows us to see doctrinal formulas as expressed in culturally available metaphors and addressed to contextual needs. If the ecumenical situation is indeed a new context in its own right, with its own metaphors and needs, it will not only permit but require a new stage of doctrinal formulation. This would become true in still a more formal way if the churches were to gather in an ecumenical council, a possibility I discuss at the end of this chapter. But the movement from the old view of conflicting doctrines as inevitably church-dividing to this new ecumenical consciousness is a phenomenon in the history of doctrine itself. It is more than a matter of seeing things through the eyes of philosophers such as Wittgenstein and human scientists such as Geertz, or even of theologians such as Lindbeck himself.

I doubt in fact that the advent of human science perspectives on religion has had much to do with the ecumenical phenomenon. At most, it has helped us see what is happening. Few dialoguers in Faith and Order (very few indeed outside the Protestant camp) have read Wittgenstein, Geertz, or Lindbeck. Human science perspectives, of course, may be something "in the air." Theologians are hardly immune to general intellectual and cultural trends. But Lindbeck is really saying that his perspective illuminates something he finds going on in ecumenical discussions, whether or not the discussants consciously hold the cultural-linguistic position or have even heard of it. Speaking of the relevance of his view to recent "bilateral" agreements, he writes,

> It could be shown that this account approximates a pattern of reasoning often found in ecumenical agreements, not least on the Lord's Supper. Doctrines may be talked about in these agreements as if they were propositions or, in some cases, nondiscursive symbols, but they are treated as if they were rules or regulative principles.[8]

Lindbeck does not in fact try to show what he says "could be shown," but he refers to a whole series of dialogues on the Eucharist, especially those involving Lutherans and Roman Catholics,[9] in many of which he has participated personally. Presumably the same applies to the work of Faith and Order. It would be fascinating actually to analyze some of this work and to see what it means to say that doctrines are treated "as if they were rules or regulative principles." What is the evidence? Are we speaking of something specific that can be pointed to in the text, or are we merely saying that the text is consistent with a cultural-linguistic explanation whether that was the intent of the dialoguers or not?

I believe that for Lindbeck the cultural-linguistic approach merely puts contemporary words to something that has been true of Christian doctrine all along. Without denying that doctrines make substantive assertions, we can say that they in fact have *functioned* like principles of grammar and syntax. We may legitimately read the creeds not for the particular terminology they use to convey their content but for the essential encoding or ordering visible in that terminology. Lindbeck, drawing on Lonergan's studies of the development of the trinitarian and christological dogmas, argues that Athanasius himself saw the Creed of Nicaea, "not as a first-order proposition with ontological reference, but as a second-order rule of speech. For him, to accept the doctrine meant to agree to speak in a certain way."[10] Moreover, the creeds were not so much a matter of adapting (watering down, accommodating) Christian truth to the terminology of late Hellenistic philosophy as they were the incorporation of that cultural material *into* an ever more clearly held framework of the governing logic or grammar of the faith itself.

The creeds do not state that grammar literally as a set of rules, but they do instantiate the pattern. They show it in use. They leave it to each new generation to decide what new content and language, provided it follows the pattern, is needed for its situation. To know the Christian tradition well, then, is to know it as a native speaker knows his or her language. The essential thing is that I can go on, writing sentence after new sentence, each of which exhibits the principles of my tongue's grammar but says the new things that need to be said.

The ecumenical situation clearly demands that new things be said. Sometimes, as Lindbeck points out, one only finds out what the rules are in the attempt to say these new things. Only as an ecumenical consensus begins to develop does it become possible to see how the ancient doctrinal rules apply, and only then does it become possible to pose "precisely the right question . . . in precisely the right way" so that it becomes "revelatory of the underlying structure."[11] There is evidence, I believe, that certain rules of grammar have been gotten right in the ecumenical debate, and these represent permanent gains. I think of BEM's treatment of infant and believers' baptism as representing two perspectives or emphases in a single process of "Christian initiation" rather than as opposed and incompatible doctrinal views. Or one might cite the acknowledgment, again in BEM, that "apostolic succession" can subsist in different polities, and that churches may choose to emphasize different outward signs of the same inward reality.

The final arbiter of validity in the ecumenical tradition-making process is the same today as it has always been: "reception" by the people. It is they, presumably, who are the "native speakers" of the tradition's characteristic language. They represent the *sensus fidelium*. They decide if there is con-sensus, whether, in the end, an innovation in the expression of tradition conforms to historic "grammatical" usage. (Here, by the way, the Orthodox populist tradition makes the point far more clearly than does the Protestant standard of *sola scriptura* or the Roman Catholic stress on magisterium. But, as Lindbeck says, this is a principle which works best where the church is undivided.) But who are the people we have in mind? It is clear that church members today are hardly the well-informed, pious, and united population that term *sensus fidelium* romantically implies. Where does membership begin and end? Think of the crowd in St. Peter's Square. Lindbeck acknowledges, "most Christians through most of Christian history have spoken their own official tongue very poorly."[12] What is more, as the next section of this chapter will stress, there are many relatively new interpretations of the faith which have begun to be represented in the Faith and Order process only recently. It is not clear that these faith communities are as yet fully involved in the creation of new tradition as this has been described in these pages. Many are critical of the process itself, finding it Western, complacent, insensitive, and potentially oppressive in new ways.

Yet if the true people of God for purposes of reception cannot be identified with any known community, the Faith and Order process nonetheless *presupposes* such a reality. Or perhaps it would be more exact to say that the Faith and Order process *postulates* the reality in question as a transcen-

dental or regulative principle in the Kantian sense. The work
of Faith and Order requires for its possibility the governing
sense of a reality which does not yet exist in the world of
phenomena, but which is required to complete or underwrite
the logic of the process itself. This reality can be described in
a variety of ways. It is the comprehensive communion implied
when we speak of the church universal. No such reality exists
in our actual experience. But ecumenical dialogue speaks of it
constantly. It is that to which we refer when we speak of the
faith's catholicity. It is the communion of saints, the invisible
company of all those who by the Holy Spirit are instruments
of God's purposes for humankind. It is the human race itself
to the extent that it has come within the energy field of God's
reign, the people as the place of God's own "dwelling" among
human beings.

The practical difficulties of verifying reception in such
terms are no doubt insuperable. But I am not thinking of
opinion sampling. What I am saying, rather, is that to "receive" the products of ecumenical work, the churches need to
have accepted the regulative idea behind that work. They
need to embody the *sense* of a larger people of God in their
ecclesiological reasoning. They will be appropriate evaluators
of ecumenical documents if they already understand themselves to be signs and sacraments of a people representing
God's transformative presence in the world.

To put the matter yet another way, for what community
of faith are the doctrinal products of ecumenical discussion
intended to be regulative? If doctrines are rules, they must be
rules for someone. Yet the ecumenical communion for which
all this theological work is being done does not yet visibly
exist. It is not simply the company of those active in the World
Council of Churches or otherwise friendly to ecumenical
causes. It is not simply all the baptized. All this work is being
done to be received as regulative for the churches themselves,
but not just for purposes of business as usual. Ecumenical
documents are intended as regulative for the churches in
order that they can be signs, sacraments, and instruments of
the people of God whose transcending sense these documents
should ultimately be intended to express.

3. Converging Horizons: An Intercontextual Method

I have interpreted in the preceding pages what could be called the "classical" method of Faith and Order. That method is devoted for the most part to finding formulas in which the traditional confessions and communions can find common ground. But of late a new kind of challenge has appeared. How does the ecumenical dialogue take account of the testimonies of Christian communities focused on locally defined issues—justice, peace, freedom, and the like—as experienced by particular ethnic, national, and gender-related advocacy groups? Liberation theologies, Christian feminism, the voices of gays and lesbians, culturally specific hermeneutics of every kind: each of these represents a claim that the Spirit is at work not only among those who represent these interests inside church bodies but also in the broader movements of human spirit to which these advocates are related.

Clearly we are speaking of some of the most significant social phenomena of our time, movements which have attracted millions of adherents and produced substantial art, music, and literature as well as traditions and strategies of political advocacy. There is no room in this book to describe each movement with its particular forms of expression. That is regrettable, for suffering human beings cannot be summed up in generalizations. Only by sharing experience in solidarity with any particular group does one begin to understand its perspective on the world. Fortunately for the churches, there are many faithful communicants, as well as leaders, who are ready to bear personal testimony to what these movements mean for them. The records of this testimony are readily available in numerous publications,[13] and one can experience it personally in many a congregation or scene of Christian involvement in political action. Here human spirit and Holy Spirit meet in complex and fascinating ways.

These perspectives point to dimensions of catholicity that dare not be ignored. They do so in at least two ways. Each represents not merely liberation for a particular category of people, but also a perspective on the liberation of all people.

Together they stand for catholicity in a new sense of the term. The "all" in Vincent's aphorism must now refer to faith as understood within *all* the experiences of human life, not merely those which have previously come within the ken of theologians. Above all, I think of the great variety of experiences of oppression, exclusion, repression, poverty, hopelessness, as well as views of life from the standpoint of cultures that have not made much impact on the Western academic tradition in which theologians are typically trained. Without taking account of all this, much that is indispensable for grasping the human condition as a whole is simply left out.

How is all this being brought into the ecumenical traditioning process, and with what effect? Faith and Order began a half generation ago to avail itself of an intercontextual method that looks at and seeks in solidarity to share the testimonies that come from communities such as these around the world, bringing them so far as possible into conversation with the developing ecumenical tradition. Intercontextual method does not mean that contextual theology is the only theology, or that "situation" becomes theology's primary source. Rather, two moves are involved. Testimonies to specific local or issue-oriented efforts to overcome human brokenness in the light of the gospel are brought into the effort to recover and extend the common Christian tradition. And, in return, insights gained in that tradition-making process are brought to bear upon the efforts of these communities to address their particular concerns. The clear implication is that the churches of the Western world, with their university-related theological faculties and deep relationships to dominating cultures, come to represent one context among others. While the long Faith and Order tradition has been related to that Western context, intercontextual method in effect now decenters the conversation. Now insight can come from any source. All are on an equal basis.

Intercontextual method, under that name, came relatively late to Faith and Order, after many years of assuming that peace and justice issues belonged somewhere else in the institutional structure. For ecumenical organizations such as the

World Council of Churches (WCC) there are still territorial issues involved. Are not the theologians trespassing into the area of Church and Society, and probably missing the point much of the time as they do? What, some ask, can Faith and Order do with issues like racism and sexism beyond blunting their cutting edge by assimilating them into esoteric ecclesiastical dialogue, burying them under mountains of prelatical prose? Yet when one looks at the history of Faith and Order, one finds ample precedent for such concerns. From the Fourth World Conference on Faith and Order (Montreal, 1963) to the meeting of the Commission on Faith and Order at Louvain, 1971, and beyond, the issue of the relation between the unity of the church and the unity of humankind has been on the Faith and Order agenda as well as that of other WCC bodies.[14] The Sixth Assembly of the WCC (Vancouver, 1983) authorized a Faith and Order study of "The Unity of the Church and the Renewal of Human Community." The resulting work sought to bring testimonies from several arenas of liberation struggle into the unity-fostering dialogue process. Since 1985 this effort has included a series of regional consultations intended precisely to hear the testimony of Christians working at the forefront of struggles to renew the human community in justice and inclusivity. Justice issues have been studied at Singapore (1986), Porto Alegre, Brazil (1987), and Harlem, U.S.A. (1988). Questions concerning the community of women and men have brought groups together in Prague (1985) and Porto Novo, Benin (1988).

All this has begun to bear fruit in what might thus far be described more as an editorial than a theological process. But something more than cutting and pasting will soon be needed.[15] The 1990 "Unity of the Church and the Renewal of Human Community" document incorporates edited and enlarged versions of previous documents, notably the 1985 essay on "The Church as Mystery and as Prophetic Sign." Quotations and references from the issue-oriented studies are sprinkled illustratively through the older material. Chapters with the titles "Unity and Renewal and The Search for Justice" and "Unity and Renewal and the Community of Women and

Men" have been added. The repeated "ands" say much about the technique in use, it is a form of incorporation by accumulation. This is not to say that the resulting document lacks either coherence or integrity. Far from it. But the result is repetitive prose through which few readers without professional motivation will persevere. And it is not yet clear that a new understanding of the very form and nature of the church's thinking has gained ecumenical acceptance, as eventually it must if we are to realize a sense of the global human conversation at work in the church, and of the church at work in the human conversation.

Still, something new is already happening. In the past, tradition has not often sought to embrace local and issue-focused forms of witness. It has tended instead to dissolve them conceptually into ontological generalizations. It is helpful to see the new development from the point of view of the German philosopher Hans-Georg Gadamer whose celebrated book *Truth and Method*[16] wrestles with the question of how human beings of different historical periods or cultural contexts can understand one another. Gadamer's watchword is "fusion of horizons." A "horizon" describes the limit of what can be seen by a particular observer located at a particular point in space. If two observers are to have anything in common, their horizons must "fuse', or at least overlap. But, says Gadamer, this will not happen unless the two perspectives share some common stock of tradition. So it is in ecumenical discussion. Faith and Order tests its fresh articulations of tradition in which historic traditions live on for their capacity to sponsor at least a "convergence," if not "fusion," of horizons, this time not only between past and present and between the different historic communions, but also with all the new expressions of faith in movements of human inclusion and liberation. The new horizons of faith have their impact upon the growing ecumenical tradition: pressing it, extending it, enriching it.

All ecumenical creation of new tradition, we now realize, is driven by the need to test whether a common fund of language can be conceived within which differing experiences can meet. And we need to know whether the encounter itself can generate still more language whose connection with the classical stream of tradition is evident to all its "native speakers." To revert to Lindbeck's language, if doctrines are less like propositional truths and more like grammatical rules for faith and practice which "native speakers" instinctively know, then the rules found essential to the integrity of the church in particular times and places may come to have the force of doctrine for the time and place concerned. Lindbeck speaks of doctrines that are "conditionally necessary." Could they be understood as of the *esse* of the church and its tradition for this or that particular situation? Could they be seen as binding, announcing a *status confessionis*[17] for here and now, in the full recognition that in another situation the same insight might be expressed in quite a different way and perhaps not have the same salience and importance? Or perhaps that the insight is fundamental enough eventually to become part of the catholic faith itself? Such possibilities, it would seem, are clear implications of intercontextual method. Out of hearing the witness of many communities of faith, the larger faith community then begins to find those affirmations which it can affirm to be of the *esse* of the faith in its full catholicity for our time. Have any new insights reached such a degree of acceptance by the whole church that they are now rules for all new articulations of Christian faith: principles to be upheld "everywhere . . . and by all" if not "at all times?" If so, we are enriching the definition of catholicity. Several principles certainly have gained this status in modern times. My list would include the rejection of slavery in all its forms, the duty to resist tyranny, the "preferential option for the poor," the rejection of all kinds of racism and sexism, the conviction that we must care for the earth. Perhaps these are still controversial for some. Attempts to add other rules to the list certainly are. What about the prohibition of abortion, or the refusal to participate in war?[18]

In the use of intercontextual method such issues surface as they never could in Faith and Order's traditional agenda. These issues have come together in the WCC's current emphasis on "Justice, Peace, and the Integrity of Creation." The ecumenical movement is far from finished with these themes. But meanwhile there is growing acceptance of another formula for catholicity: the understanding of the church as sacrament, sign, or instrument of human beings' union with God and with one another.

4. Sign, Sacrament, and Instrument: Testing a Terminology

In the combined processes of tradition building and testimony interpreting just described, at least one new conceptual (and potentially doctrinal) resource has not only emerged but also achieved some degree of reception, at least in circles familiar with ecumenical dialogue. I refer to language, first found in *Lumen Gentium*, which depicts the church "by its relation to Christ" as "sign," "sacrament," or "instrument" of God's reconciling and uniting work in the world. This terminology could serve to link the growing ecumenical tradition concerning the nature of the church with testimonies from the "periphery."[19] It could open as yet unexplored vistas on the notions of signification, sacramentality, and, as this book insists, communal sense making as the churches begin to play more effective roles in the human conversation as such.[20]

The importance of this terminology looms large in the doctrinal sense when one realizes that the tradition, even after all these centuries, has not yet worked out an understanding of the church which links it clearly to the economic Trinity, and particularly to the presence of God in the world through the configuring work of the Holy Spirit to form a people. As I have shown in chapter 4, there has been a tendency to think about the church politically, using models from the civil order, and to equate ecclesiology with polity or canon law. Now, however, the use of the term sign opens the way for seeing the faith community as itself an expressive or signifying medium. This move brings the community very close, given continuing prophetic criticism, to being another form of the Word. Likewise the church draws close to being a sacrament; a place where the human *polis* is transsignified, as Pannenberg says,[21] so that it says something different, makes another kind of sense.

Let Protestants who fear that the extension of the term sacrament to the ecclesial body makes the institution immune to criticism, overbearing, or absolutistic, remember that the Word in its transit through the human world is subject to the same misunderstandings and distortions. To the extent that Scripture is the churches' book and the communication of the Word depends on the churches' interpretation of it, it is difficult to see any real advantage in *sola scriptura*. The one principle is as ideal and literally unworkable a criterion as the other. It is interesting to see a certain hesitation on the Roman Catholic side too about the term sacrament in reference to the church. Whether this reluctance reflects concern about possible confusion with other uses of the term or of fear of creeping triumphalism, it no doubt lies behind the charmingly inexact expression in *Lumen Gentium*, "kind of." How is the church "a kind of sacrament"? If one remembers that in the present treatment (as in Eastern Orthodoxy) not the hierarchy but the people are the sacramental reality, the picture becomes quite different. The language of sacrament, sign, and instrument becomes not a danger to the churches but a challenge to them to think how they may fulfill what the language implies.

The passage in *Lumen Gentium* deserves quotation for purposes of reference once again.

> By her relationship with Christ, the Church is a kind of sacrament or sign of intimate union with God and of the unity of all humankind. She is also an instrument for the achievement of such union and unity.[22]

The record of ecumenical reception of this formula—in these exact words or near facsimile—is impressive, but also at times ambiguous. Much depends on the various contexts in which the terminology is used. Quite different ecumenical approaches have been able to make use of it. The ecumenical debate in a real sense converges on these words as hinge concepts in understanding the relationship between church and world. This is a form of reception, but one limited mainly to ecumenical documents and technical theological work. It is not yet reception in the larger sense of established usage in the grammar and syntax of the people. As long ago as the Second Assembly of the WCC (Evanston, 1954) one reads of the church as "bearer of hope, the sign and witness of God's mighty acts, the means of His working," and as the "sign of that which he is doing and will yet do." But in 1968 at Uppsala, a sentence appears destined to be quoted often afterward: "The church is bold in speaking of itself as the sign of the coming unity of mankind."[23] This gave rise to a Faith and Order study begun in 1969 in which the Uppsala sentence was to be evaluated. The immediate outcome of this decision appears in the report of the Faith and Order Commission in Louvain, 1971. The church,

> is a sign by which God's all-embracing love is visible in this world. It is not only a symbolic image. It is a sign, because the living Christ wishes to be, and is, present in its midst. It is a sign. But it is also no more than a sign. The mystery of the love of God is not exhausted through this sign, but, at best, just hinted from afar. So just as the Church can be understood in this way as a sacrament or a sign, its oneness can also be understood as a sign.[24]

A WCC document of 1972-73 elaborates.

> Signs point to a reality, an event, a meaning with which they are not identical but whose presence they make real and effective. Being intimately linked with the reality they represent, they remain signs only as long as this presence is effective and recognized as such.[25]

These materials, Günther Gassmann says,

> represent the most thorough theological examination to date of the concept of the church as sacrament, sign, and instrument in ecumenical debate. It is truly remarkable that, in the

course of a difficult and controversial study, which produced
no conclusive results, a new ecclesiological perspective should
have been investigated so intensively and continually new
descriptions of it reached. In it the study made a significant
contribution to the ecumenical debate. Whenever the concept
of the Church as sacrament sign and instrument appears in
various ecumenical texts after Accra, 1974, it can basically be
traced back to that study.[26]

Despite a demurral by Ernst Käsemann, the Salamanca
report[27] sees the terms sacrament, sign, and instrument as
possible means of arriving at a description of the unity of the
church. The terms sacrament and sign refer in the first instance to the mystery of God's revelation in Jesus Christ. They
have in the course of history also been used for the community
of those who believe in him.

> Because this community is an integral part of the mystery of
> God's action in bringing about his kingdom, it is, in a deriva-
> tive sense, "sacrament" and "sign" in history, reflecting God's
> purpose and promise to all people. As the Church communi-
> cates the gospel, it is a "sign" in the sense of instrument. It
> contributes to the salvation and communion of people with
> God in Jesus Christ.[28]

The gradually broadening acceptance of this terminology
does not necessarily go hand in hand with agreement about its
use. Several perspectives and contexts can be identified. Some
writers are matter of fact. If division and conflict in the church
are signs and reflections of divisions in the world, so unity
achieved would signify God's purpose to unite humanity in
Christ. Other drafters stress unity as a spiritual gift, obscured
by divisions, but still with power as a sign of hope to the
world. Still others are mission-oriented. The church is a sign
of the kingdom of God in the sense that it is called to be an
instrument of the kingdom by continuing Christ's mission, by
living in a way that is credible. And finally there are those
who warn us not to measure the church by its worldly goals.
The unity of the church is a gift of the Spirit. It has doxological

and sacramental integrity which cannot be measured in terms of secular efficacity.

A fundamental question, then, is whether the sacramental and the socio-ethical dimensions implied in the sign concept can be held together. Can one speak of the consequences of the church's signifying presence in the world and at the same time do justice to the church's inherent being as sacramental reality in its own right? I submit that sign theory more deeply pursued and appropriated into theological formulations can make it possible consistently to say both these things at once (see my argument in chapter 3). The churches themselves are sacramental realities in that they transsignify elements of sense in the world in which they have discerned works of the Spirit, making that work visible in their forms of life. They thereby body forth the mystery of God's salvation. And this transsignifying is certainly also ethical in character. It is often accomplished by taking stands on issues of importance to human well-being.

The capacity of sign terminology to assist in bringing about the convergence of otherwise divergent points of view can also be seen in other areas of concern. A salient example is to be found in the 1991 report of the International Reformed-Roman Catholic Dialogue Commission.[29] Here the issue concerns the theological underpinning of ecclesiology. On the Reformed side, the report develops the traditional protestant understanding of the church as *creatura verbi*, the creation of the Word of God. But then it goes on to say:

> The community of faith is thus not merely the community in which the gospel is preached; by its hearing and responding to the Word of grace, the community itself becomes a medium of confession, its faith a "sign" or "token" to the world; it is itself a part of the world addressed and renewed by the Word of God.[30]

On the Roman Catholic side there is then an articulation of the church as "sacrament of grace." This cites copious patristic and conciliar references for usage of the term sacrament to describe the church as such, but warns that "the Church is a sacrament by derivation, by the fact that it is a sign and instrument of Christ." Christ is the true sacrament of grace. The church may be called so only by analogy. The church is an "instrument in Christ's hands." The document continues:

> The Church, then, is only a sacrament founded by Christ and entirely dependent on him. Its being and its sacramental acts are the fruit of a free gift received from Christ, a gift in relation to which he remains radically transcendent, but which, however, he commits to the salvation of humankind.[31]

The notions of the church as creation of the Word and as sacrament of grace draw closer together in the realization that each of these formulations in its own way points to the church's expressive, signifying character. As the document puts it, these conceptions "can in fact be seen as expressing the same instrumental reality under different aspects, as complementary to each other or as two sides of the same coin."[32] The Faith and Order study of "The Church as Mystery and as Prophetic Sign" culminated in 1990 in a document titled *Church and World: The Unity of the Church and the Renewal of Human Community*.[33] The term sacrament applied to the church as such has now virtually disappeared and has been replaced with the term "mystery" (translating the Latin *sacramentum* in the sense of the once hidden but now revealed *mysterion* of God's purpose for the world). The adjective "prophetic" is now appended to the word sign. Instrument as a technical term no longer figures prominently. What is going on now? The first impression is that the clarity and force of the words of *Lumen Gentium* are now being buried under plethora of different formulations each designed to please one interest or another. It is all but impossible to summarize the message of this document simply. While particular passages are clear, their overall sense is elusive.

The study turns on the relationships between (1) the rule of God in creation and history, (2) the church as visible and invisible expression of the mystery of God's redemptive purpose, and (3) the church as prophetic sign or instrument. No longer are the three terms sign, sacrament, and instrument simply ranged side by side. Rather the paragraphs point to the dynamic interaction of the realities to which these terms refer within the overarching category of God's saving purpose for all humankind. The exposition of these interacting realities goes forward as the conversation among historic traditions and the listening to new forms of witness also continue.

The notion of the kingdom, or realm of God's rule, plays a central role. Both the prophetic literature and the gospels are invoked in a rich exposition which makes no attempt to address the critical difficulties attending such use of the biblical text. The kingdom is expounded largely as an ethical vision for this world, in which eschatology is conceived in largely this-worldly terms without forgetting that justice and peace are gifts of the grace of God, and that one must pray for the Lord to come. The implied doctrine of salvation tends toward a christological universalism. The prophetic themes of wrath and retribution lead to the establishment of "what is right and just."[34] A new, inclusive covenant will be established, a restored human community will bring peace, justice, and harmony among persons and nations. In Jesus this kingdom is already "in our midst." "The reality of the kingdom is embodied in the person and work of Christ, crucified and risen."[35]

We are called to conversion, faith, and renewal. There are clear consequences:

> Discipleship in the kingdom of God consists in patient and persistent efforts to match human circumstances with God's promises, and God's promises with human circumstances . . . renewal begins with the members of the church; it is never for themselves alone. The renewal of the church is always for the sake of the human community for which the church is a sign and foretaste of the kingdom of God which comes to us both as judgment and as promise.[36]

A central issue raised in this document concerns the relationship between mystery and sign. Of what, we ask, is the church a sign? Is it a sign of the mystery? If so, how is the mystery of God's saving presence signified? The terms are interrelated and complementary. "The church as sign is an invitation to the world to let itself be permeated by the divine mystery."[37] And further, "In the New Testament the word "mystery' designates God's primal intention to accomplish the salvation of all humanity through Jesus Christ."[38] And further,

> when the word "mystery" is applied to the church, it refers to the church as a reality which transcends its empirical, histori-cal expression—a reality which is rooted and sustained and shaped by the communion of the Father, Son, and Holy Spirit."[39]

We are told that the "saving communion with Christ which the church already enjoys" is one "upon whose final scope no limits are set; it will be a question of the eventual inclusion of the whole world."[40] And again we read:

> The word "sign" can make clear that the church is there for others . . . . The concept of "sign" indicates especially the essential relation between church and world . . . . If the adjective "prophetic" is attached . . . it is in order to recall the dimensions of judgment and salvation, and the eschatological perspective which inheres in the notion of "mystery."[41]

This language is at least compatible with the vision in these pages of a people of God shaped by the power of the Spirit. The term people of God gives us a name for the mys-tery insofar as it is present in history as the social reality of God's humanity. It is the ecclesiastical and transecclesiastical communion of those in whose lives and associations the Spirit is at work, bringing the kingdom to expression on the stage of history. The churches are signs of this reality. And if the churches are signs, then everything about them—unity, holi-ness, catholicity, apostolicity—contribute to their sign charac-ter. The new move is to see the qualities of the church as not merely ontological (having to do with its being or *esse*) but also as expressive. Subtly, and surely without conscious intention, this theological innovation participates in what has become known in philosophy as the "linguistic turn." The church becomes an expressive medium, a signifying element in the language nexus which is the essence of our shared and evolving humanity. What, finally, do the churches say? The idea expressed most frequently, in the words of Günther Gassmann, is that the churches, in dialogue together, are "the sign of the coming union of all human beings in God's kingdom, the redemption of creation and the fulfillment of all things."[42]

Differences of viewpoint remain on many points. Is this union, redemption, and fulfillment to be expected within history or beyond? In what way is the church's signifying power related to the presence and work of Jesus Christ? What is the relationship between the sacramental nature of the church itself and the sacraments celebrated within the church? But certainly sign language has already provided many with new ways of articulating the purpose of the church's presence in history. It has given many traditional formulas new content. It has also brought different ecclesiological understandings such as the notion that the church is "creation of the Word" and the understanding that it is "sacrament of grace" closer together.

Where will this discussion go next? This Faith and Order study document now goes to the churches for study and comment. It will flow into the new study, just beginning at this writing, of the doctrine of the church. I believe that this work points to the need, and the possibility, of a truly universal "council of the people."

5. Drawing the Threads Together: An Ecumenical Council?

What result has this discussion now reached? I have been trying to reframe the notion of catholicity in a new dimension of meaning. Classical understandings of catholicity addressed the questions of their time, but today they are too narrow. Ignatius of Antioch simply meant the whole church as opposed to local churches. Vincent of Lérins saw catholicity in terms of a doctrinal consensus "everywhere, always, and by all."[43] Augustine gave *ecclesia catholica* a meaning corresponding to the worldwide sway of Rome. Churches over the years have employed the term to depict their own possession of whatever they regarded as the *essence* of ecclesial reality: that which is found everywhere that Christian faith is lived in a fullness of communal existence. Catholicity is an important concept today because—along with the notions of unity, holiness, and apostolicity—it expresses the encompassing frame of reference in which churches relate to one another and to the world. It refers to the shared but diversely defined sense of universal Christian identity which makes the ecumenical movement possible.

I argue that today we can discern in ecumenical discussion an understanding of catholicity more encompassing than anything found in the classical models, an understanding which corresponds to what I have called the sense of a people of God. Catholicity now begins to mean the totality of God's presence and people-configuring work in the world, in relation to which the churches do their practical reasoning, configure their lives, and relate to each other in testimony to the world. The most important outcome of the work of the Faith and Order movement (and to some extent the bilateral dialogues) has been a broadening and deepening of the discussion's total frame of reference. Human-science resources, as I have used them to set forth my argument, illumine this ecumenical work and help explain how it is possible.

I have shown, first, that ecumenical dialogue generates new expressions of tradition for a uniquely global situation, while leaving older traditions intact for their own contexts. This catholicizes the context of doctrinal reflection. I have then described the intercontextual method by which new kinds of faith community, in touch with a range of human concerns seldom before given theological consideration, become equal partners in the conversation. This acts out a catholicity of inclusion. Finally, I have shown that the terms sign, sacrament, and instrument have gained currency for describing the churches' relationship to the totality of God's dwelling and acting in the human situation. Which clarifies the way visible churches should understand their participation in a catholicity defined by the universal reign of God.

The word catholicity now needs to refer to all these dimensions of inclusiveness and world involvement in Christian faith. It is not so much an attribute *of* the churches as it is a quality of God's reconciling work in which the churches are called to participate. The ecumenical movement is an instrument conceived by the churches to organize and enhance their participation in this encompassing reality. I argue that God's reconciling work in the world needs to be understood not only as a mystery hidden before all ages but now revealed, nor only as a kingdom present and yet to come, but also as the calling of a people to be the place of God's dwelling and acting in the Spirit.[44]

My argument has lifted up the people metaphor because it does things the mystery and kingdom terminologies do not. The tradition has always needed words to show that God's reconciling activity transcends visible churches, but the terminology chosen has tended to make that transcending activity mysterious and inaccessible. The people metaphor, by contrast, portrays God's active worldly presence in a form neither located out of sight in a "mystical body" nor relegated to an unfathomable future. The sense of a people of God conveys a this-worldly, concrete, present reality which the churches are called to discern and signify. It is a way of speaking concretely about God's community-forming presence in history as the context of the churches' life and action. One can speak, with Joseph Haroutunian, of "the people of God and their institutions."[45]

Hermeneutically conceived forms of human science have played a helping role in this discussion. Just as George Lindbeck believes that the cultural-linguistic method brings out something that has always been true about the functioning of doctrines in the practical reasoning of faith communities, I claim that a perspective which sees social realities as expressive or signifying brings out something that has always been true about the functioning of churches in the context of the larger community of humankind. Churches are lived, even if fragmentary, decipherings of the larger human community that bring out the shapes of God ruling there in the power of the Spirit.

The people metaphor thus enriches the array of other metaphors found in ecumenical documents by affirming that God's rule is present in actual human persons, actual movements of the human spirit, which may or may not be visibly connected with the churches, and yet are integrally related to the message the churches convey. Without this metaphor there is a tendency either to identify the "mystery of salvation" substantially with the visible church (as *Lumen Gentium* says, the "mystical body . . . subsists in" the Roman Catholic Church[46]) or to speak of God's electing grace as creating a "church invisible" (Augustine, Calvin, and much of the Protestant tradition). The latter term leaves the impression that we have no responsibility for what is not our doing and what we cannot see: the elect will find their way into the church in God's good time. My concern, which I believe is of significant ecumenical importance, is to say that we must be *responsible* to a people of God coming into existence all around us in life configurations that may never identify with the churches as they are today. We should be seeking to discern that people-forming energy of the Holy Spirit in movements of human spirit. Such movements cannot be ignored. They not only share this planet and this moment in history with us, but they also are represented *within* the churches. However the churches understand their own particular forms of life and mission, they share this genuinely catholic responsibility equally, and therefore they also have ecumenical responsibility for one another.

How might this responsibility for one another be concretely expressed? From its beginning, the ecumenical movement has looked forward to the convening of a genuinely ecumenical council.[47] I mean this not in the sense that the

word "council" bears in "World Council of Churches" (where
it refers simply to an organization in which many of the
"churches" hold membership), but rather in the sense of
"Council of Nicaea." Not since the year 787 has the entire
church met in an assembly subsequently recognized as having
full conciliar authority: as having made decisions for the entire church on earth. Such a move in modern times still awaits
the overcoming of doctrinal and jurisdictional obstacles, the
growth of a level of mutual trust which does not yet exist, and
eventual readiness on the part of the churches to "receive"
the council's results. No doubt a future "council" in the full
sense of the word will have an organization and composition
different from those of the "seven ecumenical councils" of
ancient times. It will recognize much greater pluralism of
expression in the churches, much greater local autonomy. It
will not issue condemnations or anathemas. It will not define
new doctrines. It will focus on great affirmations concerning
God's purposes in history, human responsibility for justice,
peace, and the renewal of creation, and other concerns not yet
grasped. It will take fully into account the existence of other
faiths and will affirm that Christian faith cannot properly be
articulated unless Christians are in a dialogue of spiritualities
representing the full range of human faith expression.

On the way to such a council we must begin to consider
the nature of this last-mentioned conversation. It already involves the churches in the public world, the world of the
human *polis*. This larger conversation is already present in the
churches, and the churches are already present in the wider
dialogue. What contribution do they, or could they, make?
The final chapter takes up this inevitable question.

VI

Churches in the Human Conversation

Some images must not go away. In the opening pages of *The Life of the Mind*,[1] Hannah Arendt recalls the sight of Adolf Eichmann in a Jerusalem courtroom, charged (as transportation organizer for Hitler's death camps) with complicity in the murder of six million Jews. How can we, the enlightened children of modernity, make sense of such systematized evil? We think at once, Arendt says, of powerful forces: pride, envy, depravity, hatred. These are certainly part of the picture. Yet this man Eichmann seemed oddly unideological, unthreatening, even uninteresting. Thinking of him, Arendt gave the English language a new expression: "the banality of evil." She writes, "The deeds were monstrous, but the doer . . . was quite ordinary, commonplace. . . . There was no sign in him of firm ideological convictions or specific evil motives." What was the problem, then? "Not stupidity," she says, but *thoughtlessness*."[2]

1. A Refreshing of Perception

One of the great powers of Hannah Arendt's writing, George Kateb tells us, is her

> ability to refresh perception. She tries to get us to look again at subjects on which there already exists perhaps too much writing and therefore too much confident understanding. By her further reflection, she tries to save these subjects for our further reflection.[3]

We need from time to time to save certain subjects for the further reflection that always must go on about the kind of society in which we live. This reflection must focus on society's potentiality for evil as well as for hope. We cannot possibly forget, even if we try, what happened in Germany and its conquered territories from roughly 1934 to 1945. The stream of Holocaust literature keeps coming, as any reader of the *New York Times Book Review* or the *Times Literary Supplement* can attest.[4] A figure like Elie Wiesel bears personal and eloquent witness to what it meant and means. The Holocaust is not only a remembered series of events, but also a central symbolic expression of the reality of evil. It is a reality with which we must wrestle in any attempt to talk about our hopes for the human community. This reality must somehow keep breaking through our ordinary, everyday, life perceptions and come to our thinking attention.

Nevertheless, enough is enough: we cannot keep thinking about the Holocaust every minute of the day. We have to live. "If we were responsive to this claim all the time" Arendt remarks, "we would soon be exhausted."[5] And so we defend ourselves rhetorically. Arendt again:

> Cliches, stock phrases, adherence to conventional, standardized modes of expression and conduct have the socially recognized function of protecting us against reality, that is, against the claim on our thinking attention that all events and facts make by reason of their existence.[6]

The irony is that too much talk of the Holocaust can itself become accessory to the self-protective defensive process. Too much exposure to it can actually aid and abet our addiction to defensive conventionality. The very quantity of the literary and documentary output threatens to dull the active imagination. We remember indeed, but we cease to *think*. What should be a symbol to make us aware can end by doing the opposite. The Holocaust can itself become cliché, a conventional reference, part of the furniture of the mind, almost a symbolic vaccination against its own enormity as something still to be faced seriously. We are not so different from Eichmann. It could even be that he has helped to make us what we are.

I will argue that such thoughtlessness, Eichmann's and ours, is above all a failure to see fellow human beings as members of a communal network of covenantal obligation. It is an absence of thoughtful attention to the intrinsic claims of those about us. It is a lack of the minimum level of sensitivity in the human spirit needed for establishing and maintaining an inclusive body politic. Under such conditions some persons are not recognized as members of the community, and hence can be treated as objects or even as commodities. They are not part of the dialogue, not members of the species-defining conversation. In the most comprehensive meaning of the language used in this book, such thoughtlessness is the absence of a sense that all human beings—of whatever religion, nationality, race, sex, or economic class—belong to a global people which in turn belongs to God.

What Eichmann and his colleagues lacked was not basic intelligence. Nor was their failure an incapacity for philosophical reflection. Absent from Eichmann's imagination was the ability to think of other persons as human beings and fellow citizens, to think in even an ordinary, nonphilosophical way about what he was doing to them. For him the common life was symbolically a void: a place for purely technical rationality. His world had in it no symbols of, or for, an inclusive human life together. He does not seem even to have harbored what H. Richard Niebuhr calls an "evil imagination."[7]

Arendt's point is that in this case evil began not with an evil imagination but with an *empty* one. Evil has the opportunity to enter where there is no richly understood and inclusive sense of a shared social world. Mythologies of domination and race may not even be needed until after the fact, if then. All that is needed is inattention to the human beings in front of one's nose.

The world in which the churches today are called to bear their witness contains much senseless pain and suffering, some of it unthinkingly or deliberately inflicted by other human beings who recognize no covenantal obligation to others. It is a world which calls for more than philosophical or religious *explanation*. Such a world calls for practical and political *action* to build reliable structures of inclusive community. Arendt was committed to responsibility in and for the *polis*: the "public square," the arena of practical reasoning for the purpose of ordering human affairs. In Arendt's thought, the world of the *polis* as sphere of human relatedness and obligation has an almost sacred quality. For her, "freedom" and "worldliness" in this political sense are what makes life worth living. She warns us not to let either philosophizing or theologizing become "a substitute world, a world elsewhere."[8] Preoccupation with purely intellectual matters could place us (who cannot imagine behaving as Eichmann did) in complicity with those who let evil into the world in their own unthinking ways, even if the results are not so immediately apparent. An absorption with philosophical reflection, just as much as an inability to reflect at all, can be the enemy of the "ordinary thinking," the alertness to where one's actions lead, needed for maintenance of simple human decency in a life spent together on this planet.

In his play *No Exit*, Sartre has one character say, "Hell is other people." Many of us more than half believe it. If there is a lesson to be learned from the Holocaust, it may be that the existence of a truly human community cannot be taken for granted, that the *polis* is something to be worked for, that anything like a genuine and inclusive human conversation is something that must be achieved over and over again. To think of the human world as a realm of fellow citizens today requires more than academic analysis, or even empathy; it requires a will to solidarity which *receives* others as fellow- or sister-human beings.

In large measure this needs to be done through social *institutions* which embody the sort of covenantal relatedness of which I am speaking. Robert Bellah and four collaborators have made this point persuasively in *The Good Society*.[9] Educational, economic, legal, medical, political, and other structures, especially those of intermediate size, create and maintain settings of civility in which human beings can live and grow. Yet the argument of this book suggests that institutions today are less and less able to guarantee that the social realities and relationships they are meant to foster will really be there. Thus I think that justice sometimes happens, but not always. It is not ensured by the existence of a "justice system," nor are education, health, and a host of other social objectives. A certain minimum level of civil dialogue is needed in society for institutions themselves to flourish, and we often fall below that level. It is quite possible that the great system managers of today, those who run communications and commercial empires far more complicated than the railroad system of the German concentration camp network, are thoughtlessly sending many human beings to shortened, materially and spiritually impoverished lives. System management is different from institution maintenance. The system is inhuman while the institution is the expression of the human and the sustainer of the *polis*.

How may the churches help promote a people-fostering, inclusive conversation today, and hence not only make genocide less likely, but also lay foundations for a global lifeworld capable of sustaining the institutions human beings need? The churches need to appropriate the sense of a people of God in their own self-understandings. If they do, they will also reach out to help sponsor a "conversation of humankind." I contend that it is of the essence of the churches' mission work to make such an inclusive human conversation possible, and to sustain it in the long term. The pages that conclude this book seek to develop this theme in four steps. First, I try to work out a view of the contemporary human condition as, in essence, a state of material interdependency in the absence of covenantal communion. Second, I look critically at a secular attempt to see the human community as a field of "communicative action," that of the German social philosopher Jürgen Habermas. Third, I consider criticisms and possible modifications of this position, borrowing ideas from Hans-Georg Gadamer. And finally, I attempt a constructive statement, informed in part by Peter Hodgson's *God in History*, but also drawing on the World War II story of the people of the French village of Le Chambon-sur-Lignon, who banded together under the leadership of a Protestant congregation to save the lives of Jews.

2. Is the Conversation Possible?

We now need a more careful analysis of the capacity (or lack of it) of contemporary humankind for conversation. For some the very word may have an effete, elitist, ring. But I mean it in the down-to-earth sense of communication that brings together, includes, and builds relationships of mutual understanding and trust. There is something covenantal about conversation. If it is possible at all it implies confidence among the participants that truth is being told, that the dialogue is more than dissimulating charade, that there are limitless possibilities of communication and comprehension. I am aware, of course, that this term has come down in recent philosophy from Michael Oakeshott to Gilbert Ryle, and thence to such neo-pragmatists as Richard Rorty, and over the last few years to David Tracy who makes much of the term in *The Analogical Imagination*[10] and in *Plurality and Ambiguity*.[11] Conversation begins to mean something close to the heart of being human. It is hard to imagine atrocities where real conversation is going on; which is perhaps why prisoners and hostages have the instinct, or the good sense, to talk as much as they can with their captors. But how much of the idea of a *comprehensive* human conversation is, so to speak, mere talk? Is the contemporary human condition such that dialogue can be the primary category? We need to look at what is actually going on among human beings today and ask what sorts of conversation are possible and what they mean. What, in all its complexity, *is* this contemporary human condition about which we hear so much that is both trite and true?

First, a word about what we are doing. To speak of humanity as being in a particular condition, that is, in a certain systemic state of affairs as opposed to having a certain "nature" or "essence," is a relatively recent habit. It points to a modern departure from the long tradition of static and abstract conceptions of the human. From Plato to St. Augustine, from Aristotle to Aquinas, from Calvin to Rousseau, from Jonathan Edwards to Reinhold Niebuhr, we are heirs to a succession of attempts to say what human nature essentially *is*, to find categories which capture the human essence. Today we move toward a more dynamic way of thinking. We cannot avoid awareness of relativity and change, or of the pluralism of human visions and cultures; hence the notion that human beings, even if their nature cannot be brought within a single definition, may be thought to share a certain historical moment or situation. Humanity may *have* no predetermined essence. What we will be is perhaps also an open question. But it may still be possible to say that we share a certain "condition" here and now. The old notions of nature and essence are replaced by the sense of dwelling together in a common planetary space/time. Despite vast differences of ideology and culture, we share common global circumstances of nature and history that invite reflection on the state of the human system today and on that system's possible future states. And the most salient characteristic of our situation could well be a paradox. We live in ever expanding networks of interdependency, and yet have not yet achieved an interhuman imagination, a common human sense, a capacity for conversation across cultural and political boundaries which could make global community possible.

Interdependency as such is of course not new. Life in small-scale cooperative units has been our species characteristic from the start, resting as it probably does on the long period between birth and maturity under parental care needed by us (and other primates) for the very continuation of the race. We have been interdependent beings in this sense for millennia. What *is* new is the global reach of interdependent relationships, the energy level (in kilowatts, megatons, and so forth) of the moves we are capable of making, and the virtually instantaneous character of action and reaction born of the information age. The new interdependency refers to a range of empirical facts known to all. No ideological lens is needed to see these things; they are with us beyond any possibility of doubt. Our interdependency today is systemic, with aspects of cognition, communication, and control. Consider the mutual implication and interrelationships of the world's economies. Movements on the Tokyo stock exchange can send financial shock waves around the globe, triggering reactions in Hong Kong, Singapore, Zürich, London, and New York. The success or failure of Third World economies in generating wealth with borrowed funds has impact on the solvency of banks in Chicago and Texas. Public media bring us instantly into touch with persons and events the world over. Even in the cognitive world, science not only speaks a common, largely culture invariant, experimental, and mathematical language, but scientists on different continents increasingly depend on each other for data. News of a successful experiment is flashed across oceans, instantly understood, repeated if possible, hailed if confirmed, and sometimes received as a common achievement of humankind. Much of this, of course, is sheer gain, when directed toward worthy goals.

But the creation and expansion of these networks of interdependency have outpaced all our efforts to achieve corresponding forms of collective human imagination, moral ways of seeing each other as codwellers and coactors on this globe. Existing bodies of moral insight are usually tied to specific religious, ethnic, and political communities. Besides, we have witnessed an impoverishment, even a pollution, of the "public philosophies," the forms of common life sense, we do possess. Instead, our new networks of interdependency coexist with expressions of alienation, isolation, and radical autonomy. We witness today the vigorous development of individualism, privatism, nationalism, racism, much of it expressed in aggrandizing behavior: what Robert Adams calls the "squalid scrimmage of appetitive impulses characteristic of a commercial, mechanical society."[12] Robert Bellah, following Alexis de Tocqueville, has studied these tendencies in North American society, where individualism and self-seeking have become a secular religion.[13] Bellah's insight is that American individualism has reached a point at which it denies the existence of any moral claim in the network of relationships, old or new, in which human life is set. On the contrary, individual self-seeking uses the information and control networks for its own purposes. The "state of the system" is then one in which centers of initiative considering themselves autonomous operate within a system of relationships in which everything is in fact interconnected, in which every action by a powerful person, or ethnic group, or nation state, has an impact on the entire human race. But the impact is ignored, or seen to be without ethical or spiritual consequence. Indeed if any thought is given to the impact at all, the thought of communication between those responsible and those affected is far from most persons' minds. Instead, it is often assumed that some invisible, usually technological, hand will somehow adjust for what has been done.

It also begins to be clear that political life as such has less and less to do with the maintenance of meaningful human communication. Gaining and keeping power today is more often than not a matter of distorting truth in the process of manipulating voters' emotions. The political campaign is no longer a communicative process. Issues as such are seldom discussed. And government is often reduced to maintaining minimum (and sometimes subminimum) conditions for the conduct of life: sanitation, police protection, welfare, economic regulation, and the like. It is not clear that organs of government stand for anything in themselves beyond a certain umpiring of competitive interests functioning both inside and outside the boundaries of legality.

One suspects that such attitudes are not limited to North

America. America's particular cultural and economic circumstances have given a certain naive self-satisfaction to its world-impacting, world-ignoring decisions. But comparable autonomy and capacity are beginning to exist elsewhere, if in different cultural frames of reference, and indeed are actively pursued as obvious goals of human fulfillment. One need only think of Western European firms which manufacture and sell weapons, or the substances needed to make nuclear warheads or poison gas. Or consider the growing tribalisms and nationalisms that, if they do not represent individualism as we know it in the West, certainly do represent a search for power with global consequences. And not all initiatives are inherently power seeking or violent. They may have been begun simply to create jobs and stimulate economic development. Still, a development such as that of the deforestation of the Amazon basin is in no sense Brazil's business alone. It will inevitably be felt as change in the composition of the atmosphere everywhere on earth.

We are witnessing a paradoxical alienation of modern human beings from their own achievements. This is manifest not merely in particular events and situations. It seems to be gaining a systemic foothold in the structures of common life. There is, for example, our strange love-hate relationship with the natural sciences and the technology which flows from them. On the one hand, the sciences not only make our global interdependency possible, they provide us with metaphors of reality which, even if based on limited public understanding of the actual state of scientific theory, dominate the worlds of ordinary language. Within limits, the world of science is a global conversation in its own right. But on the other hand, we feel a growing distrust of scientists and professionals of all kinds. We know that they dispose of technical knowledge and concepts dauntingly beyond our ken, and also that they represent self-interested priesthoods of expertise which need funds so vast that only centers of entrenched power can provide them. Science has helped create many of our problems; we also depend on science to resolve these difficulties. If we are not uneasy about such ironies, we should be.

Likewise there is a paradox in our relationship to the industries of mass communication. Our sense of common humanity is powerfully fed by images generated by the global media. We have a sense, unique to this time in history, of the simultaneity of human activity everywhere. We can witness distant human beings in action in "real time." Real values, real sympathy, real understanding, can thereby be shared over chasms of cultural difference. But at times we experience an information overload so egregious that human response becomes impossible. Especially when communication is manipulated by political interests we see the triumph of image over substance. We may in the end know less rather than more. Media images become forms of entertainment which fail to encourage human engagement. Mass communication may have deepened, rather than relieved, our tendencies to individualism and clannishness.

And finally there is a paradox in the relationships between caring and control. We have the ability to collect, store, and disseminate vast amounts of information not only about public matters but about each individual. "Humankind" is no longer an abstract idea. It would be possible today, given the political will, for each human being to be listed in a single constantly updated information bank. We could know precisely, empirically, at any moment what was meant by "the human race." On the one hand there is great potential here for caring. The storing of medical and genetic information alone could be a great boon. Yet the possibilities are equally great for using such information for totalitarian control. Our imagination of each other could come to be controlled by powers with reasons of their own for keeping us at odds with our neighbors.

All this leads us to ask whether there *is* a "conversation of humankind," or the possibility of one, in the world just described. Can there be a genuinely *public* world in our time? Is there a realm of human interaction in which all can be players, in which all can have influence on the character of the whole? The conditions of contemporary human life are such that one wonders. It may turn out that there is no genuine public arena in the sense that Hannah Arendt understood and revered it. The term "public" is common enough. Most people suppose they understand it. But a world which is instrumentalized, manipulated, and controlled, be it ever so interdependent, is not *truly* public. It is, rather, a world defined by the competition of powerful private and governmental *interests*: that is, a world in which the "public" imagination is in fact shaped by hidden, and not so hidden, forces that destroy its genuinely open, shared, inclusive character.

The sum of all this is simply put: humanity is one in the sense of being interconnected by numerous interrelated and technologically based energy and information networks, but it is not one in any way that could be called spiritual or ethical. Science and technology are profoundly paradoxical in their impact. They offer unprecedented opportunities for achieving a global network of shared human concern. But they also exacerbate old problems, and give rise to new ones, which threaten to drive humanity apart. What is needed is a moral vision of the human prospect couched in terms which can wrestle in a practical way with humanity's strangely interdependent alienation from covenantal communion. The conversation endlessly talked about by philosophers and theologians needs to be restored. The social institutions which embody the human spirit and see to human needs must find new energy and life.

I am arguing in this book that an ecclesiology embodying the sense of a people of God could help the churches gain such a dialogical vision of humanity and the power to aid its achievement in history through perduring forms of human association. But we must approach that possibility by first studying a parallel secular claim, that of critical social theory oriented toward emancipatory action, as found in the research and writing of the Frankfurt School, and particularly of its second-generation social philosopher Jürgen Habermas.

3. Restoring the Conversation: "Communicative Action"

Jürgen Habermas seeks to address issues such as those I have just set forth in his theory of "communicative action."[14] Habermas has devoted his career to studying the conditions of possibility of genuine human dialogue, and hence of what we have called a public world. His work takes the form of a "critical" social theory. The word critical has a long history, at least from Kant forward. Here it means essentially that participants in the community-forming process are able to gain a certain leverage on it, a certain distance from it in reflection, which enables them to recognize distortions in the generative process of sociality: notably distortions brought about by exploitation and domination. For Habermas, this critical leverage is the work of an autonomous reason itself critically derived from the Enlightenment type, a reason which overcomes alienating traditions such as that of Christianity, and yet, as I will later argue, learns something from that tradition as well. Critical inquiry is called to the defense of the human world as a genuinely public conversation, in other words, one not distorted by powerful ideological interests or the exclusion of potential participants.

Early in his career, Habermas traced the gradual emergence of both the reality and the concept of publicness in the rising bourgeoisie of late seventeenth-century England. At that time, the public realm came to be distinguished both from the private sphere and from the state. It became the realm of general discourse, the discourse of such public spaces as the London coffee house. In Habermas this analysis of emerging publicness is at the same time an analysis of modernity. He follows Hegel in identifying civil society, a realm distinguished over against both the family and the state, as the distinctive creation of the modern world.[15] But if modernity has created the conditions of genuinely civil discourse it has also given rise to conditions which threaten that sphere through the control and intervention of the administrative-bureaucratic apparatus of the modern state. Habermas denies that modern administrative regulation necessarily wipes out the possibility of communication between ordinary social actors. But he is clear that the public realm needs both analysis and defense.

In more recent work Habermas makes a basic distinction between the "lifeworld" and the "system." Lifeworld in Habermas has some of the sense it does in Husserl: it is the network of lived assumptions, values, beliefs, customs, and relationships which make up the fabric of life, including the generally unthematized images and metaphors that help shape that life. It is the common experience, the shared flow, of social existence. But it is apparent that the lifeworld, especially today, is shaped by the institutional and political products of instrumental reason and by the communication, distribution, and control grids that serve such institutional and political structures. The "system" has its "steering mechanisms": for Habermas they are money, power, and the market. The system can "all too easily become uncoupled from the 'lifeworld' and attain the status of a self-justifying, self-perpetuating phenomenon to whose inevitability the human community can frequently be persuaded to bow."[16] But by rights the reverse should happen. The system should be an instrument of the lifeworld's values. It should be under the control of the community's human purposes. As it is, "the human cultural values that are central to the lifeworld lie exposed to the depredations of the technocratic barbarism of the system."[17]

Under these conditions, society is the victim of what Habermas calls "systematically distorted communication." At this point one sees the philosopher's debt to Freud. The system represses what might otherwise come to expression in the lifeworld, or at least it distorts what congruency might otherwise exist between linguistic symbols, action patterns, and public expressions of meaning. "A barrier is formed between the publicly participating ego and the repressed realm of the unconscious, so that causally determining motives no longer correspond to linguistically apprehensible intentions."[18] Habermas suggests that the distortions of communication correspond to the varying degrees of repression which characterize the institutional system within a given society; and that in turn, the degree of repression depends on the developmental stage of the productive forces and on the organization of authority, that is, of the institutionalization of political and economic power."[19]

Among other things, this analysis is concerned to penetrate the veil of ideology and to elucidate the mechanisms of repression which characterize a particular society.[20] The reasoning which leads Habermas to these conclusions is presided over by what appears to be a regulative principle or postulate: the sense of human society as ideally a community of undistorted discourse, which Habermas calls "the ideal speech situation." This is an ideal for human discourse in which there are no barriers to full communicative interchange, to untrammeled "communicative action." As Habermas puts it, this situation exists when "if and only if, for all possible participants, there is a symmetrical distribution of chances to choose and to apply speech-acts."[21] All potential participants in such a discourse have the same chance to initiate and sustain dialogue through questions and answers, claims and counterclaims. No preconceptions remain excluded from consideration.[22] All have the same chance to express their attitudes, feelings, and intentions.[23] The notion of an "ideal speech situation" would open the possibility of revising, or replacing, a linguistic system if that system were seen to contain built-in bias. Something of this sort has in fact been done in certain social groups with the elimination or suppression of sexist language.

What is the reality status of this Habermasian notion? It is, of course, a theoretical ideal against which "systematically distorted communication" is defined and measured. We have called it a regulative principle in the sense given that term in chapter 3. Yet it does not exactly fit Kant's description, for the "ideal speech situation" is not the regulative assurance of coherence in a given field of discourse in the sense of Kant's "rational psychology" or "rational cosmology." It is, Habermas says, something anticipated in *every* act of linguistic communication, not merely those in certain areas of concern. It is "an unavoidable reciprocal presupposition of discourse."[24] It is a open question whether an actual social situation might come to embody this ideal, or whether it will remain only an expression of the implied logic of human communication.

It is not impossible, Habermas thinks, that an "ideal speech situation" might be approximated in real life. If it were ever achieved, it would be a realm of unrestrained and universal human interaction, an arena of discourse free from all constraint, whether accidental or systematic, with an equal distribution of chances to participate, and in which the only force is the force of the better argument. One can see at once that this would mean a field of discourse in which all forms of "subjugated knowledge" could be fully expressed and heard, in which the language in use would have no characteristics, such as sexist terminology, or patriarchal assumptions, tending to disadvantage any individual or class of participants.

Such a situation, furthermore, would not be merely communicative or rhetorical. It would imply, indeed require, a correspondingly ideal form of social life. This would mean a form of life whose institutional and practical organization allowed dialogue that was free, symmetrical, and unconstrained. Participants in the dialogue would need to be socially located in such a way that they could express their intentions openly and without fear of reprisal. Everyone would need to share fully in the power to set agendas, to open or limit debate. There could be no privileges and no disabilities in setting the terms of the conversation. In short, the "ideal speech situation" would require a society free from domination, and free from ideologies which could introduce systematic distortion of the dialogical field.

But as matters stand, this ideal, in the quaint language of social science, is "counterfactual." It does not exist, and is not about to exist soon. It is, as noted, an ideal type, a postulate, a regulative principle of an unusually comprehensive sort, which introduces a critical perspective and an emancipatory energy into political life. Where does the emancipatory energy in this proposal come from? Habermas will admit that he draws not only on logical analysis but also on the Enlightenment as a tradition of understanding. He knows that as a late twentieth-century West German he participates in a recently achieved but now powerful and successful tradition of religious and political liberty. But Habermas argues that the substance of the Enlightenment vision as expressed in Western democracy, and hence the energy of the demand for freedom and inclusiveness, can be derived logically from an analysis of the a priori conditions of discourse as these are worked out in his theory of communication. In brief, the fact that people enter into discourse implies that consensus is thought possible, otherwise there would be no reason to begin. But confidence in the possibility of consensus is rationally grounded only insofar as the discourse presupposes and anticipates the full inclusion of every possible viewpoint and experience. To take part in discourse at all is to acknowledge that freedom of expression is sacred and that mutual understanding can be achieved. As Charles Davis puts it, "the very structure of speech involves the anticipation of a form of life in which autonomy and responsibility are possible."[25]

4. The Theological Use of Critical Theory

It is understandable that theologians have found the Habermasian vision of communicative action and the ideal speech situation enticing. It is so near to being a secular analogue of the kingdom of God, with an emphasis on inclusion of otherwise disadvantaged participants in the dialogue, that a number of theologians have attempted to form intellectual alliances for building a new vision of the church in relation to God's presence in history.

The German political theologian Helmut Peukert,[26] for example, has attempted to take advantage of this parallelism, arguing that only a religious framework can sustain the human solidarity needed for communicative action to become a reality of history. Furthermore, a notion of universal solidarity must account theologically for the deaths of those who have preceded us and whose lives contributed, without gain to themselves, to the freedom we enjoy. They are united to us in relationship to God and through the solidarity implied in faith in the resurrection of Jesus Christ. Likewise, Francis Schüssler Fiorenza has made considerable use of Habermas in his *Foundational Theology: Jesus and the Church*,[27] a work that sees the church as a community of interpretation, a realm of communications which raises distinct validity claims. The relation between interpretation and truth conditions has implications for foundational theology, which must be about the task of retrieving and interpreting its own religious tradition. Schüssler Fiorenza writes a "foundational theology" which is ecclesiological in form and which, if the word "foundational" is given its full philosophical sense, appears to make claims beyond those offered in the present book.[28] And finally there is Paul Lakeland's *Theology and Critical Theory: The Discourse of the Church*.[29] This work seeks to deepen the self-understanding of the Roman Catholic Church "through the application of Habermas's critical theory to certain aspects of its functioning."[30] It also explores the possible consequences of intellectual partnership between theology and critical theory as it develops the idea of the Christian community as a realm of ethical discourse.

I suspect that attempts such as these to relate critical social theory to ecclesiology are the beginning of a trend which this book now joins and seeks to further. We will see more such works in the next few years. But it may not be possible to adapt Habermas's perspective for theological purposes without modifying it in several respects. I offer here some comments in that direction. These fall in three categories: (a) Habermas's views on religion and its social function; (b) modifications of the "theory of communicative action" to permit religious traditions to join the dialogue, and (c) the public world as an arena of practical reasoning open to dialogue about the underlying commitments of the participants.

(a) Habermas on the Social Role of Religion

What does Habermas himself say about religion in its social role? He has gone so far as to acknowledge the historical contribution of religious communities in envisioning the ideal of human communication he now seeks to defend rationally. Religious worldviews, he says, have in the past functioned to connect the sense of personal and communal identity with dominant social institutions. Religious institutions have sometimes been in their own ways *loci* of something resembling "communicative action." They have been "place holders" (reminding us of Bonhoeffer's *Stellvertretung* or principle of "deputyship") for the rationality of society. But their function in this respect is now superseded by other forms of social organization. Habermas does not argue that religion is in process of disappearing in modern society. It continues to be one of the important elements in the lifeworld. But the "Protestant ethic" has become secularized. Ethical judgments once maintained in religious contexts have been carried over to nontraditional and rational settings. Sheila Briggs has put the matter vividly:

> Religion seems for Habermas to have exhausted its social evolutionary potential now that the processes of social and cultural differentiation have created the conditions for a communicative ethics making claims for universal validity not on the basis of religious reasoning but of the competence with which members of modern societies can engage in speech acts.[31]

Habermas finds that today's religious communities have little utopian energy left in them. They have no capacity to envision a future society built on human solidarity. He seems to ignore the contemporary theologies of liberation with their objectives of sponsoring socially transformative discourse. He does not exclude the possibility of religious motivation among the social actors involved in emancipatory projects, but this is very different from allowing that *theological* arguments could provide normative grounds for emancipation. Indeed, theological arguments are unlikely to fare very well in the communicative evaluation of validity claims because, as the discourse of particular traditioned communities, they are not universalizable. In the Habermasian scheme such arguments would seem to derive from distinctive commitments not shared or sharable by all. Their particularity would rule out their being able to be judged universally as "better arguments."[32]

Thus it turns out that for Habermas, the representatives of Black, or feminist, or Third World liberation theologies are welcome discussants among others in the ideal speech situation. Apparently, however, they are not encouraged to come with contributions representing either their particular religious commitments or the subjugated kinds of knowledge possessed by their constituencies. Neither is recognized as valid in the precincts of Enlightenment rationality. The ideal speech situation, which at first glance looks so much like a secular analogue to the kingdom of God, is, at least in the hands of its inventor, nothing of the kind. It represents at least as much oppression—this time by a dominant rationalist tradition—as have religious traditions themselves. Moreover, Habermas's vision of communicative rationality excludes from the public arena precisely the sorts of language we need for dealing with paradox, tragedy, and evil on the one hand, or with aspiration, possibility, and hope on the other. Such limit conditions of human experience are far better articulated in the various religious traditions of the world than they are in a realm of Enlightenment-style rationality. Above all, Habermas's notion of an ideal speech situation offers little defense against figures such as Adolf Eichmann whose thoughtlessness comes from having no depth tradition to think *with*. In principle, of course, an ideal speech situation includes the voices of those who would otherwise be victims. But there needs to be more than a rational principle of inclusion to defend us against powerful system managers and the evil they do. There needs to be some positive and powerful *metaphor* of inclusiveness, something like the sense of covenantal peoplehood defended in these pages, defining the arena of common life.

(b) Traditions in Dialogue

Yet Habermas remains important to us as the contemporary philosopher par excellence of the human conversation, of the public world. Is there any way of modifying his vision to make it more theologically fruitful? Can religious traditions, including liberation traditions, have their place in the larger human dialogue? To answer this question we must wrestle first with a prior one. Is the ideal speech situation really derivable simply from the nature of communicative action as such? Many critics of Habermas, including his teacher Hans-Georg Gadamer, would contend that such an ideal cannot be generated simply by the application of reason to human discourse as we know it. Rather, reasoners in the ideal speech situation, however public their styles of discourse, are always giving expression to some *tradition* in which freedom and inclusiveness have been experienced in at least a rudimentary way. Traditions of free discourse are transmitted and maintained only as existing, historical, forms of life. One becomes part of such a tradition not through public discourse alone, but by participation in a community which embodies it. It seems plain that Habermas himself is influenced by his experience of living in a political tradition of democratic values, and in a university tradition of rigorous care in the marshalling of evidence and argument.

But Habermas would argue that, however powerful these forms of life may be as lived traditions, all that is of public value in them can be sustained by the force of arguments independent of tradition as such, independent even of the tradition that arguments should be tradition free! Indeed, in the ideal speech situation the only legitimate force is the persuasive power of reasoning itself. Argument, then, (not therapeutic, or bureaucratic or any other form of common speech) is the model for discourse in the field of communicative freedom. But we have already seen that no form of discourse is without its metaphorical underpinnings. Lakoff and Johnson (see chapter 3) contend persuasively that *all* human language is metaphorically constituted, including the language by which we characterize discourse itself. Habermas casts discourse basically in the form of argument, as if the notion of argument were value free. But for Lakoff and Johnson the notion of argument is the lead example of metaphorically constructed conceptualization. A study of actual language-in-use demonstrates that, at least in the English-speaking world, argument is conceived as a form of "war." The very idea is grounded in metaphors of mortal conflict. Hence to say that the only force is the force of the better argument may well be to introduce elements of coercion at the metaphorical level which supposedly have been removed at the level of social structure. I would contend that there is no way to describe the nature of discourse in the ideal speech situation without introducing some such implicit metaphorical content. One might as well, then, be open about the presence of tradition in this matter. The issue is not whether or not a tradition of discourse is present. We need to ask *which* tradition is present, and whether its presence is openly acknowledged. The ideal speech situation as purely rationally derived seems to imply the claim that Habermas has found some Archimedean point beyond the distortions of actual human communication as basis for his vision. But what and where is that point? Either the academic and democratic traditions are covertly at work where argument alone is supposed to reign, or there is some transcendental or even eschatological assumption behind the scenery.

Habermas's recourse to an Enlightenment-style rationality in his concept of communicative action is in one sense already a reply to Gadamer's treatment of tradition in human dialogue—both the dialogue between past and present and that among different contemporary spheres of understanding. Habermas has tried to define an objective rational framework for human science. His view, despite his own demurrals, has been seen by many as a new foundationalism.[33] Gadamer, a generation older, has ironically enough been a father of today's "postmodern," antifoundationalist views. Building on the thought of Heidegger, Gadamer argues that poetic language itself is the field of disclosure of Being. Following this line, we could say that since the churches are language communities, they are not only *ways* of being, they make present or disclose aspects of Being itself. That is why I have argued that churches in their various ways disclose the community-forming work of the Holy Spirit in the world, the people in whose life God has a "dwelling place." The truth to which the churches bear witness lies in their linguistically enabled forms of life rather than in theological propositions which have a merely regulative function with respect to those forms of life. For Gadamer, the experience of art, liturgy, or participation in the play of communal interactions governed by regulative ideas, brings one closer to the kind of "truth" available in human communities than does the ideal of rational argument found in Habermas's *Theory of Communicative Action*.[34]

Gadamer is realistic where Habermas is not. Gadamer knows that we come to the playing field of common understanding already formed by our particular histories. We come with "prejudice." This word is not used prejudicially! It means, simply, pre-judgment. Gadamer also speaks of "effective historical consciousness" which means that we are already formed by the stream of history in which we participate. If we are inquiring into the past, we must reckon on the direct or indirect impact on us of the very events we are seeking to understand. If we are trying to interpret the acts of others, our history-formed consciousness as interpreters will play a role in the process. The meeting of persons and traditions is the famous "fusion of horizons," where the socio-historical location of the interpreter is as important as the location of the texts or forms of life to be interpreted. I believe that the public world is precisely a place where many such perspectives at least provisionally come close enough to one another for a kind of practical reasoning or *phronesis* to take place.

Do all these circumstances, which make understanding possible, permit the forming of a *principled* public world or *polis*? Gadamer would say that insofar as the participants in dialogue share some minimal tradition of discourse, perhaps embedded in a common language, there could be something very much like Habermas's arena of communicative action. The difference would be that reason would not be conceived as a criterion derived in some self-evident way from the fact of discourse as such. The forms of rationality operative in the discourse would borrow from those already presupposed by the discussants, insofar as they could be located within the region of horizon fusion making the dialogue possible. The difficulty here is that it is hard to imagine how the redemption of validity claims by distinguishing between better and worse arguments can go very far unless there is already wide agreement on the criteria to be applied. Furthermore, Habermas would ask, where is the critical element? Without some commonly held critical principles, some "hermeneutic of suspicion," how are discussants to know when the traditions they represent are in fact exclusive or oppressive, and hence prone to produce distorted forms of reasoning? Particularly today, with traditions unsure of themselves and already subject to ideological distortion, with radical pluralism emerging in once homogeneous cultures, can the fusion of horizons be a sufficient conceptual basis for constructing a public world?

(c) The Practical Redemption of Validity Claims

Horizons of discourse fuse in a world of practical decision making. I may understand my Moslem neighbor on a limited basis, but he (or she) and I bring our assumptions about the meaning of life to the resolution of problems we share because we live on the same street, or because our children attend the same school. How are we able to communicate? What is happening as we decide?

The notion of *phronesis* or practical reasoning can help us.[35] Aristotle used this term to refer to deliberation in search of the practical wisdom needed for the governance of public affairs. The term today comes increasingly into use in hermeneutical, neo-pragmatist and liberation circles to mean shared reflective practice in a context of competing visions and claims. The notion of *phronesis* may best describe the kind of reasoning possible for members of traditioned communities who bear testimony to their faith commitments by participating in public deliberation about issues of the common good. While their symbol systems and metaphysical constructs may differ, Roman Catholics, Protestants, Jews, Moslems, Buddhists, secular humanists, and all the rest may express their respective commitments by engaging with each other in the sort of practical reasoning which keeps the public sphere honest and open.

Charles W. Allen[36] persuasively argues that *phronesis* is a conception of reasoning which offers a middle road between the claims of those whom he calls "tribalists" (Nietzche, Kuhn, Foucault, Lindbeck) and "objectivists" (Descartes, Kant, Husserl, Ogden, Tracy). Allen's definition of *phronesis* departs from the aristocratic overtones found in Aristotle. He writes, "Phronesis is the historically implicated, communally nurtured ability to make good sense of relatively singular contexts in ways appropriate to their relative singularity."[37] Such reasoning, Allen tells us, needs a community of trust and loyalty in order to flourish. It is subject to the limitations of the historical context with its unacknowledged conditions and unintended consequences. It needs to have an element of critical distancing. In other words, it needs the capacity for self-correction. It operates in particular situations, which may in many ways be unique. And finally, it makes sense (a favorite expression of Paul Ricoeur) in a way related to whatever is the subject matter or problem at hand.

Allen further argues that *phronesis* is not merely one way of making sense. For human beings it is the primary way. The implication is that more technical sorts of reasoning, with their implicit or explicit transcendental claims, always function within some sort of broad phronetic consensus about what we as human beings at any given time or place are trying to do. This claim parallels Gadamer's notion that the human sciences, which study such broad representations of human purpose in communal context, are prior in the order of knowing to the natural sciences, which reason in such a way as to carry out these human purposes and whose reasoning is influenced by the communally maintained reality sense. This vision has the further implication that for *phronesis* to be fruitful there must be at least *some* already existing sense of things, some way of putting the world together, some moral commitment to a vision of the good society, some notion of life's meaning characteristic of a particular place or epoch.

Allen assists our argument further with a suggestive play on words. "Tribalism," he says, is a "radical confessionalism," in which, with H. Richard Niebuhr, we cannot avoid stating "what has happened to us in our community, how we came to believe, how we reason about things and what we see from our point of view." My claims, whether religious or not, are radically influenced by my standpoint, in other words influenced to the roots "all the way down." But likewise my claims will be confessionally radical, by which Allen means that we have a commitment in the process of *phronesis* to get to the bottom of everything we say and do as members of traditioned communities. In the human dialogue, that is, we must be committed with *confessional* force to a self-critical stance. We must come into the dialogue both knowing where we come from and realizing that we cannot say in advance where the dialogue will lead. We come to *phronesis* in the public world in effect inviting criticism from those equally committed to the public world who come from somewhere else.

But once practical decisions begin to be made in the public realm it may be legitimate to ask whether the prior commitments which the actors bring to the arena are in any way relevant to the public discussion. Is the public discussion and its outcome relevant to the truth status of our confessional presuppositions? William Werpehowski[38] argues that it is reasonable for discussants to explore together the commitments which underlie the agreement they have reached about practical issues. For example, Christians of various persuasions as well as adherents of other religions or of secular faiths may be able to agree about the shortcomings of the relationship between patients and physicians in our culture. They may further agree that technology, and even the struggle against death itself, should be subordinated to a relational approach that overcomes disrespect and inhumanity and seeks a genuine human bond with those who suffer. They might then, at the next stage of discussion, ask what faith assumptions, what assumptions about the nature and destiny of the human, support the de facto agreement they have reached. Christian participants in the dialogue could contribute their conviction that "covenant, and a very particular sort of covenant, is the basis of creation."[39] They could bear testimony to the conviction that the inner meaning of the physical universe is found in relationships of covenantal fidelity through which God becomes present in space/time.

Eventually, Werpehowski thinks, it could be shown that the worldview implicit in such practical agreements coincides with the biblical vision, and there finds its most adequate and indeed profound expression. If persons from many faith communities really *can* reach practical agreements, then it is in order for Christians to propose their own vision as the best account of what lies behind such agreements. Given the successful outcome of a process of *phronesis* or practical reasoning, Christians can claim they have the better argument. Not the better argument in Habermas's sense which presupposes an Enlightenment-style agreement about rationality, but the better argument for explaining transcendentally what is involved in something already pragmatically agreed. In several ways this proposal resembles Habermas's vision of communicative action. But what confessional presupposition best warrants such a dialogical view of human life? A Christian participant in the public dialogue about the human good can offer "an anthropology of cohumanity, which presents human creatures as fulfilled in covenants of mutual assistance, which in turn reflect the work of the triune and covenanting God."[40] Presuppositions held by traditioned communities, Werpehowski argues, can lend greater *coherence* to beliefs held in the public realm. This may be true even if there are other belief systems such as Marxist or secular humanist positions competing to offer clarifying presuppositions. Given a measure of *practical* agreement about the good for humanity, the way is open for discussion of what that practical accord presupposes.

If this makes sense, we can say that the truth of Christian presuppositions, doctrinally expressed, lies not only in their ability to regulate the life of truth-bearing communities, but also in their ability to fund common human agreements, regions of *public* consensus, about social goals which move humanity toward fulfillment. It makes sense for Christian affirmations to have their truth tested in the public arena, for the Christian tradition affirms that God is at work in the *world*. It is there that the dramatic work of the triune God, which leads from creation to consummation through the unfolding of a covenantal vision of humanity, takes place. The test of the truth of Christian doctrine is that it should order the community of faith to participate insightfully and energetically in the *phronesis* of the *polis*, the "fear and trembling" through which this divine dynamism works itself out in the search for justice and peace, and for the integrity of the creation itself. Doctrine participates in truth not only through its regulative function within the churches, but also by ordering the churches' instigative, shaping, interpreting work in the arena of human life.

The sense of a people of God here reaches the end of its biblical trajectory. It becomes the name for *humanity* going through this phronetic, truth-testing process on the way to being finally ordered by the configurative power of the Spirit, whose identity we know in Jesus Christ. But this theological realization of humanity does not happen all at once or massively at any one time or place. It happens here and there in what Peter Hodgson calls gestalts of freedom and hope. It is the task of the churches to function as sacraments and signs that this is going on, as well as to be instruments in the process itself.

5. Gestalts of Freedom and Hope

Wherever many cultures, sub-cultures, and interests are able to join in practical reasoning toward measures for achieving the good society, we see the appearing of the *polis*. For nearly every political philosopher—from Plato and Aristotle to Hannah Arendt and Jürgen Habermas—the *polis* is something which approaches the sacred. The ancient, medieval, and classical Protestant worlds saw it as achievable in established orders of life under legitimate rulers. Today, however, we must think of the *polis* as an ideal rarely fulfilled. It is less a stable order than an ecstatic achievement which happens from time to time when a representative variety of interests comes together around a vision for human life together.

This is why, as I have already said in this chapter, I am so ambivalent about many of our social institutions. The good society cannot exist without them. Yet the institutions we have in no way guarantee the achievement of the values they are supposed to protect precisely because they do not exist in a coherent political order capable of sustaining the human conversation they need in order to survive. The *polis* today is not so much an established fact as it is a possibility constantly present but seldom realized in the complexities of political life. Such moments of meeting and understanding are not to be taken for granted. Their occurrence is often the result of much work and devotion, and yet there is no guarantee that any amount of human effort will bring such moments about.

The "March on Washington" of August 28, 1963 (described in chapter 3) expressed a discernment of common interests among many different racial, ethnic, economic, or political groups. It was an enactment of those interests through a gathering which heard Martin Luther King express his vision for the body politic: "I have a dream." Such ecstatic meetings, such instances of what Emile Durkheim called "collective effervescence," are fleeting moments for a level of communicative action which do not often characterize the public order as a whole. I believe that such moments are among the gestalts[41] whose description Peter Hodgson derives from the thinking of Hegel and Troeltsch and in whose reality he sees God's presence in history. Instead of Habermas's communicative action, Hodgson uses the term "communicative freedom." He writes:

History is a process of victories and defeats, of configurations and deconfigurations; yet it is empowered and lured onward by a transfiguring practical ideal, a gestalt of freedom, the image of a communion of solidarity, love, mutuality of recognition, and undistorted communication. The gestalt that lures and empowers history is the gestalt of God. It appears as such when the historical field has been cleared of all pretensions, of all autonomously based projects and powers, and when human projects and powers are seen rather to be the bearers, the vehicles of God's presence, of God's strange empowering kind of power.[42]

Hodgson writes in explicitly theological terms that may seem to exclude legitimate dialogue partners. Yet there are hints in Habermas and other secular writers (Rorty, Arendt) that this configuration of public life, whatever terminology is used to describe it, defies purely historical explanation. It is not simply a playing out of nostalgia for a long-lost communal ideal such as that thought to have existed in ancient Greece. Nor, if experience teaches us anything, can it be simply engineered into existence as a planned social scheme. There is, in fact, something about it that cannot be accounted for purely rationally. Richard Bernstein points out that Arendt spoke of "the 'miraculous' quality" of the action which creates a *polis*, of how a body politic "can make its appearance against all odds." Habermas himself tells us that communicative reason develops "a stubbornly transcending power even when it is violated and silenced again and again."[43] "Is it inappropriate," Hodgson asks, "to suggest that precisely this is how God's presence and power are experienced in history, if they are experienced at all?"[44]

History, then, is a fabric in which "redemptive divine presence" and "transfigurative human praxis" are "interwoven." One could go a step further with the weaving metaphor to suggest that the fabric has a subtle pattern, which, in the right light and from the right angle, one can see. This is the divine gestalt, the shape of "love in freedom," the shape given concretion by "certain images associated with the ministry and death of Jesus, images of compassionate freedom and liberating love."[45] Where does this notion of gestalt come from? Hodgson finds it first in Hegel's *Philosophy of Religion*, where it refers to the historical configuration of the "divine idea" in the form of an "objective spirit." He finds it then in

Troeltsch's notion of *Gestaltung*, or the forming of "historical individuals" in the sense of coherent configurations of historical factors. We have seen two traditional examples in the course of this book: the great medieval synthesis and the phenomenon known as the "Protestant ethic." The various liberation theologies could be on their way to articulating another great historical whole, provided that they are persistent and establish communication between their varied expressions. It is too early to tell if this will happen. Hodgson's specific move is to renounce the search for gestalts of freedom in the massive, world-historical sense of the word, and to look for it in scattered, fragmented forms in, with, and under, so to speak, the manifest structures of society. The theological move from theoretical constructs to a focus on praxis parallels this move from the "divine idea" in German idealism to the notion of historical forming or shaping: a move in which we are assisted by Troeltsch's historical realism.

Hodgson expresses his thought in a variety of ways. Here is an example:

> God is present in specific shapes or patterns of praxis that have a configuring, transformative power within historical process, moving the process in a determinate direction, that of the creative unification of multiplicities of elements into new wholes, into creative syntheses that build human solidarity, enhance freedom, break systemic oppression, heal the injured and broken, and care for the natural. A shape or gestalt is not as impersonal and generalized as an influence or presence, since it connotes something dynamic, specific, and structuring, but it avoids misleading personifications of God's action. What God "does" in history is not simply to "be there" as God, or to "call us forward," or to assume a personal "role," but to "shape"—to shape a multifaceted transfigurative praxis. God does this by giving, by disclosing, in some sense *being*, the normative shape, the paradigm of such a praxis. This is what I mean by the divine gestalt.[46]

One does not see this divine configuration in history easily. It takes much work, as Hodgson says, echoing Hegel.

Undoubtedly the need is for engagement. Such gestalts are best seen by being involved in the search for a truly public realm for practical reasoning in the human interest. Do the divine gestalts, if we can discern them, fit into any sort of continuity or pattern? Are they perhaps best identified by standing within the story, and then by asking how and where the story continues? Do we not always stand on the brink of decision, asking ourselves what we must do if we want to be part of the continuation of the narrative? If so, maybe the answer lies in searching, in objective uncertainty, either for places where the gestalt seems to appear or for ways in which our own action can instigate its appearance?

What should be the role of churches in relation to such possibilities of discernment and vision? I have argued in chapter 5 that the churches are already meeting places of many interests and cultures. The human conversation goes on *in* the churches, requiring them to evolve an intercontextual method for understanding their own social being. Ecumenism is the churches' necessary response to this reality. It is indispensable preparation for participation in the practical reasoning of human society as a whole, and indeed puts the churches in an almost unique position. To the extent that they have dealt with their own reality as places of meeting for many cultures and interests, they can contribute insight to the larger human dialogue. They can provide places where some of the needed practical reasoning about the good for humanity can go on. They can help create spaces in human society where larger, more visionary questions about the purpose of human life can be asked.

This place making or space making can go on in at least four easily visualizable ways. First, the churches can create spaces for such forming of human life in the Spirit by direct *instigation*. They can take the initiative of organizing forces in the civil community for a spiritual task when no one else will either discern the possibility or have the courage to do something about it. A threshold space for God ruling comes into being where people inside the congregation and outside are given the leadership, the organization, and the spiritual support to do something they would not otherwise do, and therefore to become, for a moment at least, the community they would not otherwise be. Human beings combine to create a threshold space for the appearing of a people of God, a gestalt of the Spirit. The church can seed the worlds of business, the professions, government, or the media with people ready to do this when the opportunity comes.

Second, the churches can open space for such a threshold by *discernment* and *articulation*. The church can identify the configurations of the Spirit in activities already taking place which may be little known, or out of touch with each other, or in need of recognition and support. Such discernment is often, but not always, the result of members' engagement in the situations concerned, and may owe something to their encouragement or instigation. But often the spiritual dimension of what is going on in the public world is so diffuse, so scattered, that it is not easily identified for what it is. Like some of the ancient Inca designs spread over acres of hillsides in Peru, it cannot be seen from the standpoint of any single location on the ground. By discerning the patterns of the Spirit and by articulating their meaning, especially when seen as a configuration of elements rather than as isolated events, churches can make the outlines of a people of God identifiable and perhaps publicly visible. They can say to the world what is happening in the larger lineaments of its daily life.

Third, the churches can open space for the appearing of the people by providing means of *communication* and *networking* between movements of the Spirit. A church building is often a meeting place, and sometimes a sanctuary, for a wide range of community groups. Can advantage be taken of this to help these groups meet each other and discover what they have in common? Churches can also hold open space for spiritual networking among people and movements otherwise widely separated. The Christian churches together are already a global communications medium, whose power of discernment, if not of dissemination, easily rivals that of the electronic media. Relationships between movements with which churches are in touch, in diverse cultures or geographical areas, can be maintained through this communications capacity to which oppressed groups, denied access to commercial and governmental media, may turn for support.

And finally, the churches can maintain space in society for *questions* which no one else thinks to ask, or is able to ask given their society's limited imaginative means. Sometimes such space is held open by a terminology or a tradition of discourse, which has been long forgotten by most secular decision makers but which can come to life again when certain otherwise intractable questions begin to exercise the public mind. It has been said that not least among the achievements of the documents of the U.S. Catholic Bishops' Conference on nuclear deterrence and the economy was to provide a moral terminology around which diverse and perhaps otherwise incommensurable viewpoints could at least converse. From such convergence, gatherings in the Spirit may emerge. Where there is no convergence, a space can be held open in the culture for a particular kind of question to be asked until its meaning *is* understood .

In these ways and others, the churches have the opportunity to function as signs, sacraments, and instruments of God at work in human life. As I have said, I believe that this understanding is compatible with what Peter Hodgson is arguing, namely, that gestalts of the kind described are means by which God is present in human history by the power of the Spirit. Under present human circumstances that presence is always fragmentary and elusive, but it is God's way of taking form in the midst of human life. It follows that only by being in touch with these situations and moments of meeting, which are also constituting events in the formation of the *polis*, can the churches legitimately claim to be speaking language about God and not merely projecting their own values upon the cosmos. Both ecumenical and political relationships are thus indispensable for the churches' claims that they are carriers of divine revelation, that they represent God ruling in human history.

I have consistently argued that the people of God are those at any given moment who are involved, knowingly or not, in the fulfillment of God's purposes for the human race. They *are* the human race insofar as it is as yet caught up in the work of the Spirit, which prepares the way for the king-dom. I contend that such language gives a kind of metaphori-cal, visual concreteness to what in Hodgson's writing remains philosophical and abstract. We are indeed talking about "shapes of freedom," which are situations in which the true *polis* of humanity momentarily appears as diverse human beings meet and make practical decisions. It is clear that neither political structures nor churches can predict such mo-ments, much less control them. What is important, however, is that the *idea* that such moments and meetings are possible, the *sense* that they are manifestations of the historical pres-ence of God, should be operative in the churches' thinking. The churches need to take into their self-understandings the *sense* that this is how God calls into being a people whose possibility in the world the churches are summoned sacra-mentally to represent. The sense of a people is both a strong metaphor to bring this home and the name of a fundamental ecclesiological idea.

Let me try to make vivid what this could mean. Various examples could be offered, some of them trite from overuse: Mother Theresa gathering and caring for the poor in Calcutta, Martin Luther King galvanizing people of good will in Bir-mingham and Atlanta. These instances are too well known and perhaps not *enough* subject to scrutiny because they command such general assent. I will offer a less well-known instance in which a pastor and congregation instigated a larger human gestalt of freedom and hope: the rescue of Jews by a French Protestant community during World War II. The tale is told in a book *Lest Innocent Blood Be Shed* by the Jewish ethicist Philip Hallie.[47] The story is simple. The Prot-estant congregation of the small French town of Le Chambon-sur-Lignon, under the leadership of its Pastor, André Trocmé,[48] set up a network of persons in the region—Protes-tant, Roman Catholic, and otherwise—to protect Jews from capture by the Gestapo. Le Chambon became a send-off point on the underground railway leading into Switzerland, a city of refuge in the sense of Deut. 19: 7-10, from which the name of the book comes. Trocmé and his congregation organized a network of responsible ones whose function was just the opposite of Eichmann's rail network. The "responsible ones" hid Jews in their homes, saw to it that messages traveled rapidly when the Germans appeared for a roundup, knew what they needed to know and no more. Members of this action community included members of the congregation, but also many others. This community of sanctuary defied and even morally infiltrated two far more powerful structures, the governmental structure consisting of local representatives of the Vichy regime and later of the German occupying force, and the ecclesiastical authorities of the Reformed Church of France.

One notes an absence of theologizing or philosophizing as such: doing was the thing. Trocmé's often pacifist, but also basically Reformed, language from the pulpit was no doubt instrumental to the doing, although not by way of constant justification of the sanctuary operation. Rather, Trocmé's preaching seems to have built up the congregation in its spirituality and basic understanding of life, in the light of which the protection of persons in mortal danger simply seemed the natural thing to do. Trocmé's wife, Magda, apparently spoke for many. When a Jew would appear on her doorstep in the dead of night there was no question. "Naturally," she would say, "come in and come in!"

It is the writer Philip Hallie who philosophizes. When he does so, the question is straightforward and unavoidable. His story tells "how goodness happened here." Ethics, Hallie tells us, is a question of character. Here, in a sense inclusive of a wide range of theological understandings and identities, was a community of *shared* character. Hoping that under similar circumstances he and his family would do what the Chambonnais did, Hallie seeks to make this community in principle universal, yet invisible until circumstances arise in which it appears. He writes:

> It is not a community with palpable laws and a seat in space. And it is not a homogeneous community. It has atheists in it, and Jews. It is a community of ethical belief.[49]

I have meditated over these words. I find that I agree with what they say, even if I would use different language. Churches, synagogues, and other religious communities have the role of making this ethical diaspora of the Spirit visible where and as they can. Such a larger people of God has no palpable laws. It does not possess a seat in space. But it is real, and the sense of it is what faith communities, in their various ways, are called to express.

It is clear that in Le Chambon the appearance of this ethical community on the stage of history was instigated by a single Protestant congregation with the indispensable leadership of its pastor. If there was any visible sacrament or sign of this wider community of character, it was the congregation with its open door, the "beautiful gate" that led into the tiny courtyard of the presbytery, the home of Magda and André. The rest was invisible to the eye. It had to be.

Is there a more adequate account of the meaning of what happened in Le Chambon than the one Hallie offers? Does the notion of a universal ethical community call for a more explicit transcendental ground? Saving these Jews meant taking them into a network of co-recognition of human claims, of the most basic kind of symbolic intercourse, involving the recognition of a language community taking form in such a way as to disclose the Being that we represent as a human community. Or could one say that here the Spirit, the final giver of life and meaning, came to objectivity? Here was a gestalt in history, an acted-out intentional network for saving the lives of human beings. Trocmé's congregation instigated it, made the potential discernible, brought about the conditions for its realization. This was a vocation, quite simply, of disclosing the people of God in process of coming to be, the forming of a gestalt of limited duration at a given time and place where that people appeared. In that forming or shaping of life, not in the exact words chosen in the pulpit, lay the larger truth of what André Trocmé preached, and of what the Chambonnais did.

Is it justifiable to articulate this larger, yet thoroughly practical truth in theological terms? At the beginning of this book, I argued that in Scripture the people of God is understood as the historical appearing, the temporal taking-form, of God's ruling, shaping, determining, presence in human life. The people of God is always understood, of course, in the perspective of actual communities whose limited metaphors restrict the ways in which the larger reality can be understood. While recognizing that God can only be understood from some such point of reference, this argument seeks in principle to remove the metaphorical limitations: to show that what is meant involves much more. God becomes tangible, knowable, in the form of a universal human community which is the place of action of the Holy Spirit. Humanity as such is the setting for an ordering of thinking and acting corresponding to the rule of God in the universe itself.

What sort of theism does this involve? We can say only that God in this sense is *represented* in the doctrines of the different religious communities: that many diverse constructions of the meaning of God emerge, which tend to correspond to the configurations of power and imagination at work in different communal settings. The *reality* to that these constructions point is the reality which appears in the universal human community, the dwelling place of the humanity of God. Hence the truth of different representations of God is fully tested only in the public, interactive realm, not in arguments which may be made within the confines of particular communities taken alone.

In a sense one cannot go further than this. The doctrinal, liturgical, and artistic representations of God in particular religious communities are far richer than meanings for the word "God" that have public currency in our secular world. God is more compellingly *represented* imaginatively in particular communities of faith than in the public realm where such representations are *tested*, where the divine reality actually comes to *be*. In the latter realm, there may *be* no generally acceptable language for the theological meaning of the emerging community of humankind. The whole people *of* God may have no common language *for* God. That is why particular communities of faith are so important. Their God language is profound, yet incomplete. They keep open spaces in which the *question* of adequate language for God can continue to be asked.

Here, then, is the final ecclesiological criterion: how and where do the universal people of God appear in history? What is the role of communities that gather to be signs or sacraments of that appearing? Depending on its situation, a Christian body can signify such an appearing in many ways. Each of these ways involves the holding open of a particular kind of actual or metaphorical *space*: space in which the orders of this world are rendered transparent or open to the possibility of being transformed and fulfilled as instruments of the Spirit at work. So we come full circle. The space represented by St. Peter's Square, circumscribed by Bernini's permeable arcades, filled with all sorts and conditions of human beings who are in touch with other human beings who in turn are in touch with still others until the whole world, of every race, religion, and form of belief or unbelief is represented. This space becomes a metaphor of space for the Spirit to do its configuring work. Here is a representation, one of many, of the people of God in process of formation, of the reality in history that the organized churches exist to serve. In the elaboration and realization of such a perspective lies the heart of the ecclesiology needed for our time and for the future of humankind.

Notes

FOREWORD

1. See Richard J. Bernstein, *Philosophical Profiles: Essays in a Pragmatic Mode* (Philadelphia: University of Pennsylvania Press, 1986), 21ff., 45ff.

INTRODUCTION

1. The idea behind this formulation came from a conversation with Robert Bellah.
2. I am thinking of Jacques Derrida, Paul de Man, Richard Rorty, and others. See William Placher, *Unapologetic Theology: A Christian Voice in a Pluralistic Conversation* (Louisville: Westminster/John Knox Press, 1989), especially 24ff.
3. This term, made prominent by Paul Ricoeur, appears first in *The Symbolism of Evil* (Boston: Beacon Press, 1967), 352. "For the second immediacy that we seek and the second naiveté that we await are no longer accessible to us anywhere else than in a hermeneutics; we can believe only by interpreting." The notion is discussed in detail by Mark I. Wallace in his recent book, *The Second Naiveté: Barth, Ricoeur, and the New Yale Theology* (Macon, Ga.: Mercer University Press, 1990). See also my discussion in "Paul Ricoeur on Biblical Interpretation," in Ricoeur, *Essays on Biblical Interpretation*, ed. Lewis S. Mudge, (Philadelphia: Fortress Press, 1980), 6ff.
4. My use (apart from quotations in which the original usage is preserved) of such terms as "church," "the church", "the churches," "the church universal" needs to be clear. "The churches" are the visible institutions ordinarily called by this name, taken in the aggregate without reference to their differing views of the meaning of the term "church" or of other bodies' status in light of those views. Bodies holding membership in the World Council of Churches illustrate but do not exhaust the genre. By "the church" I mean the total social reality, in history and beyond, however visibly institutionalized, effected by Jesus Christ in the power of the Holy Spirit. "The church" translates the common New Testament term for the Christian movement as a whole, *to ekklesia*, which in turn translates the Hebrew *qahal*

or *qahal Yahweh*, "those belonging to God." It is what the New Testament means by "the body of Christ" and other terms. Likewise "the church" means the "the holy catholic church" as defined in the third article of the Apostles' and Nicene (Constantinopolitan) Creeds. Today this term has no exclusive referent: it cannot mean any given ecclesiastical body or group of bodies. Yet it is indispensable, carrying with it the sense that the church is intrinsically one and that it is by definition a reality of history. I make sparing use of "the church" in these pages precisely because it is so difficult to say what this reality is or where it is to be found. The usage, indeed, always implies a question, as yet unanswered, posed to "the churches." The terms "church universal" or "the church catholic" are not different from "the church" as such: these expressions merely emphasize the universality or catholicity which inheres by definition in "the church." The word "Church" (with upper case "C") is used here only when the reference is to a particular body, e.g., "The Presbyterian Church" or "The Roman Catholic Church."

5. *The Compact Oxford English Dictionary* (Oxford: Clarendon Press, 1971) affirms that ecclesiology concerns the nature of the church, but tells us that this term "now, usually" means "the science of church building and decoration." Obviously, the possibility of misunderstanding lies close at hand.

6. I am using the term "fundamental theology" in the sense given it by David Tracy in *Blessed Rage for Order* (New York: Seabury, 1975) and *The Analogical Imagination* (New York: Crossroad, 1981), but drawing somewhat different conclusions. For Tracy, the defining characteristic of fundamental (not "fundamental-*ist*") theologies of every kind is "a reasoned insistence on employing the approach and methods of some established academic discipline to explicate and adjudicate the truth-claims of the interpreted religious tradition and the truth-claims of the contemporary situation" (*Analogical Imagination*, 62). As Tracy says, the discipline employed is usually philosophy of some kind or the philosophical dimension of some other discipline. In my case, the discipline is a philosophical approach to human science or critical social theory. The feature of the human world on which philosophical attention is focused is thus the existence of traditioned communities which are experienced by their members as making transcendent reality present in shared forms of life.

My focus on this philosophical discipline and on these human phenomena calls in question Tracy's neat distinction between fundamental, systematic, and practical theology as distinguishable arenas of discourse addressed to different audiences. To say that the existence and texture of the community of faith is the primary datum for reflection is to bring the interpretation of traditional content (the task of "systematic theology") and reasoned action in the world in consequence of tradition (the subject of "practical theology") *into* fundamental theology itself. If communities of faith (which by living their traditions model the moral and spiritual unity of human consciousness) are to be met with in time and space, that fact is as important a clue to the nature of reality as the orderliness of nature or the presence of a moral imperative in the human heart.

The term "fundamental" is sometimes confused with "foundational." The latter word refers most often—and always in this book—to a philosophical position which claims to have found a perfectly certain starting point for our knowledge of reality. Descartes' aphorism, "I think, therefore I am," is the classic example of foundationalism. A fundamental theology may be built upon a foundationalist philosophical perspective, but such a theology may also be constructed on a nonfoundationalist basis. The existence of faith communities which signify the potential unity of humankind as a community of spiritual discourse requires, at the very least, a confidence in what George Steiner calls the "necessary possibility" of God. If I affirm more than this, as I do, it is on the basis of confidence that my Christian religious tradition of faith in God gives faithful expression to my experience of basic trust, or consent to being, or conviction that I am addressed not only by words but by the Word. Truth in the philosophical sense lies in a dialogical process, moving toward the realization of a global community in the Spirit. It does not refer to any "apodictic" certainty which the philosopher can offer with confidence that his or her argument rests on some alleged epistemological bedrock.

7. The term is one frequently used by the American philosopher Josiah Royce in *The Problem of Christianity* (Chicago: University of Chicago Press, 1968), cf. especially vol. 1, 172ff., 183; vol. 2, 219, 428.

8. I have come across the new book by Konrad Raiser, *Ecumenism in Transition: A Paradigm Shift in the Ecumenical Movement?* (Geneva: World Council of Churches, 1991) too late to take it properly into account. But it is plain that Raiser makes a proposal which converges in some respects (but not in others) with the argument of this book. Raiser focuses on the biblical image of "household of life" or "household of God," treating it as designating a spiritual reality more comprehensive than any existing ecclesiastical body can claim to represent. At the very least, it means the whole company of the baptized and all those whom God has called by a baptism of the Spirit. See also chap. 5, n. 44.

9. Elisabeth Schüssler Fiorenza favors the term "people of God" for similar reasons. The "people" image calls attention to the *ekklesia* as "the actual assembly of free citizens gathering for deciding their own spiritual-political affairs." Schüssler Fiorenza continues, "Since women in a patriarchal church cannot decide their

own theological-religious affairs and that of their own people—women—the *ekklesia* of women is as much a future hope as it is a reality today. Yet we have begun to gather as the *ekklesia* of women, the people of God, to claim our own religious powers, to participate fully in the decision-making process of the church, and to nurture each other as women Christians." *In Memory of Her: A Feminist Theological Reconstruction of Christian Origins* (New York: Crossroad, 1989), 344.

10. Some of the early manuscripts read, "and they will be God's peoples." The plural form underlines that for some interpreters the vision goes beyond Israel or the church as *a* people to include what is elsewhere called "the nations."

11. I have this on the testimony of colleagues who knew Haroutunian well. I have not been able to find this exact phrase in his writings, but it is fully consistent with the argument and style of his *God With Us: A Theology of Transpersonal Life* (Philadelphia: Westminster Press, 1965): "There has been much effort on the part of Christian thinkers to 'rediscover' the nature and function of the church, and the total effect of this effort has been a genuinely renewed understanding of the church as a people first and as an institution second." And further, "The church has emerged as a community with its institutions rather than as an institution for the religious benefit of the people" (48). My argument goes beyond Haroutunian's in finding the people of God also among adherents of non-Christian faiths and among persons of no organized religious tradition at all.

12. Hyung Kyung Chung, "Come Holy Spirit, Renew the Whole Creation," an introduction to the theological theme of the Seventh Assembly of the World Council of Churches, Canberra, Australia (February 8, 1991).

13. E.g., the Pope's remarks in the encyclical letter *Dominum et Vivificantem*, on "The Holy Spirit in the Life of the Church and the World," (Vatican City: Polyglot Press, 1986), 7, 92-104.

14. See Lewis S. Mudge, "An Ecumenical Vision for the Year 2000," *The Christian Century* 96 (September 19, 1979).

I. A MEDITATION IN ST. PETER'S SQUARE

1. Cf. Introduction, n.11.

2. Wolfhart Pannenberg, *The Church*, trans. Keith Crim, (Philadelphia: Westminster Press, 1983), 9ff.

3. Josiah Royce, *The Problem of Christianity* (Chicago: Henry Regnery Co, 1968), Vol. 1, 172. "The power that gives to the Christian convert the new loyalty is what Paul calls Grace. And the community to which, when grace saves him, the convert is henceforth to be loyal, we may here venture to call by a name which

we have not hitherto used. Let this name be 'The Beloved Community.' This is another name for what we before called the Universal Community. Only now the universal community will appear to us in a new light, in view of its relations to the doctrine of grace." See also Vol. 1, 173, 183, 352, 357; and vol. 2, 219, 428.

4. Base communities are by now well known. First remarked as a phenomenon of Latin American Catholicism by the Latin American Bishops' Conference at Puebla, Mexico, in 1979, these "Christian communities of the common people" are an ecclesial expression of the "preferential option for the poor" already expressed at the Bishops' Conference in Medellin in 1968. The Puebla meeting characterized them as "a Church that is trying to incarnate itself in the ranks of the common people on our continent, and that therefore arises out of their response in faith to the Lord" (para. 263), quoted in Sergio Torres and John Eagleson, eds., *The Challenge of Basic Christian Communities*, (Maryknoll, N.Y.: Orbis Books, 1981). Somewhat similar communities have now appeared in other parts of the world, but those of Latin American Catholicism remain the paradigm case.

5. Leonardo Boff, *Ecclesiogenesis* (Maryknoll, N.Y.: Orbis Books, 1986).

6. Wayne A. Meeks, *The Moral World of the First Christians* (Philadelphia: Westminster Press, 1986), writes, "If we were to describe John's prophecy in conventional literary terms . . . we would say that he has made his description of the heavenly reality a parody on the power and ceremony of Rome. The effect on the reader, however, is just the contrary: Rome is presented as a parody of heaven. Its pomp is sham, its power a diabolical artifice, its power a bold front concealing its predestined destruction" (p. 145).

7. Walter Wink, *Unmasking the Powers: The Invisible Forces that Determine Human Existence* (Philadelphia: Fortress Press, 1986), 97.

8. Ibid.

9. Ibid., 97-98.

10. Paul Minear, *Images of the Church in the New Testament*, (Philadelphia: Westminster Press, 1960).

11. Avery Dulles, *Models of the Church*, (New York: Doubleday Image Books, 1978).

12. Paul Ricoeur, *The Rule of Metaphor* (Toronto: University of Toronto Press, 1977).

13. Minear, *Images of the Church*, 24.

14. Robert Bellah, *The Broken Covenant* (New York: Seabury, 1975).

15. *Lumen Gentium* in *The Documents of Vatican II*, ed. Walter M. Abbott, S.J. (New York: Guild Press, American Press, Association Press, 1966), 9ff.

16. *Gaudium et Spes* in *The Documents of Vatican II*, 199ff.

17. George A. Lindbeck, *The Future of Catholic Theology: Vatican II—Catalyst for Change* (Philadelphia: Fortress Press, 1970), 34ff.

18. Dulles, *Models of the Church*, 57.

19. Paul Lakeland, *Theology and Critical Theory: The Discourse of the Church* (Nashville: Abingdon Press, 1990), 118.

20. *Lumen Gentium*, 14ff. and n.1, 14.

21. Ibid., 23. The phrase "subsists in" (Latin *subsistit in*) has been the subject of much debate. It appears that the Council fathers desired a softer word than *est*, i.e."is," to describe the relation between the church founded by Christ and confessed in the creeds and the Roman Catholic Church, "constituted and organized in the world as a society." The meaning of *subsistit in* must be inferred from the many other references to the work of grace outside the organized body of Roman Catholicism, including the material concerning the "people of God" discussed here and the treatment of other ecclesial bodies in the "Decree on Ecumenism." There seems little to be gained from research into the meaning of the Latin as such. Cardinal Ratzinger is said to have argued that the form *subsistit* comes from the Latin *substans*, the root from which we derive the philosophical term "substance." If this is true we have something very close to a Latin version of *homoousios*, "of one substance with," applied now to ecclesiology rather than to the relation between the first and second Persons of the Trinity. But I think this is both a philological and a theological error. *Subsistit in* will mean whatever the political and theological relationships at any given time between Roman Catholicism and other Christian bodies allow it to mean.

22. Ibid., 24ff.

23. Ibid.

24. Ibid., 33, n.51.

25. Ibid., 29.

26. Ibid., 32.

27. Ibid., 238.

28. Ibid., 209.

29. Ibid., 15.

30. Lindbeck, *Future of Catholic Theology*, 34.

31. *Gaudium et Spes*, 209.

32. The German word *Gestalt*, meaning a "totality" or a "whole," is a key term in Peter Hodgson's *God in History: Shapes of*

Freedom (Nashville: Abingdon Press, 1989), *passim*. I will make further reference to Hodgson's argument, particularly in chapters 4 and 6.

33. Dietrich Bonhoeffer, *The Communion of Saints: A Dogmatic Inquiry into the Sociology of the Church* (New York: Harper and Row, 1963), 134, 146-47.

34. I owe this perception to Peter Hodgson, *God in History*, 209. "God was 'incarnate', not in the physical nature of Jesus as such, but in the gestalt that coalesced both in and around his person—with which his person did in some sense become identical, and by which, after his death, he took on a new, communal identity."

II. AN UNRAVELING OF ASSUMPTIONS

1. 1. I am indebted in my discussion of Ernst Troeltsch to Benjamin Reist, *Toward a Theology of Involvement: The Thought of Ernst Troeltsch* (Philadelphia: Westminster Press, 1966).

2. Ernst Troeltsch, *The Social Teaching of the Christian Churches*, trans. Olive Wyon, 2 vols. (London: George Allen & Unwin, 1931).

3. Ibid., 1012.

4. Ibid.

5. Dawn DeVries has written a dissertation, *Christus Praesens: Word and History in the Preaching of John Calvin and Friedrich Schleiermacher* (University of Chicago, 1992), as yet unpublished, which studies the hermeneutical and homiletic practices of the two theologians. She finds that these two figures, historically separated by the Enlightenment, "demythologize" biblical material for illustrative purposes in remarkably similar ways. This is a finding of interest in the light of Troeltsch's well-known distinction between classical Protestantism, which he regarded as a two-centuries-long late flowering of the Middle Ages and modern post-Enlightenment Protestantism. See also Brian Gerrish, *The Old Protestantism and the New* (Chicago: University of Chicago Press, 1982).

6. Troeltsch writes, "The ecclesiastical institutions maintain themselves by their own historic weight, and, once they have been created, they can serve other ends than those for which they were originally constructed." *Social Teaching*, 1010.

7. Edward Farley, *Ecclesial Reflection: An Anatomy of Theological Method* (Philadelphia: Fortress Press 1982), 165-68 *et passim*.

8. Troeltsch, *Social Teaching*, 992.

9. Ibid., 796.

10. Ibid., 796-97.

11. See Robert N. Bellah, "Civil Religion in America" in his *Beyond Belief: Essays on Religion in a Post-Traditional World* (New York: Harper & Row, 1970), 168ff.

12. Thomas Luckmann, *The Invisible Religion: The Problem of Religion in Modern Society* (New York: Macmillan, 1967), 103ff.

13. Robert Bellah, *Habits of the Heart* (Berkeley: University of California Press, 1985).

14. Troeltsch, *Social Teaching*, 992.

15. Hans Georg Drescher, "Ernst Troeltsch's Intellectual Development," in John Powell Clayton, ed., *Ernst Troeltsch and the Future of Theology, (Cambridge: Cambridge University Press, 1976), 24.*

16. Ernst Troeltsch, *Der Historismus und Seine Probleme*, Gesammelte Schriften, Bd. III (Tübingen: Verlag von J.C.B. Mohr (Paul Siebeck), 1912-1925).

17. Peter C. Hodgson, *God in History: Shapes of Freedom* (Nashville: Abingdon Press, 1989), 48.

18. By tradition, as Edward Shils has most recently shown in *Tradition* (Chicago: University of Chicago Press, 1981), is meant both the essential content of (in this case) a religious culture, consisting both of classical documents and of classical interpretations of those documents. Tradition may be transmitted in linguistic form, either written or oral, or it may be transmitted as a body of largely unspoken custom. Either way, it may assume a variety of literary and active forms. A liturgy such as *The Book of Common Prayer*, for example, contains a significant quantity of material from Scripture as well as more recent material having classical status. It is in itself an authoritative working interpretation of that material, containing rubrics regulating the usage of the material, and is the center of a living stream of ritual and moral practice. Different religious bodies relate to their traditions in different ways and entertain different theories *about* tradition, all of which makes this field of inquiry highly complex. See also Albert C. Outler, *The Christian Tradition and the Unity We Seek* (New York: Oxford University Press, 1957).

19. Farley, *Ecclesial Reflection*. The discussion that follows is substantially informed by Farley's presentation on pages 101ff. Here and elsewhere my argument also draws upon Ludwig Wittgenstein's notion that language, with its inherent "grammar" or "logic", dwells in a certain "form of life." Farley does not connect his term "logic of triumph" with Wittgenstein, but the logic of doing so seems irresistible. As the reader will see, the present book turns conceptually on the notion that every form of life the gospel has taken on in the world has its own logic of discourse, its own kind of practical reasoning or *phronesis*, its own notion

of what "makes sense." With the increasing dysfunctionality of traditional ecclesial forms of life, the "sense" they make becomes dysfunctional as well.

20. Ibid., 104.

21. Ibid., 104ff.

22. In these paragraphs on Protestantism, I again follow Farley's argument, ibid., 125ff.

23. Ibid., 104.

24. Ibid., 126.

25. Ibid.

26. Ibid., 127.

27. See Hans Küng, *Infallible* (New York: Seabury, 1981), 195. (Reference in Farley, *Ecclesial Reflection*, 127).

28. *The Book of Confessions*, Presbyterian Church, U.S.A. (New York: Office of the General Assembly, 1966) sec. 5.130.

29. Farley, *Ecclesial Reflection*, 127ff.

30. It is notable that much of the latter part of Farley's *Ecclesial Reflection* is devoted to this question of "ecclesial duration." See 217-99.

31. See Rowland A. Sherrill, "The Bible in Twentieth-Century Fiction," and Edwin M. Good, "The Bible and American Music," in *The Bible and American Arts and Letters*, ed. Giles Gunn, (Chico, Calif.: Scholars Press, 1983).

32. By "civil religion" Robert Bellah means the ostensibly religious practices and language that accompany American civic rituals: presidential inaugurations, the opening of Congress, Memorial Day speeches, and the like. Whatever it is that permits phrases such as "In God We Trust" on the currency and requires references to God on public occasions, despite the principle of "separation of church and state," is civil religion. See Bellah's classic essay, "Civil Religion in America," in *Beyond Belief*.

33. I am indebted for this idea to a lecture by Professor Lawrence Welborn at McCormick Theological Seminary about 1986.

34. In a paper originally read in 1973 at the Pacific Coast Theological Society, then published in a symposium, *Pluralism and Textual Interpretation* (The Center for Hermeneutical Studies: University of California and the Graduate Theological Union, 1983).

35. Philip Hefner, "Theology in the Context of Science, Liberation, and Christian Tradition," in William Schweiker and Per Anderson, eds., *Worldviews and Warrants: Plurality and Authority in Theology*, (Lanham, Md.: University Press of America, 1987), 35.

36. Ibid., 34.

37. Ibid., 36.

38. I am grateful to my former colleague John Burkhart at McCormick Theological Seminary for having heard me out on this subject and having put the issue thus succinctly.

39. Langdon Gilkey, "Dissolution and Reconstruction in Theology," *The Christian Century*, 82, (February 3, 1965): 135ff. "What we had thought was solid earth has turned out to be shifting ice—and in recent years as the weather has grown steadily warmer some of us have in horror found ourselves staring down into rushing depths of dark water."

40. Van A. Harvey, *The Historian and the Believer*, (New York: Macmillan, 1965).

41. William A. Silva, *The Expression of Neo-Orthodoxy in American Protestantism*, Ph. D. dissertation, 1988, Department of Religious Studies, Yale University (Ann Arbor: University Microfilms, ADG 90-09030). Silva argues that elements of neo-orthodox theology became part of the theological consensus of mainline American Protestantism in the 1950s, but ambivalence concerning the understanding of divine revelation led to continuing tensions within the theological community, while neo-orthodoxy's inaccessibility to many outside that community narrowed its field of influence.

42. Van A. Harvey, "The Alienated Theologian," in Robert A. Evans, ed., *The Future of Philosophical Theology* (Philadelphia: Westminster Press, 1971), 113ff.

43. Sharon Welch, *Communities of Resistance and Solidarity: A Feminist Theology of Liberation* (Maryknoll, N.Y.: Orbis Books, 1985), 10.

44. Ibid., 11ff.

45. See Calvin O. Schrag, *Radical Reflection and the Origin of the Human Sciences* (West Lafayette, Ind.: Purdue University Press, 1980), 1ff. Schrag quotes testimony to this effect from Max Scheler, Ernst Cassirer, Georges Gusdorf, and Paul Ricoeur. Ricoeur writes, "The sciences of man are dispersed into separate disciplines and literally do not know what they are talking about." See "The Antinomy of Human Reality and the Problem of Philosophical Anthropology" in *Readings in Existential Phenomenology*, ed. N. Lawrence and D. O'Connor (Englewood Cliffs: Prentice-Hall, 1967), 390.

46. Michel Foucault, *Power/Knowledge: Selected Interviews and Other Writings*, ed. Colin Gordon, (New York: Pantheon Books, 1980), 81.

47. See Thomas J. Oden, *Agenda for Theology* (San Francisco: Harper and Row, 1979) and Stanley Hauerwas and William Willimon, *Resident Aliens: Life in the Christian Colony* (Nashville: Abingdon Press, 1989).

48. See Gordon Kaufman, *The Theological Imagination: Constructing the Concept of God* (Philadelphia: Westminster Press, 1981).

49. See David Tracy, *The Analogical Imagination: Christian Theology and the Culture of Pluralism* (New York: Crossroad, 1981).

50. See Richard Rorty, *Consequences of Pragmatism: Essays* (Minneapolis: University of Minnesota Press, 1982).

51. Alasdair MacIntyre, *After Virtue*, (Notre Dame, Ind.: University of Notre Dame Press, 1981).

52. Ibid., 244f.

53. In fact it is plain that MacIntyre in his more recent volume, *Whose Justice? Which Rationality?* (Notre Dame, Ind.: University of Notre Dame Press, 1988), has taken the logical step, transferring his affections from St. Benedict to St. Thomas Aquinas.

54. Margaret R. Miles, "Imitation of Christ: Is It Possible in the Twentieth Century?" *The Princeton Seminary Bulletin*, 10, New Series (1989), 9.

55. Ibid.

56. See Lewis S. Mudge, *The Crumbling Walls* (Philadelphia: Westminster Press, 1970), 67ff., *et passim*.

57. See James F. Hopewell, *Congregation: Stories and Structures* (Philadelphia: Fortress Press, 1987).

58. Harvey Cox has given an account of this episode in *The Silencing of Leonardo Boff: The Vatican and the Future of World Christianity* (Oak Park: Meyer Stone Books, 1988).

III. TOWARD A HERMENEUTIC FOR ECCLESIOGENESIS

1. My account of the August 28, 1963, "March on Washington" is based on personal experience.

2. In some ways, the "March on Washington" can be seen as the mirror image of the scene in St. Peter's Square. In Rome, many spiritual journeys and identities are daily gathered under the aegis of a particular ecclesiastical body. In Washington, many ecclesiastical bodies were brought together under the aegis of a particular spiritual journey.

3. The reference to Hegel is obvious, but our dependence on this philosopher should be kept within limits. The distinguished historian of ideas, John Herman Randall, once said that Hegel's great contribution to Western thought is this notion that spirit can become "objective." By "objective spirit" Hegel meant the historic monuments and classics of human civilization seen as products of the process by which consciousness dialectically evolves in

a dance of intersubjectivity which generates self-knowledge, the means of expressing it, shared symbols, a social will, and finally the society's enduring cultural expressions of its self-understanding: literature, art, music, architecture, the state. Hegel seeks to portray a realm of law or *Recht* in which freedom and reason are upheld by established social arrangements. Spirit has become objective. The most lucid exposition I know of Hegel's understanding of "spirit" and objective spirit is in J. N. Findlay, *The Philosophy of Hegel: An Introduction and Re-examination* (New York: Collier Books, 1958), especially 313ff. My purpose here is not to expound Hegel's views as such. The philosopher might or might not recognize himself in these paragraphs. My point is only to give credit for a basic idea where credit is due, and then to adapt the material for my own purposes. Hegel can plausibly be seen as the inventor both of pragmatism and the sociology of knowledge. His notion of the human realm as essentially and intrinsically a spiritual dialectic of life-possibilities gives us something suggestive and useful. His way of seeing Christian faith as saying ritually and symbolically what the philosopher seeks to grasp conceptually is also highly suggestive. As the sequel will show, I have also learned from Peter Hodgson's portrayal of Hegel's notion of *Gestalt*, or life-configuration, as developed in the *Phenomenology of Spirit*, trans. A. V. Miller, (Oxford: Clarendon Press, 1977), 104-107, 264-65, 410-16. References in Peter C. Hodgson, *God in History: Shapes of Freedom* (Nashville: Abingdon Press, 1989), 274.

4. Alexandre Kojève, *Introduction to the Reading of Hegel*, ed. Allan Bloom, trans. James H. Nichols, Jr., (New York: Basic Books, 1969), 3ff., *et passim*.

5. Benedict de (Baruch) Spinoza, *Ethics* (London: Oxford University Press, 1923), Pt. III, Prop. VII, 144. See also the discussion in Stuart Hampshire, *Spinoza* (Harmondsworth, England: Penguin Books, 1951), 76ff.

6. Paul Ricoeur's "effort to exist and desire to be," unlike the formulations of existentialists driven by despair, or suffering the dread and anguish of existence, stems from a fundamental affirmation of life as the gift of grace. He identifies his passion to exist with faith in the meaningfulness of existence. I owe this helpful formulation of what many have said less well to Kevin J. Vanhoozer, *Biblical Narrative in the Philosophy of Paul Ricoeur: A Study in Hermeneutics and Theology* (New York: Cambridge University Press, 1990), 6. For the phrase itself, see Ricoeur, *Freud and Philosophy* (New Haven: Yale University Press, 1970), 46.

7. In the classical philosophical tradition, what is *present* denotes what really exists, as opposed to that which is merely imagined. In Plato, for example, imagination brings to mind absent or non-existent things. A similar position is found in Jean-Paul Sartre.

My use of the term "presence" implies that symbolizations of reality held in being by forms of the imagination which are in power, arbitrary though they may be, are to be taken as interpretative manifestations of being, as recreations by the creative imagination of what *is*. Such interpretations of reality powerfully influence our behavior and self-understanding. They make something "present" in a sense different from that envisioned in Plato. In this, as in other ways, I take my departure from the thought of Paul Ricoeur, for whom the imagination both "invents" and "discovers" something about reality itself. Again, my formulation follows that of Kevin J. Vanhoozer, *Biblical Narrative*, 9-10. This process of invention and discovery becomes more experientially, if not metaphysically, real when certain works of the imagination play dominating roles in some social or cultural synthesis. A helpful discussion of theological meanings of "presence" can be found in Peter Hodgson, *Jesus—Word and Presence: An Essay in Christology* (Philadelphia: Fortress Press, 1971). Hodgson writes in the context of the "absence of God" theologies of the sixties and of the earlier work of Jürgen Moltmann and Wolfhart Pannenberg, theologians of hope and of the presence of the future God. For Hodgson, God is present, if at all, by means of word. "If God's presence is to be experienced afresh, then what is required is a rebirth of language" (p. 23). The word "God" in fact means "the promise of presence:" this on the strength of von Rad's translation of Exod. 3:14 as "I will be there." Hodgson's 1971 book, of course, predates deconstructionism's assault on the tie between language and being, an attack which demands the kind of comprehensive reply found in George Steiner's *Real Presences*. Hodgson's book, read today, cries out for a treatment of human spirit and Holy Spirit of the sort supplied in his more recent work *God in History*. I have tried to draw all this together with full documentation in chapter 4.

8. The term "thick description" (originated, it seems, by Gilbert Ryle) has been taken over by the anthropologist Clifford Geertz, who means by it a focus on the richness and intricacy of human signification in the world of action. Geertz describes Moroccan sheep thefts, Balinese cockfights, a Javanese funeral, so as to expose the whole range of layers of meaning involved in these activities. He writes, "Whatever, or whenever, symbol systems 'in their own terms' may be, we gain empirical access to them by inspecting events, not by arranging abstracted entities into unified patterns." See Geertz, "Thick Description: Toward an Interpretive Theory of Culture," in *The Interpretation of Cultures* (New York: Basic Books, 1973), 17.

9. George Herbert Mead, *Mind, Self, and Society* (Chicago: University of Chicago Press, 1934), 13ff., 51ff., 363ff. I am indebted to a discussion of Mead in Gibson Winter, *Elements for a Social Ethic* (New York: Macmillan, 1966), 17ff., 85ff.

10. See Robert S. Corrington, *The Community of Interpreters* (Macon, Ga.: Mercer University Press, 1987), 1-29.

11. Roland Barthes, *Systeme de la Mode* (Paris: Editions du Seuil, 1967) and *Mythologiques* (Paris: Editions du Seuil, 1957).

12. Ludwig Wittgenstein, *Philosophical Investigations* (Oxford: Blackwell, 1956), sects. 248, 373, 664, *et passim*. I owe these references to Anthony Thiselton, *The Two Horizons: New Testament Hermeneutics and Philosophical Description with Special Reference to Heidegger, Bultmann, Gadamer, and Wittgenstein* (Grand Rapids, Mich.: William B. Eerdmans, 1980), 386-87.

13. Paul Ricoeur, *The Rule of Metaphor* (Toronto: University of Toronto Press, 1977), especially 65ff.

14. George Lakoff and Mark Johnson, *Metaphors We Live By* (Chicago: University of Chicago Press, 1980), especially 3-9.

15. Ibid., 4.

16. Ibid., 5.

17. Paul Ricoeur, "The Model of the Text: Meaningful Action Considered as a Text," in John B. Thompson, ed., *Paul Ricoeur: Hermeneutics and the Human Sciences*, (Cambridge: Cambridge University Press, 1981), 197ff. I am aware that Ricoeur's proposal to conceive human action on a textual model has received significant criticism. See, for example, John B. Thompson, *Critical Hermeneutics: A Study in the Thought of Paul Ricoeur and Jürgen Habermas* (Cambridge: Cambridge University Press, 1981), 125ff. Thompson believes that Ricoeur, like Peter Winch, is guilty of "illegitimate generalization from the linguistic sphere." Social circumstances and institutional contexts, Thompson thinks, have a reality of their own which resists reduction to a purely linguistic model.

18. The concept of "communicative action" will be discussed at greater length in chapter 6.

19. 'The true malice of man appears," Ricoeur writes, "only in the state and in the church, as institutions of gathering together, or recapitulation, of totalization." "Freedom in the Light of Hope" in *The Conflict of Interpretations* (Evanston: Northwestern University Press, 1974), 423.

20. John Dominic Crossan, ed., "Paul Ricoeur on Biblical Hermeneutics," *Semeia* 4 (Missoula: Scholars Press, 1975), 82, 104.

21. John Dominic Crossan, *In Parables: The Challenge of the Historical Jesus* (San Francisco: Harper and Row, 1985).

22. Two recent works which draw significantly on human science insights serve to illustrate the approach to faith-community formation we have in mind. In *Congregation: Stories and Structures* (Philadelphia: Fortress Press, 1987), James Hopewell

recommends an approach to local ecclesial gatherings which resembles that of the cultural anthropologist who comes upon a previously unknown tribe and who seeks to discern the nature of that tribe's coherence and self-understanding. Hopewell, along with many others today, foreswears structural-functional approaches to try to discern how the congregation gathers around and embodies the unique significations inherent in its stories, its relationships, its architectural and neighborhood-discerning mapping of meanings. Hopewell's approach is an extension of the science of ethnography. It is ethnographic in the sense that it studies the sense-making elements in the life of the *ethnos*, the "people." Hopewell tries to read the messages embodied in the tales church members tell and in the ways they conduct their common life.

Robert Schreiter's equally important book, *Constructing Local Theologies* (Maryknoll, N.Y.: Orbis Books, 1985), does something similar with its emphasis on signification: the "semiotic" study of the way in which the world with its objects becomes a field of "signs" whose usages come to be controlled by "codes" which are in turn gathered around significant metaphors and finally incorporated in characteristic narratives. Schreiter is less interested in the study of actual ecclesial gatherings and more concerned to ask how theology can actually be pursued in the local or congregational mode. But he produces a result compatible with Hopewell's, if in a somewhat different vocabulary. Schreiter takes his inspiration from theorists like Roland Barthes and Umberto Eco. The world and its objects are not just there: they signify. Human life in society is a journey through a realm of meanings ready to be activated by our touch.

23. As one might expect, the words "I believe in" with reference to "the holy catholic church" have been controversial. The phrase is not found in the Nicene Creed of 325 or in the Niceno-Constantinopolitan Creed of 381. In the Apostles' Creed the "in" is not repeated before "holy catholic church." The earliest texts of the Apostles' Creed, in fact, do not mention the church at all. Peter Hodgson, in his note on this subject in *Revisioning the Church: Ecclesial Freedom in the New Paradigm* (Philadelphia: Fortress Press, 1988), 113, writes, "It appears, then, that when reference to the church was added to the creeds, the church was first viewed as an instrumentality of belief, the place where the Spirit is at work; then it was to be 'believed' . . . but not 'believed in' in the sense that God is to be 'believed in.'"

24. H. Richard Niebuhr, *Christ and Culture* (New York: Harper Torchbooks, 1951).

25. Ibid., 244.

26. Cf. Sang Hyun Lee, *The Philosophical Theology of Jonathan Edwards* (Princeton: Princeton University Press, 1988).

27. Edward Farley, *Theologia* (Philadelphia: Fortress Press, 1983), 31, 35-36, 55.

28. For references to Aristotle, see Hans-Georg Gadamer, *Truth and Method* (London: Sheed and Ward, 1975), 19-29. See also Gadamer, "The Power of Reason," *Man and World*, III, 1970, 5-15. References in Thistleton, *Two Horizons*, 294ff.

29. Gadamer is discussing the Italian philosopher Vico, who argued the case for the importance of practical reasoning, especially attacking Descartes for his mathematization of reality and lack of a sense of history. See *Truth and Method*, 22-23.

30. This view is derived from points made by Wittgenstein in *Philosophical Investigations*. I owe this reference and this application of Wittgenstein's views to theological language to Thiselton, *Two Horizons*, 381ff.

IV. REAL PRESENCE

1. Wolfhart Pannenberg, *The Church*, (Philadelphia: Westminster Press, 1983), 157ff.

2. Van A. Harvey, *The Historian and the Believer*, (New York: Macmillan, 1966).

3. Edward Farley, *Ecclesial Man: A Social Phenomenology of Faith and Reality* (Philadelphia: Fortress Press, 1975), 6.

4. Ibid.

5. Calvin Schrag, *Radical Reflection and the Origin of the Human Sciences* (West Lafayette, Ind.: Purdue University Press, 1980), xi.

6. Ibid., 7.

7. Edmund Husserl, *The Crisis of the European Sciences and Transcendental Phenomenology*, ed. Don Ihde, (Evanston: Northwestern University Press, 1970).

8. Schrag, *Radical Reflection*, 15.

9. Michel Foucault, *Power/Knowledge: Selected Interviews and Other Writings*, ed. Colin Gordon (New York: Pantheon Books, 1980), 81ff.

10. The term is derived from the French scholarly journal *Annales* in which many of the key methodological statements of this perspective have appeared. The approach in question is both comprehensive of very wide ranges of data and given to exhaustive description of the details of everyday life. See Fernand Braudel, *The Mediterranean and the Mediterranean World in the Age of Philip II* (New York: Harper and Row, 1975), and *The Structures of Everyday Life: The Limits of the Possible* (New York: Harper and Row, 1981).

11. Emmanuel LeRoy Ladurie, *Montaillou: The Promised Land of Error* (New York: Random House, 1979).

12. Sharon Welch, *Communities of Resistance and Solidarity: A Feminist Theology of Liberation* (Maryknoll, N.Y.: Orbis Books, 1985).

13. Ibid., 7.

14. I have been informed in my formulation by the typology proposed by the sociologist, Guy E. Swanson. In *Religion and Regime* (Ann Arbor: University of Michigan Press, 1967), Swanson studied the relations between theological constructs and political systems in some forty-one independent political units in Europe at the time of the Reformation. His purpose was to discover correlations, if any exist, between the character of the regimes by which these societies were governed and the theological patterns connected with their "Reformation settlements," when decisions were made in each territory either to maintain allegiance with Rome or to embrace some form of Protestantism. See my treatment of Swanson's work in *The Crumbling Walls* (Philadelphia: Westminster Press, 1970), 95ff.

Swanson classified "religions" and "regimes" in terms of the degree to which they saw governing power as "immanent" in the institutions and forms of imagination to which this power was related. A high degree of immanence meant that institutions and symbols were virtually identified with the power beyond them and devoid of any power of their own. Politically, a highly immanental regime would be one in which every social institution was conceived a direct expression of the ruler's personality or charisma. Religiously, an immanental system would be one in which divine power was considered to inhere directly in religious objects, persons, or symbols.

"Religions" and "regimes" in Swanson's classification are less immanental as the distance grows greater between the sources of ultimate authority and the visible instruments related to them. Politically, a regime with a low degree of immanence would be one in which political decisions were made through the interaction of separate organized power interests, none of them identified with the regime as a whole. Confidence would be placed in the rationality of the interactive process designed to bring sufficient agreement out of conflict to make social decisions possible. The ultimate sovereignty would not be considered inherent in any political person, institution, or symbol, but would be thought somehow to transcend all these instrumentalities absolutely. Religiously, a system with a low degree of immanence would be one in which no ecclesiastical institution or organization, or any religious personality or symbol, would be even remotely identified with the divine authority. Considerable confidence might be placed in the logic of the religious system or polity. But God would be felt to transcend all this absolutely. Swanson coined the term "heterarchic" to refer to regimes and religions of this sort. Between the "immanental" type and the "heterarchic" type he distinguished a series of intermediate possibilities.

Swanson's work has drawn criticism, mainly from sociologists and historians who find that his specific descriptions of religion and regime in particular European political units leave something to be desired. As so often happens, an attractive theory falls short of accounting for many details in the field of evidence it is intended to deal with. In my judgment Swanson's typology is at least as illuminating and at least as close to the facts as Max Weber's proposed linkage between Calvinism and capitalism. Indeed Swanson has no need to postulate inner states such as "salvation anxiety," but simply makes the point, as I would put it, that both political and theological constructs in any society draw upon the same images, symbols, metaphors, and texts.

15. Thomas D. Parker, "The Political Meaning of the Doctrine of the Trinity: Some Theses," in *The Journal of Religion*, Vol. 60, No. 2, April, 1980, 169.

16. *City of God*, trans. Gerald G. Walsh, S.J., and Daniel J. Honan, (New York: Fathers of the Church, Inc., 1954) Book XXII, Ch. 30, 511.

17. See chap. 1, n.21.

18. *Institutes of the Christian Religion*, ed. John T. McNeill, trans. Ford Lewis Battles, *The Library of Christian Classics*, (London: SCM Press, 1960), Vol. XXI, Book IV, Ch. I, para. 9, 102-103.

19. Ibid., Book IV, Ch. I, para. 9, 102-103.

20. I trace this phrase to a lecture on Edwards by Prof. Thomas Shafer at McCormick Theological Seminary about 1982.

21. George Lindbeck, *The Nature of Doctrine: Religion and Theology in a Postliberal Age* (Philadelphia: Westminster Press, 1984).

22. Ibid., 17-18.

23. Actually there are four positions named in Lindbeck's argument. In addition to those named he speaks of an approach which combines the "cognitively propositional" with the "experiential-expressive." This hybrid approach is favored by "ecumenically inclined Roman Catholics" such as Bernard Lonergan and Karl Rahner. See p. 16.

24. Review article on *The Nature of Doctrine*, in *The Journal of Religion*, 68, (January 1988), 88ff.

25. See, for example, David Tracy, "Lindbeck's New Program for Theology: A Reflection," *The Thomist* 49 (July 1985), 460ff.

26. George Steiner, *Real Presences* (Chicago: The University of Chicago Press, 1989).

27. Ibid., 3.

28. Ibid., 4.

29. Northrop Frye, *The Great Code: The Bible and Literature* (New York: Harcourt Brace Jovanovich, 1982).

30. Peter C. Hodgson, *God in History: Shapes of Freedom* (Nashville: Abingdon Press, 1989), 37.

31. See Isaiah Berlin, *The Crooked Timber of Humanity: Chapters in the History of Ideas* (New York: Alfred F. Knopf, 1990). Berlin's title comes from Immanuel Kant: "Out of timber so crooked as that from which man is made nothing entirely straight can be built."

32. The term "appresentation" as I use it here derives from Edmund Husserl, in whose thought it refers to that which must accompany what is directly present to us in order to complete the unity we see in a given object of perception: the unity of meaning needed to identify that object as what it is. I can only see part of a red ball or a blue cube at any given time, but this is generally enough to permit me to identify what I see. The sides, back, and interior of the object presented to perception are appresented, i.e., somehow implied in the identity I bestow upon the object I see. Without what is appresented, the object is not what it is in its totality: it is not this rather than that. For Husserl, perception always involves a conferral of meaning on the object perceived. Hence in every perception there are features presented, and other (seemingly by inference) appresented. It would appear to follow that those conceptions needed to grasp the totality of an object perceived, as well as that totality of the context or background which makes it what it is, can in the Kantian sense be called "regulative ideas." Husserl goes on to apply a version of his theory of appresentation to the problem of other minds. We move from perception of another person's speech and action to the inference (or something very like an inference) that we confront an interior life, a consciousness, analogous to our own but not given to our perception as such. See Edmund Husserl, *Cartesian Meditations: An Introduction to Phenomenology* (The Hague: Martinus Nijhoff, 1970), especially 108ff. See also Alfred Schutz, *Collected Papers: I. The Problem of Social Reality* (The Hague: Martinus Nijhoff, 1971), 331ff., 347ff.

Edward Farley has taken up Husserl's notion in *Ecclesial Man*, 194-205, 215-34. Farley argues that "the intersubjectivities of a determinate social world" (p. 203) carry with them certain appresented realities. From realities directly apprehended "in conjunction with the redemptive modification and intersubjective ecclesial shaping of consciousness" (p. 217) we meet the appresentation of an historical redeemer, of the cosmos as creation, and finally of transcendent reality itself. My argument in these pages is indebted to Farley's presentation.

33. Can Lindbeck's own theory be understood philosophically in the Kantian sense? If Lindbeck is a Kantian, he must mean that doctrines are principles which direct us to look upon connection or coherence in the churches' world of understanding and action *as if* it originated in some necessary cause or condition, some otherwise unattainable truth about the world, formulated in the doctrine. Doctrine would thus preside regulatively, but not constitutively, over a realm of acted-out sense. Lindbeck would be thinking of doctrines in the way Kant understands "transcendental ideas" which function as "regulative principles." Lindbeck does not in fact say this. But may it not be plausible to treat the "sense of a people" of God as a transcendental idea in its own right—a way of referring to the unity of humankind as God's dwelling place on earth—which functions as a "regulative principle" for ecclesiology? That is the direction of my argument in this book.

34. Kant begins to develop the notion of a "regulative principle" or "regulative idea" in Section 8 of "The Antinomy of Pure Reason" which deals with "the cosmological principle of totality." All appearances or phenomena we may encounter in this world are conditioned; that is, their existence depends on something else which is itself dependent on a prior condition. There is thus a series of conditions which, so far as our inherently limited knowledge is concerned, form an infinite regress. A regulative principle is a rule which prescribes this regress in the series of conditions of any given phenomenon and in doing so forbids the regress to close by treating anything at which it may arrive as absolutely unconditioned. This is a "regulative" rather than a "constitutive" principle in accord with which we would know the absolute totality of the series of conditions. But there is no such "constitutive" cosmological principle. The absolutely unconditioned is not to be met with in experience. We can form a concept of the cosmic whole, but we cannot "intuit" it, i.e., have it in empirical experience. I cannot say anything about the world as a whole. I can only state the "rule" which determines how experience of the world is to be obtained and extended. See Immanuel Kant, *Critique of Pure Reason,* trans. Norman Kemp Smith, (London: Macmillan, 1950), 210–11, 258, 450ff., 455ff., 481, 486, 515ff., 533, 535, 546ff., 550ff., 554ff., 564ff.

35. Richardson, for example, argues in *The Doctrine of the Trinity* (New York: Abingdon Press, 1958) that the Trinity is a flawed formulation which nonetheless wrestles with a problem which must be solved somehow. How can God be both transcendent and immanent? The three terms, "Father", "Son" and "Holy Spirit" together express doxologically the way God is known in the history of salvation. But the combination is arbitrary and artificial. "Father" and "Son" represent the realms of transcendence and immanence, while "Holy Spirit" brings the two

realms together in a different frame of reference which was never properly worked out in early Christian thought and has not been to this day. The ancient solution substituted one paradox for another. The problem became to explain how God can be both three and one. Richardson asks us to name the paradox of transcendence and immanence for what it is, retaining the historic symbols for use in worship.

36. Parker, "The Political Meaning of the Doctrine of the Trinity" 173–74.
37. Ibid., 174 (italics added).
38. The God "who loves in freedom" is an expression in Barth's *Church Dogmatics* which has been taken over as a watchword in Hodgson's *God in History*.
39. Karl Barth, *The Humanity of God* (Richmond, Va.: John Knox Press, 1960), 45–46 (italics in the original).
40. Karl Rahner, *The Doctrine of the Trinity* (New York: Seabury, 1974).
40. Jürgen Moltmann, *The Crucified God* (New York: Harper & Row, 1979).
42. Eberhard Jüngel, *The Doctrine of the Trinity* (Grand Rapids: Wm B. Eerdmans, 1976).
43. Quoted in Hodgson, *God in History*, 100.
44. Ibid., 52.
45. Ibid., 106.
46. Ibid., 107.
47. Michael Welker, "The Holy Spirit," trans. John Hoffmeyer, *Theology Today*, 46 (April 1989): 5–20. I am indebted to a paper by Gregory Cootsona for calling my attention to this article.
48. Ibid., 7.
49. Ibid., 11 (italics in the original).
50. Ibid., 14.
51. Ibid., 15.
52. Ibid.
53. Ibid., 16.
54. Ibid.
55. Ibid.
56. Ibid., 17.
57. Ibid.
58. Ibid., 19.
59. Ibid.

60. Ibid., 20.

61. See Karl Barth, *Church Dogmatics*, II, 2 (Edinburgh: T & T Clark, 1957), 3ff., 195ff., 306ff.

62. Joseph Haroutunian, *God With Us: A Theology of Transpersonal Life* (Philadelphia: Westminster Press, 1965).

V. REFRAMING THE NOTION OF CATHOLICITY

1. Vincent, a pupil of the semi-Pelagian John Cassian, could have had little idea of the echo his words would gain down the ages. His purpose was evidently to defend the popular status quo in matters of belief against the seeming novelty of St. Augustine's radical doctrine of grace. But it was the Augustinian view that gained catholic status as that officially believed "quod semper, quod ubique, quod ab omnibus." Vicent of Lérins, "Commonitorium Primum" in J.P. Migne, *Patrologia Latina* (Paris, 1846), vol. 50, col. 640.

2. *Baptism, Eucharist, and Ministry*, the Lima Report, Faith and Order Document No. 111 (Geneva: World Council of Churches, 1982).

3. Vincent of Lerins, "Commonitorium Primum," col. 640.

4. Commission on Faith and Order, World Council of Churches, Zagorsk, 1973, in Geiko Müller-Fahrenholz, *Unity in Today's World* (Geneva: World Council of Churches, 1978), 85.

5. The most recent version of this study was edited by the Faith and Order Unity and Renewal Steering Group and advisers meeting in Jamaica, January 1990. This text rests upon a version reviewed by the Faith and Order Plenary Commission meeting in Budapest, August 1989, which in turn rests on a text reviewed at Stavanger 1985, based on an ur-text written at Chantilly, France, in the spring of 1985. This lengthy process, which calls for genetic inquiry into the origins of ecumenical texts, is typical of Faith and Order. It tends to guarantee that the final result has survived its share of challenges and hence represents a reasonable consensus of ecumenical opinion.

6. Lewis S. Mudge, "A Reformed Theologian Views the 'BEM' Documents," *The Reformed World*, 37, (March 1983): 131ff.

7. William H. Lazareth and Nikos Nissiotis, Preface to *Baptism, Eucharist and Ministry*, Faith and Order Paper 111 (Geneva: World Council of Churches, 1982), x.

8. George Lindbeck, *The Nature of Doctrine: Religion and Theology in a Postliberal Age* (Philadelphia: Westminster Press, 1984), 18.

9. See the list in ibid., 26, n.1.

10. Athanasius explained the principle of consubstantiality "in terms of the rule that whatever is said of the Father is said of

the Son, except that the Son is not the Father." According to Bernard Lonergan, in Lindbeck's words, "it was only later, in medieval scholasticism, that the full metaphysical import of the doctrine was asserted." See Lonergan, *Method in Theology* (London: Herder and Herder, 1972), 309, cited in Lindbeck, *Nature of Doctrine*, 94.

11. Ibid., 97. Lindbeck is actually referring here to Marian dogma, but his observation is generally applicable.

12. Ibid., 100.

13. A particularly comprehensive and compact summary of these new expressions of *ecclesia* can by found in Peter C. Hodgson, *Revisioning the Church: Ecclesial Freedom in the New Paradigm* (Philadelphia: Fortress Press, 1988), 68-88. Hodgson provides extensive bibliography.

14. The meetings in question are described with a wealth of detail in Geiko Müller-Fahrenholtz, *Unity in Today's World*, 11-99. A signal example of the concern can be seen in the structure of the Louvain meeting in 1971. The section topics tell the story. In each case "the unity of the church" is paired with themes having to do with human expression and freedom: "the struggle for justice in society," "the encounter with living faiths," "the struggle against racism," "the handicapped in society," and "the differences in culture." A brilliant description of the Louvain meeting can be found in Ernst Lange, *And Yet it Moves: Dream and Reality of the Ecumenical Movement* (Grand Rapids: Eerdmans, 1979), 30ff. Other WCC bodies were working with these issues at the same time, notably at the World Conference on Church and Society (Geneva, 1966) and the Fourth Assembly (Uppsala, 1968).

15. No criticism is implied which is not also taken to heart. I am familiar with ecumenical editing from personal experience. In putting together the 1985 theological consensus document for the Consultation on Church Union, early drafts contained a series of appendices called "alerts" related to racism, sexism, and institutional exclusivism in the church. These appendices were written by persons representing Christian groups formed around the issues concerned. Thus they bore witness to specific hermeneutics forged in processes of issue-centered ecclesiogenesis. Pungent and memorable as these statements were, their position at the end of the document left the impression that their issues had not been incorporated, but only added on. Full inclusion of these concerns in the body of the document was intensely desired by nearly everyone concerned. But to do so risked a dispersion of confrontation and a blunting of challenge. Moreover, how could one combine into coherent prose examples of theological reflection in such widely differing styles, with diverse ways of handling evidence, warrant, the drawing

of conclusions, and the like? The answer in 1985 was not fully theological in the sense of transformation of the tradition by new witness, but editorial in the sense of juxtaposition of different voices with admonitions that all be heard together.

16. Hans-Georg Gadamer, *Truth and Method*, 2d rev. ed. (New York: Crossroad, 1989).

17. The term *status confessionis* refers to a situation in which it is determined that the churches' response to some issue involves a question of fundamental fidelity to the gospel as confessed. Such a judgment was made, for example, by the German "Confessing Church" at Barmen in 1934 with respect to fellowship with the "German Christians" who supported Hitler. A similar judgment was made by the World Alliance of Reformed Churches at Ottawa in 1982 in suspending from membership two white Dutch Reformed Churches in South Africa for their theological defense of apartheid and exclusion of black and "colored" Christians from communion.

18. The question of pacifism as a possible element for inclusion in any new synthesis of the catholic faith was unexpectedly tested at Canberra (1991) when Konrad Raiser, a former member of the WCC staff, proposed a statement of absolute refusal to participate in war as an addition to the Assembly message. Even in a meeting which had included bitter criticism of the United States and its allies for their military operations in the Persian Gulf region from January to March 1991, this proposal was rejected.

19. The word periphery apparently violates the principle that intercontextual method decenters the ecumenical dialogue process, allowing no context to occupy a favored position. Still, it is the term used by the liberation theologian Enrique Dussel for the developing nations and may even have the advantage of appealing to the spirit of insurgency against ecclesiastical powers located at the "center."

20. It is worth noting that one of the earliest discussions of signification in both theological and philosophical senses is to be found in Augustine's *On Christian Doctrine*, Books I and II. Augustine is discussing the sacraments, but his treatment became one of the foundation stones of the modern science of semiotics or theory of signs.

21. Wolfhart Pannenberg, *The Church*, trans. Keith Crim, (Philadelphia: Westminster Press, 1983), 142ff.

22. *Lumen Gentium*, 15.

23. Geiko Müller-Fahrenholtz, *Unity in Today's World*, 4.

24. Günther Gassmann, "The Church as Sacrament, Sign and Instrument: The Reception of this Ecclesiological Understanding in Ecumenical Debate" in *Church, Kingdom, World: The*

Church as Mystery and Prophetic Sign, ed. Gennadios Limouris, Faith and Order Paper No. 130 (Geneva: World Council of
Churches, 1986), 4. I am indebted to this essay for a study of this
terminology whose main directions I follow.

25. Ibid., 5ff.

26. Ibid., 7.

27. The Salamanca Report and Käsemann's remarks are quoted in
ibid., 8.

28. Ibid., 8-9.

29. Report of the International Reformed-Catholic Dialogue Commission (Geneva: The World Alliance of Reformed Churches,
1991).

30. Ibid., 37.

31. Ibid., 38.

32. Ibid., 40.

33. *Church and World: The Unity of the Church and the Renewal
of Human Community*, Faith and Order Paper No. 151 (Geneva: World Council of Churches, 1990).

34. Ibid., 12.

35. Ibid., 13.

36. Ibid., 16.

37. Ibid., 27.

38. Ibid., 26.

39. Ibid.

40. Ibid.

41. Ibid., 29.

42. Gassmann, "The Church as Sacrament," 14.

43. See this chapter, n.1.

44. Konrad Raiser in *Ecumenism in Transition: A Paradigm Shift in
the Ecumenical Movement?* (Geneva: World Council of
Churches, 1991), has offered a somewhat similar perspective on
the larger reality within which the churches as institutions have
their being. He suggests the metaphor of a "household of life"
or "household of God." Parts of Raiser's proposal are derived
from writings and reports of the former General Secretary of
the WCC, Philip Potter. It is structurally similar to my own in
suggesting that the theme of "church unity," undergirded by a
"christocentric universalism" long prominent in ecumenical
work, needs to give way to greater recognition of diversity in the
Christian community and of the gathering, transforming work
of the Holy Spirit. Persons and movements beyond this community also need to be taken into account. "The ecumenical movement is to be seen wherever Christians and others are one way

or another seeking to work for the unity of mankind." (Philip Potter, "Report of the General Secretary," *The Ecumenical Review*, 25, (1973): 416-17, quoted in Raiser, *Ecumenism in Transition*, 85.) Raiser writes, "The biblically based perception of the *oikoumene* . . . is founded on the totality of relationships instead of structures; it is an expression of living interaction. . . . It lives in the certainty that the earth is habitable, because God has established his covenant with the whole of creation, and it is guided by the hope that God himself will dwell with humankind, with God's people"(86-87).

45. See Introduction, n.11.

46. See chap.1, n.21.

47. See Lewis S. Mudge, "Towards a Truly Ecumenical Council," in *Midstream: An Ecumenical Journal*, 26 (October 1987). This entire issue is focused on the question of conciliarity and the approaching turn of the millennia.

VI. CHURCHES IN THE HUMAN CONVERSATION

1. Hannah Arendt, *The Life of the Mind* (New York: Harcourt Brace Jovanovich, 1978), 4.

2. Ibid., 4.

3. George Kateb, *Hannah Arendt: Politics, Conscience, Evil* (Totowa, N.J.: Rowman and Allanheld, 1984), 188.

4. At least one periodical in America is entirely devoted to keeping consciousness of the Holocaust alive. *Dimensions: A Journal of Holocaust Studies* is published by the Braun Center for Holocaust Studies of the Anti-Defamation League, 823 United Nations Plaza, New York, N.Y. 10017. Colloquies on the subject still abound. Such a meeting, for example, took place at the Graduate Theological Union in Berkeley, California, January 26-28, 1992, under the sponsorship of the United States Holocaust Memorial Council, the Christian Scholars Study Group of the Baltimore Institute for Christian/Jewish Studies, and the G.T.U. itself.

5. Arendt, *Life of the Mind*, 4.

6. Ibid., 4.

7. See H. Richard Niebuhr, *The Meaning of Revelation* (New York: Macmillan, 1941), 72f., 83, 89 ff.

8. Kateb, *Hannah Arendt*, 91.

9. Robert Bellah et al., *The Good Society* (New York: Alfred Knopf, 1991).

10. David Tracy, *The Analogical Imagination: Christian Theology and the Culture of Pluralism* (New York: Crossroad, 1981).

11. David Tracy, *Plurality and Ambiguity: Hermeneutics, Religion, Hope* (San Francisco: Harper and Row, 1987).

12. Robert M. Adams, "The Beast in the Jungle," *The New York Review of Books*, 35, (November 18, 1988): 4. These words, for Adams, express T.S. Eliot's vision of the world around him at the time of *The Waste Land* (1922), but they seem equally applicable to our own circumstances.

13. Robert Bellah, *The Broken Covenant* (New York: Seabury, 1975) and *Habits of the Heart* (Berkeley: University of California Press, 1985).

14. Habermas's position is found in such works as *Knowledge and Human Interests* (Boston: Beacon Press, 1971); *Communication and the Evolution of Society* (Boston: Beacon Press, 1979); *The Philosophical Discourse of Modernity: Twelve Lectures*, Studies in Contemporary German Social Thought (Cambridge: MIT Press, 1987); and *The Theory of Communicative Action*, vol. 1, *Reason and the Rationalization of Society*, vol. 2, *Lifeworld and System* (Boston: Beacon Press, 1984, 1988).

15. Sheila Briggs, in the original draft of a paper presented at the 1989 Habermas Symposium at the Divinity School of the University of Chicago, p. 2. This paper is at present scheduled to appear, with revisions, in *Habermas: Modernity and Public Theology*, Don Browning and Francis Fiorenza, eds. (New York: Crossroad, 1992). I am grateful to Don Browning for sharing this manuscript material with me.

16. Ibid., 12.

17. Ibid., 12.

18. John Thompson, *Critical Hermeneutics* (Cambridge, England: Cambridge University Press, 1981), 94.

19. Ibid., 94.

20. Ibid., 95.

21. Ibid., 92.

22. Ibid.

23. Ibid., 93.

24. Ibid., 93. But Habermas asserts, in Thompson's words, "that the ideal speech situation provides a theoretical reformulation of certain ideas which are central to the tradition of Western philosophy as a whole . . . ." Habermas means such ideas as truth, freedom and justice. My argument is that the notion of humankind as a spiritual, i.e., perfectly communicative community is comparable to Kant's transcendental idea of humanity as a "kingdom of ends," and hence is morally, if not cognitively, regulative of human discourse.

25. Charles Davis, *Theology and Political Society* (New York: Cambridge University Press, 1980), 95.

26. Helmut Peukert, *Science, Action, and Fundamental Theology: Toward a Theology of Communicative Action*, Studies in Con-

temporary German Social Thought (Cambridge: M.I.T. Press, 1984).

27. Francis Schüssler Fiorenza, *Foundational Theology: Jesus and the Church* (New York: Crossroad, 1984).

28. See the discussion of foundationalism, Introduction, n.6.

29. Paul Lakeland, *Theology and Critical Theory* (Nashville: Abingdon Press, 1990).

30. Ibid., 8.

31. Briggs, Habermas Symposium paper, 7.

32. I am again following the line of thought in ibid., 8 and 9.

33. See Stephen K. White, *The Recent Work of Jürgen Habermas: Reason, Justice and Modernity* (Cambridge, England: Cambridge University Press, 1988), 128ff. "Habermas's work has often been suspected of harboring some variant of foundationalism, and yet he has just as often claimed that his is a non-foundationalist position." See, on the one hand, Richard Rorty, "Pragmatism, Relativism, and Irrationalism" in his *Consequences of Pragmatism: Essays 1972-1980* (Minneapolis: University of Minnesota Press, 1982), 173-74. A situation "in which truth is bound to prevail must itself be described in terms of examples rather than principles." On the other hand, see Rorty, *Philosophy and the Mirror of Nature* (Princeton: Princeton University Press, 1979), 380, quoting Habermas from "A Postscript" to *Knowledge and Human Interests*, trans. Christian Lenhardt, in *Philosophy and the Social Sciences* 3 (1973): "As long as cognitive interests can be identified and analyzed through reflection on the logic of inquiry in the natural and cultural sciences, they can legitimately claim a 'transcendental' status."

34. Unlike Wittgenstein, Gadamer does not think that "language games" are essentially locked up in themselves, unable to communicate beyond their own boundaries. Wittgenstein's concern is after all epistemological, while Gadamer's is ontological. Differing forms of life have in common the fact that they are disclosures of Being, and hence genuine dialogue is possible between them.

35. See the discussion of *phronesis* in chap. 3.

36. 'The Primacy of *Phronesis*: A Proposal for Avoiding Frustrating Tendencies in our Conceptions of Rationality," *The Journal of Religion* 69 (July 1989): 359ff.

37. Ibid., 364.

38. 'Ad Hoc Apologetics" in *The Journal of Religion* 66 (July 1986): 282ff.

39. Ibid., 291.

40. Ibid., 293.

41. 'Gestalt" is now close to being an English word. I dispense, therefore, with the capitalization and italics the use of a German word would require and employ the English plural "gestalts."

42. Peter C. Hodgson, *God in History: Shapes of Freedom* (Nashville: Abingdon Press, 1989), 193.

43. Quoted in ibid.

44. Ibid.

45. Ibid., 195.

46. Ibid., 205.

47. Philip Hallie, *Lest Innocent Blood Be Shed: The Story of the Village of Le Chambon, and How Goodness Happened There* (New York: Harper and Row, 1979). The story of Le Chambon is also the subject of a documentary film, *Weapons of the Spirit*, written and directed by Pierre Sauvage, who was one of the Jewish children hidden by the Chambonnais during the war.

48. André Trocmé studied at the Protestant Theological Faculty at Strasbourg, France, spent a year at Union Theological Seminary in New York, and later became pastor of the parish of St. Gervais, Geneva, and President of the International Fellowship of Reconciliation.

49. Hallie, *Lest Innocent Blood Be Shed*, 292.

Index